STUDIES IN IMPERIALISM

general editor John M. MacKenzie

When the 'Studies in Imperialism' series was founded more than twenty years ago, emphasis was laid upon the conviction that 'imperialism as a cultural phenomenon had as significant an effect on the dominant as on the subordinate societies'. With more than fifty books published, this remains the prime concern of the series. Cross-disciplinary work has indeed appeared covering the full spectrum of cultural phenomena, as well as examining aspects of gender and sex, frontiers and law, science and the environment, language and literature, migration and patriotic societies, and much else. Moreover, the series has always wished to present comparative work on European and American imperialism, and particularly welcomes the submission of books in these areas. The fascination with imperialism, in all its aspects, shows no sign of abating, and this series will continue to lead the way in encouraging the widest possible range of studies in the field. 'Studies in Imperialism' is fully organic in its development, always seeking to be at the cutting edge, responding to the latest interests of scholars and the needs of this ever-expanding area of scholarship.

Colonial connections
1815–45

MANCHESTER
1824

Manchester University Press

AVAILABLE IN THE SERIES

Colonial connections
1815–45

PATRONAGE,
THE INFORMATION REVOLUTION
AND COLONIAL GOVERNMENT

Zoë Laidlaw

MANCHESTER UNIVERSITY PRESS
Manchester and New York

distributed exclusively in the USA by PALGRAVE

Published by MANCHESTER UNIVERSITY PRESS
OXFORD ROAD, MANCHESTER M13 9NR, UK
and ROOM 400, 175 FIFTH AVENUE, NEW YORK, NY 10010, USA
www.manchesteruniversitypress.co.uk

Distributed exclusively in the USA by
PALGRAVE, 175 FIFTH AVENUE, NEW YORK, NY 10010, USA

Distributed exclusively in Canada by
UBC PRESS, UNIVERSITY OF BRITISH COLUMBIA,
2029 WEST MALL, VANCOUVER, BC, CANADA V6T 1Z2

British Library Cataloguing-in-Publication Data
A catalogue record for this book is available from the British Library

Library of Congress Cataloging-in-Publication Data applied for

ISBN 0 7190 6918 1 hardback
EAN 978 0 7190 6918 5

First published 2005

14 13 12 11 10 09 08 07 06 05   10 9 8 7 6 5 4 3 2 1

Typeset in Kuenstier
by Mudra Typesetters, Pondicherry, India
Printed in Great Britain
by CPI, Bath

For my grandmothers,
Doris Goldstraw and Margaret Laidlaw

CONTENTS

GENERAL EDITOR'S INTRODUCTION

British historians have long been anxious, for whatever reason, to separate domestic from colonial history. Recently, there has been a renewed effort to achieve this, with the publication of *The Absent-Minded Imperialists*, an impressively researched book by a distinguished historian of the British Empire, Bernard Porter. Porter argues that, at least until the later nineteenth century, the British were indeed absent-minded about (for which read largely ignorant of and culturally indifferent towards) their empire. In the realms of both high and popular culture, the British had much more significant concerns, particularly those relating to class struggles, social issues, economic matters, and relations with non-imperial parts of the globe. In all of this, the English were possibly exceptional. Other states with smaller empires may have been more imperially minded, since their empires were more closely bound up with their sense of nationalism. Moreover, within Britain itself, it is conceivable that the Scots and the Irish were more enthusiastic about empire, and the opportunities it afforded for emigration, trade, and professional advancement, than the English.

The centrality of labour, social deprivation, trade and manufacturing, as well as diplomacy and war in British politics and culture cannot be gainsaid. But there seems little reason to see these as necessarily separated out from the imperial and colonial strand that runs through them. The 'Studies in Imperialism' series has for over twenty years been largely dedicated to the exposé of this imperial thread, to the proposal that in British history empire and domestic culture – in its widest sense – should be examined within the same analytical frame. Much of this work has concentrated (but not exclusively) on the second half of the nineteenth century and the early decades of the twentieth when imperial linkages seemed to be operating most noticeably and effectively.

But now Zoë Laidlaw demonstrates the ways in which this core contention of the series can receive support from the colonial and imperial relationships in the early nineteenth century. Among other concerns, her book makes a significant contribution to the study of historical networking, revealing the extent to which military, professional, scientific, evangelical, and settler networks all operated in ways that recognised the centrality of London in imperial power-broking. The manipulation of social, familial, educational and other connections demonstrates the ways in which members of the bourgeoisie interacted with the upper class and with each other. Her analysis also confirms the manner in which the army, the missionary lobby, scientists, map-makers, and statisticians, among others, conducted their activities in such a way that the colonial dimension was a vital conditioner and energiser of a good deal of their interests. Domestic and colonial matters were often closely intertwined as policies were pushed forward into new dispensations. And although these affairs might on the face of it appear to involve a relatively small number of people, they unavoidably made an impression upon wider cultural and social, religious and political concerns.

GENERAL EDITOR'S INTRODUCTION

Laidlaw's book throws light on many other aspects of the colonial–metropolitan relationship, on developments within the Colonial Office (encapsulating a significant revision of the standard view), on pressure groups and lobbies, upon forms of patronage, and upon the information and statistical revolution that developed in the 1830s. Moreover, she escapes from earlier historians' concerns with a single colony by developing an illuminating comparison between the Cape and New South Wales. All of this is based upon remarkably extensive research in the United Kingdom, in South Africa, and in Australia. These comparative approaches, already illustrated in several books within this series, will no doubt be extended yet further in the future. Moreover, she implicitly suggests the existence of further networks, based upon ethnic affiliation (for example, the Scots and the Irish), on professionals and their associations, on missionary societies, and much else. All the best research is suggestive research and one of the considerable qualities of this book is the manner in which further ideas and areas for consideration and analysis are opened up to the reader.

John M. MacKenzie

ACKNOWLEDGEMENTS

Inevitably, this exploration of colonial connections has drawn on my own global networks – networks that connect family, colleagues and friends, and convey finance, information and advice.

I began this book in Oxford, and its central ideas were thrashed out between Rhodes House Library, the Blackwells café, and Holywell Manor. I would like particularly to thank John Darwin, who supervised my doctoral research and, with his characteristic dry wit, helped to guide, inform and expand my ideas during numerous conversations; and also Peter Marshall and David Washbrook, whose perceptive comments helped to transform that research into this book. There have been many other fruitful conversations – in Melbourne, Oxford, London, and Sheffield – which have contributed immensely to my understanding of both nineteenth-century Britain and the colonies. Support, advice and ideas came from Mike Braddick, Carl Bridge, Peter Burroughs, Jo Duffy, Julie Evans, Clare Griffiths, Pat Grimshaw, Catherine Hall, Karen Harvey, Mark Hickford, Hartley Mitchell, Dawn Nell, Ian Phimister, Andrew Porter, Simon Potter, Dara Price, Simon Skinner, Christoph Stumpf, Helen Tilley, and Ben Zachariah, as well as my colleagues at the University of Sheffield and the students who took 'The Empire in Victorian Britain' in 2003 and 2004. Without Alan Lester, David Philips, Damon Salesa, Michael Stumpf and Damen Ward, each of whom read parts, or all, of this book, it would never have been finished.

I am indebted to the archivists and librarians at Rhodes House Library, the Bodleian Library, the British Library, the Public Record Office, the Liverpool Record Office, Cambridge University Library, Durham University Library, the School of Oriental and African Studies, the Institute of Commonwealth Studies, the Foreign and Commonwealth Office Library, the National Library of South Africa, the Cape Archives, the Cory Library at Rhodes University, the University of Cape Town, the State Archives of New South Wales, and the Mitchell Library, for their assistance and guidance.

An earlier version of parts of chapter four appears as 'Closing the gap: colonial governors and their metropolitan agents', in Simon J. Potter (ed.), *Imperial communications: Australia and Britain* (London, 2005); while some sections of chapter six appeared in 'Integrating metropolitan, colonial and imperial histories – the Aborigines Select Committee of 1835–7', in T. Banivanua Mar and J. Evans (eds), *Writing colonial histories: comparative perspectives* (Melbourne, 2002). I am grateful to the Menzies Centre and the University of Melbourne for granting me permission to use this material.

While working on this book, I was funded by the Commonwealth Scholarship Commission, Balliol College, the Beit Fund, and the University of Sheffield.

I would like to thank my family, Elizabeth, David, Xanthe and Margaret Laidlaw, Annedore and Rudolf Stumpf, the Goldstraws, and the Ulmanns, for their generous encouragement and support over a much longer period than merely the last seven

ACKNOWLEDGEMENTS

years. Finally, it's unlikely that my most favourable critic and favourite companion realised just how familiar he was going to become with the former colonies, or their history, when he met me in October 1997. Michael Stumpf has not only borne it all with good grace, but has provided inspiration, critical commentary and sustenance. It could not have been done without him.

ABBREVIATIONS

APA	Australian Patriotic Association
BFC	Bourke Family Correspondence, Mitchell Library
BP	Bourke Papers, Mitchell Library
BL	British Library
CA	Cape Archives
CO	Colonial Office, National Archives
CUL	Cambridge University Library
DP	D'Urban Papers, Cape Archives
DSAB	*Dictionary of South African biography*
GRE	Papers of Henry George Grey, 3rd Earl Grey, Durham University Library
HRA	*Historical Records of Australia*
LMS	London Missionary Society
LRO	Liverpool Record Office
ML	Mitchell Library
MP	Macarthur Papers, Mitchell Library
NLSA	National Library of South Africa, Cape Town
OHBE	*Oxford History of the British Empire*
RGS	Royal Geographical Society
SOAS	School of Oriental and African Studies
TFB	Thomas Fowell Buxton Papers, Rhodes House Library (Bodleian Library)
TLM	Papers of Thomas Livingston Mitchell, Mitchell Library
WO	War Office, National Archives

CHAPTER ONE

Introduction

> I may forget the railroads, I may forget the steam engines, but I shall not forget what I have seen tonight. I have seen a little company of men – not taller than I am here – touch the spring that moves the world.[1]

Dyani Tshatshu, a minor Xhosa chief, reportedly made these comments while observing a House of Commons' debate in 1836. Tshatshu was in London to give evidence to a parliamentary committee on the relationship between Britain and her indigenous colonial subjects, an inquiry particularly inspired by the conflict between Xhosa and Europeans in southern Africa. Tshatshu was brought to London by people who shared (and probably shaped) his conviction that imperial intervention could profoundly affect colonial governance, but his sense that London was the critical hub of imperial rule was not uncommon in the 1830s. Both those who hoped for imperial intervention and those who denied its validity continually returned to the question of how imperial power was exercised and how it might be influenced.

In its exploration of imperial power, *Colonial connections* has three aims. First, it examines the operation of colonial rule in the settler colonies before self-government, an examination which entails the close consideration of both metropolitan and colonial spheres, and a focus on the imperial networks which connected them. The study of networks draws attention to both individuals and structures within the empire; this is important for an era of small formal government when non-governmental lobbyists could play a critical part in decision-making. Considering the networks used to govern the colonies during the first half of the nineteenth century additionally alerts us to the patronage and information they conveyed, while highlighting the problems, as well as the benefits, of rule via close personal connection.

Second, while *Colonial connections* covers the thirty years after Waterloo, it is particularly concerned with changes to colonial governance in the 1830s: a decade of metropolitan upheaval and colonial crises which has prompted long-standing historiographical concern. Thus the book follows a generation of colonists, metropolitan officials and colonial administrators who remembered the consequences of the American Revolution, if not its course; who matured during the Napoleonic Wars; and whose lives were shaped by the upheavals in British politics and society during the 'Age of Reform'. Apart from European and domestic concerns, this generation saw major challenges to imperial rule in the settler colonies and beyond, including the emancipation of slaves, Canadian rebellions, southern African wars, the expansion of British India and 'systematic colonisation'. The response of the Colonial Office to these issues, and to its own role in the mid-1830s, provides another focus for the book. How was the imperial government to reconcile settlers' increasing demands for greater self-government with metropolitan conceptions of their unreadiness and unsuitability for it? How could it counter domestic concerns about imperial control, expenditure and responsibility? For the metropolitan administration, the failure of personal networks – which had provided a means of exerting control over the colonies between 1815 and 1835 – would shape the solutions proposed.

Historians have questioned the conceptual centrality in imperial history of the metropole or nation, but the importance of Britain, and particularly London, to both nineteenth-century contemporaries like Tshatshu and subsequent historians determined its inclusion as a site of investigation.[2] The third aim of this book is to stress the perceived and actual importance of the metropole to colonial governance before 1845, and to examine changes in the influence of metropolitan and colonial impulses and concerns. When did the metropolitan approach to colonial government change, allowing settler colonies to gain a greater degree of self-government? How did colonial settlers shape and support their demands to have maximum effect on metropolitan government? The growth of colonial societies, metropolitan officials' sense of vulnerability, and intellectual developments all played a part in transfers of power. But these questions also highlight the importance of control over information, in order to exercise or influence power, which is seen in every section of the imperial arena, metropolitan or colonial, and reflects similar patterns in domestic government.[3]

In pursuing these themes, *Colonial connections* engages with broad questions about British imperialism in the early nineteenth century, but also allows the existing historiography of empire to be integrated with late twentieth-century work on nineteenth-century Britain. It investigates imperial power, asking where such power lay, and how it was exercised, influenced and perceived, and suggests that the study of networks of personal communication adds new depth to the question of colonial governance.

Although this book draws on evidence from across the British Empire, three sites – Britain, the Cape Colony and New South Wales – are of particular importance. The centrality of Britain has already been asserted. New South Wales and the Cape Colony were chosen because they constituted sufficiently similar, yet distinctive, colonial sites.[4] The two crown colonies shared a similar span of British settlement (although the Cape had a longer, Dutch, colonial history). Both relied in 1815 on bonded labour which was to be extinguished, or severely threatened, by 1845, and both faced an uncertain future, with questionable economic viability and fragmented social bodies. Although both colonies experienced considerable upheaval in the established imperial order between 1815 and 1845, neither received the same degree of metropolitan scrutiny as colonies in British North America or the West Indies. Yet the two colonies were also quite distinct: the experiences of slave society and penal settlement entailed different ways of considering race and indigenous peoples, for example. Dutch colonisation of the Cape had left an institutional and legal, as well as a social, legacy, while in Australia the questions of whether English law should be transplanted, and to what extent it applied to indigenous peoples, were key. In politics, New South Wales would move more quickly towards responsible colonial government than the Cape Colony.

Colonial connections provides the opportunity to bring together new imperial and British historiography, in order to examine the somewhat neglected area of colonial governance, where 'governance' implies a concern with processes of government and administration in the broadest sense. Since the late 1990s more colonial and imperial historians have taken seriously Cooper and Stoler's exhortation to place colony and metropole 'in one analytic field', producing pan-colonial and comparative studies, as well as interrogating the relationship between Britain and the empire.[5] This interest has been encouraged partly by historians' interest in the transmission, appropriation and modification of indigenous culture and ideas by the British and vice versa.[6] Other studies are inspired by a desire to understand complex phenomena such as slavery, migration, convict transportation, indigenous peoples' experiences of imperialism and missionary activity – all of which operated across and beyond the British Empire. Others, including the publications of the 'British World' historians, the multi-volume *Oxford history of the British Empire* (*OHBE*) and its companion series, and the work of the 'new imperial historians', represent a concerted attempt to revivify imperial history, or to examine more critically the nature of 'Britishness' in an imperial setting.[7]

The focus on 'Britishness' has been underpinned by a number of excellent studies of nineteenth-century British polity and society published since the 1980s. New perspectives on patronage, government centralisation, 'Old Corruption', the political sphere, evangelicalism, statistics and the 'classifying imagination' are all amenable to incorporation into conceptions of nineteenth-century empire.[8] Since 2000, several works have attempted to reconcile these understandings of British society with colonial activity, while bringing all under one umbrella of empire. This project has perhaps been pursued most diligently, although not always identified as such, for the empire before 1800 – when the opportunity to examine 'the Atlantic World' or the sphere of the East India Company encourages an integrated approach.[9] For the nineteenth century, one successful approach to juggling a variety of locations and ideas has been the employment of 'networks' or 'webs' to illuminate both critical connections and structures of empire. Alan Lester's work on the connections between the Cape Colony and Britain posits the existence of competing colonial discourses which were conveyed, explicated and strengthened by their transmission through imperial networks.[10] The personnel of these networks overlapped, muddying the discourses as well as strengthening them, but their existence underlines the widespread contemporary recognition of imperial connections as key for any individuals interested in affecting colonial governance, whether missionaries, settlers, merchants, officials or metropolitan-based interest groups. Tony Ballantyne's *Orientalism and race* is unusual both in its explicit discussion of material and intellectual webs, and in its examination of the connections between more than two imperial sites. Ballantyne has also attempted to overcome the frequent imbalance between discussions of metropole and colony, by taking 'a mobile approach', an analysis that is not firmly rooted in one space.[11] This book follows Lester and Ballantyne in working with the idea of imperial networks, although it attempts a more comprehensive articulation of the concept. Using networks does have some limitations: networks are difficult for the historian to trace, and must usually remain only partially revealed. The networks considered in this book heavily favour colonial and metropolitan elites over the less well-connected in the colonial world. Nevertheless, they provide a useful way of thinking about empire.

Despite this movement towards colonial and metropolitan integration, nineteenth-century colonial governance has received relatively little attention since the 1980s. Perhaps this has stemmed from the concern to reinstate the experience of 'ordinary' colonisers and colonised, and from an aversion to the metropolitan-centred and triumphalist imperial history written in the early decades of the twentieth century. Later work falls into two categories: that which takes a metropolitan perspective – usually focusing on the Colonial Office; or single colony studies, typically produced in those locations.[12] Studies of the Colonial Office routinely detect a profound change in 1836, when James Stephen assumed the permanent under-secretaryship of the department, bringing with him a 'bureaucratic revolution' which ended 'Old Corruption'. These works, while containing much of interest, display a limited appreciation of the broader colonial sphere.[13] The historians who focused on single colonies, on the other hand, were often quite parochial in outlook, more often falsely identifying colonial practices as exceptional than identifying what it was which made each colony different.[14] Yet an understanding of colonial governance, considered in its broader imperial context, can provide a framework for studies of both particular colonial societies and cultures of imperial rule.

This book starts from the assumption that a critical transition did occur in the 1830s: the transition from a residual desire to exert autocratic imperial control (connected with Whiggish notions of elite superiority as much as with Tory paternalism) to a pragmatic acceptance that effective management of the move towards greater colonial self-government was necessary. Two markers of this change were the relocation of patronage from the metropole to the colonies, and an altered perception of information and its uses. Imperial administrators continued to assert metropolitan centrality, but their reliance on affective, nuanced, networks of personal connection and information critical to colonial rule up to the mid-1830s changed as more emphasis was placed on impersonal bureaucracy and system. Colonists, meanwhile, realised from the early 1840s that time spent pursuing their goals in the colonies, as well as in Britain, was increasingly profitable.

Colonial connections is divided into three parts, tracing colonial governance between metropolitan and colonial spheres, and across time. 'Metropolitan concerns' introduces, and then dissects, some of the networks of patronage and information which were critical to colonial governance, and examines changes in Colonial Office organisation and policies between 1815 and 1836. 'Colonial struggles' deals with the development, implementation and effects of networks of personal communications in New South Wales and the Cape Colony up to 1845. Colonial governance is examined at three levels in this section: one chapter focuses on governors, considering the particularly awkward place they occupied as mediators between the metropolitan government and their colonial subjects; a second examines the much larger pool of colonial officials who struggled to gain security and execute their duties far from home; while the third looks at those outside government – both in Britain and the colonies – who attempted to influence colonial policy and administration. The final section, 'Agendas for imperial reform', returns the focus to Britain, examining how the pressure placed on the metropolitan government during the 1830s led to a reassessment of the role of personal communications, and consequent changes to the way in which imperial networks operated. This discussion considers the impact of a changing information order – in particular the rise of statistics – on colonial governance, and examines the way in which colonial and metropolitan concerns converged and cross-fertilised.

Colonial connections argues that those who exercised colonial power generally employed political or constitutional ideas reactively and pragmatically rather than allowing them to shape their actions, at least in the period 1815 to 1845. Assessing the relative importance of the individual, as opposed to systemic or ideological concerns, is therefore central to this book. The concern for the individual means that *Colonial connections* veers away from a detailed analysis of the work of colonial theorists except where it can be seen to have direct relevance. There is a limited engagement with those theorists and writers like Herman Merivale and George Cornewall Lewis, who presented themselves as detached in the period under consideration; like Roebuck, Molesworth, and Wakefield, who hoped to alter imperial policy; or like the 3rd Earl Grey, who retrospectively hoped to justify it.[15] What Stokes wrote of Macaulay could perhaps be applied more generally to the Colonial Office: his 'shrewd blend of altruism and self-interest . . . represented the permanent political instinct of British colonial policy'.[16]

In general terms, a growing adherence to ideals of 'good governance' and centralisation, stemming from concepts of utility, sat alongside the desire for colonies to be subordinated to imperial authority – and the fear, post-1776, that they would not submit.[17] While the Benthamite utilitarians, the Colonial Reformers, and the free traders, had much to say specifically about empire as the century progressed, it is not clear that their ideas had a great or consistent influence on those directly engaged in the government of colonies in the 1820s and 1830s, beyond the increasing preoccupation with rational and measurable approaches to government.[18] The influence of the humanitarians, and evangelical religion, in the same period was perhaps more profound, if only because it was more diffuse and thus less threatening.[19]

Although this book is concerned more with the mechanics than with the aims or ideological basis of colonial government in settler societies, and with power rather than authority, this is not to say that issues surrounding colonial authority, and the ideological basis of imperial government did not matter. Indeed, they provide a framework within which to view colonial governance. It is therefore important to outline briefly the assumptions about government that were made by metropolitan and colonial administrators. The historiography dealing with the justifications for imperial rule, and the constitutional basis for its form, and their development, is both rich and extensive. While the imperial historians of the 1970s – J. M. Ward, Peter Burroughs and Ged Martin – provided a more nuanced account than their predecessors, W. P. Morrell and Reginald Coupland, Mark Francis's 1992 work has further developed an analysis of the authority vested in colonial governors, as well as the ways in which that authority was manifested. Francis's claim that the language used to discuss political ideas and imperial ideologies was impoverished, and therefore constrained, can conversely be interpreted to explain the flexibility of these ideas, and their availability for reactive and pragmatic use.[20]

Central to ideas about colonial government between 1815 and 1845 was the uneasy existence of two constitutional positions, sometimes embraced by the same theorists and statesmen. On one hand, it was widely accepted

[6]

– by metropolitan and colonial governments, and in legal and political writing – that colonial constitutions, because they derived ultimate authority from the British crown, were subordinate to the British constitution.[21] On the other hand, in metropolitan and colonial practice the ideal seemed to be the reproduction of British forms of government in the colonies, based partly on notions of English birthrights and partly on the belief that British institutions were the best.[22] But if colonial societies were to be genuine transcripts of British society, how could they be also subordinate to the metropole? This tension forms a background to the cases examined in this book which more immediately deal with the practice of colonial governance, with the claims of settlers for greater representation or self-government, and with the legitimate scope and employment of gubernatorial power.

Within this fundamental ideological confusion, a set of working assumptions – seldom consciously examined, but implicit in most government action – guided metropolitan and colonial administrators. These assumptions, perhaps because of their practical nature, and uneasy position within the constitutional paradox of colonial rule, had little positive content. First, metropolitan administrators attempted to adhere to an ideal of 'good government', which was the same for colonial societies as metropolitan. In the wake of the Napoleonic wars, good government involved not only retrenchment, but also a belief that administrative and fiscal efficiency were ends in themselves. The desire to distance the Colonial Office and imperial administration from the taint of 'Old Corruption' both helped to satisfy the aim of retrenchment, and was a means of limiting parliamentary and public criticism of government.[23] In the 1830s and 1840s, as the Colonial Reformers became more vocal in their parliamentary attacks on the imperial establishment, and imperial crises attracted more public attention, the desire to avoid disapprobation sometimes overshadowed the original aims of efficiency and probity.

A second set of assumptions – about settler societies, and how they should develop – was also important. Just as notions of good government could be translated from Britain to the empire, so was the intention to develop settler societies on a British model. Although understandings of British society proved remarkably flexible, metropolitan administrators, particularly, argued that property in the colonies, as in Britain, should be protected, and that its possession should form the basis of political power. Whig conceptions of reform, dating back to the eighteenth century, and reinforced by the loss of the thirteen colonies, suggested that, when they were sufficiently advanced, it was appropriate to relinquish local control to colonial societies. Throughout the period this book examines, however, the prevailing metropolitan sense was that Britain's settler societies were unready to govern themselves. They were politically immature, and lacking in the natural divisions of society so important for ensuring a successful balanced constitution. Factional interests were perceived as too strong to be overcome, in British North America, the Cape Colony and the penal colonies of Australia.[24] In such a situation, it was Britain's unwelcome duty to balance an element of settler representation with the exertion of imperial power, embodying the norms of good government in the imperial representative, the colonial governor.

Both sets of assumptions underlined the contemporary belief that the metropolis was central to the exercise of power. This is not to say that ideas, influence, or personnel flowed in only one direction: this book supports work which demonstrates how all moved back and forth between London and the empire, and also between colonies.[25] Nevertheless, power was perceived to lie firmly in Britain until the advent of self-government.

The domestic and imperial crises of the 1830s did not substantially undermine these sets of assumptions. However, as will be seen, Colonial Office concern about metropolitan scrutiny of its actions; the growing realisation that settler colonies could only be controlled against their will expensively and haphazardly; and shifting attitudes to the nature of metropolitan government, in the wake of the 1832 Reform Act and the Bedchamber crisis of 1839, did encourage the metropolitan administrators of empire to reconfigure their aims for settler societies. If local self-government was to be granted (and it should be stressed that, at least up to 1845, this was seen only as occurring over the long term), the British government had to do its best to manage the transition, making it look like this was a desired outcome, and preventing the colonies from damaging British interests.

Notes

1 Quoted in TFB, vol. 15, p. 172, Thomas Buxton to Edward Buxton, 17 January 1837.
2 Burton, 'Who needs the nation?'
3 MacDonagh, *Early Victorian government*, p. 6; Cullen, *Statistical movement*, pp. 19–27.
4 The comparison between New South Wales and the Cape Colony is also embraced in McKenzie's *Scandal*, pp. 1–14.
5 Cooper and Stoler, *Tensions of empire*, p. 15.
6 Bayly, *Empire and information*; Hall, *Civilising subjects*; Lester, *Imperial networks*; Ballantyne, *Orientalism and race*; Salesa, 'Race mixing'; Ward, 'Politics of jurisdiction'; Drayton, *Nature's government*.
7 Bridge and Fedorowich, *British world*; *Oxford history of the British Empire*; Ridden, 'Making good citizens'; Colley, 'What is imperial history now?'.
8 Harling, *Old Corruption*; Bourne, *Patronage*; Eastwood, 'Province of the legislature'; 'Age of uncertainty'; 'Social legislation'; Hilton, *Age of atonement*; Ritvo, *Platypus and the mermaid*; Poovey, *Making a social body*; *Modern fact*. MacDonagh's 1977 *Early Victorian government* was an earlier work to pick up some of the same themes.
9 Armitage and Braddick, *British Atlantic world*; Gould, *Persistence of empire*; Hamilton, 'Melville'; Mackillop, 'Fashioning a British Empire'; Bowen *et al.*, *East India Company*.
10 Lester, *Imperial networks*, pp. 1–8.
11 Ballantyne, *Orientalism and race*, pp. 2–4, 9, 14–16.

12 Morrell's two volumes on British colonial policy are more reliable than most examples of the former: *British colonial policy in the age of Peel and Russell* and *British colonial policy in the mid-Victorian age.*

13 Hall, *Colonial Office*; Cell, *British colonial administration*; Young, *Colonial Office*; Blakeley, *Colonial Office.*

14 For an example of such false exceptionalism, see Fitzpatrick on Governor Arthur in *Franklin*, p. 104. For historians lamenting an isolationist stance in colonial history, see: Stewart, *Origins of Canadian politics*, p. 8; Macintyre, 'Australia and the empire', pp. 180–1; Bayly, *Imperial meridian*, p. xiv.

15 Merivale, *Lectures on colonization*; Lewis, *Government of dependencies*; Roebuck, *Colonies of England*; Molesworth, *Selected speeches* and *State of the colonies*; Wakefield, *Letter from Sydney* and *England and America*; Grey, *Colonial policy.*

16 Stokes, 'Macaulay', 49. See also Cell, *British colonial administration*, p. xi.

17 See MacDonagh, *Early Victorian government*; Harling, *Old Corruption*; Eastwood, 'Province of the legislature'; Marshall, 'Empire and authority', 116–18.

18 Winch, *Classical political economy*, pp. 25–39; see also Stokes, *English Utilitarians*; Finer, 'Transmission of Benthamite ideas'; Ray, 'Administering emigration', ch. 6.

19 Hilton, *Age of atonement*, pp. viii–x; See the debate over the influence of humanitarianism on government action between MacDonagh, *Early Victorian government*, p. 7; *Government growth*, p. 321; Hart, 'Nineteenth-century social reform', 48–57; Dunkley, 'Emigration and the state', 373–6.

20 Francis, *Governors and settlers*, pp. 4–7.

21 Ward, *Colonial self-government*, pp. 40–1, 92–5 and *passim*; Francis, *Governors and settlers*, pp. 7, 15, 26–9.

22 Francis, *Governors and settlers*, pp. 15, 17; Neal, *Rule of law*, pp. 54–5, 167–9; Ward, *Colonial self-government*; Cell, *British colonial administration.*

23 Harling, *Old Corruption*, pp. 9–14; Burroughs, 'Imperial institutions', p. 173.

24 Ward provides the best account of debates on this notion, *Colonial self-government*, chs 3–4.

25 Ballantyne, *Orientalism and race*, pp. 14–15; Drayton, *Nature's government*, pp. xiii–xv.

PART I

Metropolitan concerns

CHAPTER TWO

Networking the empire

To find a cousin is better than a mistress in every port. (Governor Richard Bourke, 26 October 1834)[1]

Networks of personal connections were of critical importance to colonial governance in the early nineteenth century. This chapter examines the way in which the study of imperial networks illuminates colonial history, considering first their nature and structure before turning specifically to three of the most important networks for this book. Together with the discussion of the Colonial Office in chapter three, it provides a metropolitan context for the remainder of *Colonial connections*.

Networks – whether of people or phenomena – have both enjoyed popularity and been subjected to extended sociological and mathematical analysis since the 1990s.[2] Imperial historians have begun to draw on the study of networks, although as yet there has been no satisfactory theoretical assessment of their nature or importance for imperial history.[3] Historians engage with social networks that are only partly revealed and which change over time, which renders most mathematical representations – reliant on analysing static, completely revealed, networks – meaningless. Nevertheless, the terminology employed by graph theorists to describe the importance of particular nodes (or individuals) in a network and the strength of the bonds between them, does (if used carefully) help to identify key features of the imperial networks under scrutiny.[4]

As they describe the multiplicity of connections within the British Empire, the networks examined in this book are inherently interesting. Their greatest historical significance, however, lies in their role as mechanisms consciously utilised by their members. This might entail the transmission of information, or patronage, or money, through the personal connections a network encompassed. That contemporaries thought about networks and attached considerable weight to them, is demonstrated by the evidence of both network insiders and outsiders. For example, a missionary in the Cape Colony, vilified by European settlers because he was married to a Khoi woman, and working more than five hundred miles from Cape Town, drew comfort from the knowledge that the information he passed to his colonial supervisor would find its way through missionary connections in the Cape Colony and in Britain to the heart of metropolitan government.[5] On the other hand, a senior military veteran stationed in the Mediterranean believed that he had never achieved promotion to a civil governorship, despite decades of service, because he had not fought in the Iberian Peninsula or at Waterloo, and was therefore outside the most useful military network of the 1830s.[6]

Although employed assiduously and consciously, networks were referred to in other terms in the early and mid-nineteenth century: overtly as 'connections', or more obliquely through the recognition of shared politics, professional camaraderie, or the obligations of friendship and family. Imperial historians, long interested in connections across and within colonies, if not in 'networks', have also found a variety of ways of describing these links. Ballantyne, for example, prefers to use 'webs' when discussing 'systems of mobility and exchange', as they emphasise transverse connections between colonies as well as radial connections between colony and metropole.[7] This is an important observation, but the term 'network' perhaps better captures the complex and irregular systems of connection examined here than the regular, two-dimensional image of a 'web'.

Some of the networks examined in this book were very extensive, with members scattered across the entire empire. Others were smaller, connecting one colony with the metropolis, one colony with another, or simply individuals within only one colony. Each type of network contributes differently to this discussion. Networks connecting metropolis to colony were the mainstay of day-to-day colonial governance, transmitting influence, patronage and information. The members of networks operating within a single colony often had to find means of presenting their arguments, and acquiring influence, in Britain. Trans-colonial networks encouraged the transmission of ideas, and experience, through the empire. While less significant to the daily grind of government than networks linking Britain to the colonies, these inter-colonial connections offer other insights to the historian. The personal correspondence between governors, for example, could contain a rare open discussion between equals about the challenges of colonial governance; while the letters of separated family members encouraged comparisons between colonies.

The nature of the bonds between network members was by no means uniform. 'Weak ties' are important in the study of mathematical networks because they link groups otherwise self-contained, and thus have the potential to expand a network greatly. In this study, 'weak ties' correspond essentially to the connections between *acquaintances*. These could represent the critical connection which allowed a particular source to reach beyond its immediate geographical location: for example, providing the means of transmitting settlers' views to the metropolitan government; or, equally, distributing the patronage held by a senior metropolitan figure to the extended family of a protégé. Weak ties could also, if cultivated, lead to the further integration of two networks, in other words turning weak ties into stronger links. The possibility of such integration underlines the fact that very few networks were ever distinct: just as most individuals had a variety of identities – settler, humanitarian, British, Australian, say – so they belonged to multiple sets of connection.

Colonial connections is also concerned with the 'strong ties' of *friendship* and *obligation*. The stronger the bond between individuals, it is argued, the greater their chances of manipulating a network to their advantage. Although an acquaintance might provide a vital link on one or even several occasions, a stronger connection would encourage repeated and more determined action. One way in which bonds were strengthened was the existence of multiple connections between the same individuals: for example, two men who were in-laws and also former comrades. Thus, just as many individuals belonged to more than one network, sets of individuals had more than one network in common.

Two basic varieties of bonds between individuals are considered in *Colonial connections*: those which gave rise to symmetric relationships; and those which did not. In the first category (which includes many family relationships and connections between missionaries in the field or military comrades) individuals were roughly equal in standing and power. When one individual acted on behalf of another within a social network it was because of friendship, family obligation or common outlook. Hamilton identifies the favours which 'gentlemen' undertook simply from a sense that: 'Gentlemen did such things for each other; indeed, they did them frequently.'[8] Such favours could include individuals giving friends access to their more influential connections; or providing a base from which to conduct a campaign (for example, a London-based woman lobbying the Colonial Office on behalf of her brother in a distant colony). Asymmetric relationships were those where one individual was subordinate to the other. Examples of asymmetric relationships include those between a high-ranking officer and his former aide-de-camp, or between a metropolitan civil servant and a colonial recipient of his patronage. While subordinate parties hoped to benefit in terms of political, social or professional advancement, patrons aimed to both 'maintain and elevate their station and . . . maintain the appropriate social order'.[9]

Not all individuals within a network carried the same weight: not only in the sense of asymmetric relationships; but also in terms of the number and strength of their connections. Thomas Fowell Buxton, for example, the parliamentary anti-slavery campaigner and co-founder of the Aborigines

Protection Society, had many contacts in British colonies, among missionaries, church leaders, scientists and administrators, as well as a broad range of connections – through his family, religion and parliamentary status – in Britain. Buxton therefore was not only a central node in the network of humanitarians, but was also able to integrate this network with several others. Sir Herbert Taylor, private secretary to two kings, aide-de-camp to the commander-in-chief, military secretary at the Horse Guards, and adjutant-general, was likewise exceptionally well-connected within military networks. As will be seen, for an individual who hoped to influence the mechanisms of colonial government, some sort of connection with the Duke of Wellington, or Robert Hay, the permanent under-secretary of the Colonial Office, was particularly valuable.

Of the networks that affected colonial governance in the mid-nineteenth century, some, like those connecting veterans of the 1808–14 Peninsular campaign, university and school alumni, or extended families, were created independently of the empire, and were closed, in the sense that previously unconnected individuals could not become part of them (except by marriage, or birth). A second class comprised networks connected with the business of imperialism itself: networks of missionaries, merchants, or colonial administrators (informal legal, ecclesiastical and administrative professional networks also existed), which developed with circumstance and colonial posting. A final category was the most accessible to outsiders. These networks depended on shared concerns, as much as profession or position. Growing networks of amateur scientific collectors, naturalists, and ethnographers belong in this category, as do the networks of individuals who provided (often, at least initially, unsolicited) information on colonial circumstances and societies to the Colonial Office. As will be shown below, determined individuals could quite easily connect into these networks, by becoming providers of specimens or information.

How a network was maintained depended partly on which of these three categories it fell into. Connections formed in the Peninsular Wars simply existed, although, unsurprisingly, they were generally accorded more weight by those subordinate in any relationship. While veterans maintained many close friendships through the frequent exchange of letters, it is not uncommon to find letters asking for a favour, or passing on information, written after twenty years' silence. Family connections operated in a similar way. On the other hand, networks built on the transmission of information – whether scientific or political – required more frequent maintenance. Letters were exchanged on a regular basis, and appearances in London by colonial-based individuals also entailed a concerted series of personal meetings. The expansion and cultivation of useful connections, as will be seen throughout this book, was a business taken seriously and pursued avidly by all involved.

The centrality of London

The networks which had most influence in colonial governance transmitted information, position and power via well-developed links to high-profile individuals in Britain, and particularly London. Contemporaries who sought to employ networks without such links were well aware of the disadvantages they faced. Imperial networks could not function without their colonial members, who provided information and local patronage; but their links to Britain were critical. Despite the extreme distance and isolation of the colonies – and the latitude this sometimes allowed – colonial governance in the period up to 1845 was characterised by imperial appointments and metropolitan centrality.

This investigation underlines the importance of Britain, and particularly London, as a hub of imperial activity and imagination. Historians have been right to emphasise the flow of ideas, attitudes and personnel not merely out to the colonies, but also back to the metropolis, and this book provides much evidence that supports such arguments. But in matters of colonial governance, Britain was central, if not always dominant. Among the circles who governed the empire, Britain was not a land abandoned, out of reach, or forgotten. While many officials hoped to make their fortune in the colonies, they generally intended to return to Britain after a period of service (at least in this era before more senior appointments were made from within colonial society). Governors remained peripatetic: their terms were officially limited to six years in the early 1830s, with the express intention of keeping them 'disinterested'.[10] Between 1815 and 1845, then, the majority of elite colonial civil servants kept Britain firmly in mind, not just as a mental touchstone, but as the society to which they would, ultimately, return. And, as the words of the Xhosa, Dyani Tshatshu, at the beginning of this book demonstrate, this perception of metropolitan centrality was not confined to expatriate Britons.

Other facets of colonial societies in this period contributed to the importance of Britain. Metropolitan newspapers were keenly awaited and often the news they carried to Sydney or Cape Town was then reprinted in the colonial press, despite being months old.[11] Finance and trade, although growing rapidly as both the Cape and New South Wales developed their own colonial markets, were still heavily tied to Britain. Keegan has demonstrated, for example, that much Cape trade was dominated until the end of the 1830s by London merchants who sent their brothers and sons to establish branches in Cape Town. These Cape firms in turn placed junior agents in the Eastern Cape, as the economy there grew.[12]

The development of commercial banking in both the Cape Colony and New South Wales also demonstrates the multiple links connecting London and the colonies. In the Cape protracted attempts to establish a private commercial bank from the mid-1820s onwards were conducted largely by John Ebden in the Cape Town Commercial Exchange, in collaboration with the London-based Cape of Good Hope Trade Society. Ebden had first lobbied the metropolitan Colonial Office on the subject in 1825; while the Trade Society's chairman, Abraham Borradaile, lobbied the metropolitan government consistently during the 1830s, assisted by an Eastern Cape settler, Thomas Philipps. Philipps also advocated banking facilities for Grahamstown and the Eastern Cape when he came to London to present a petition to parliament in 1834. The Cape of Good Hope Bank finally opened in 1837, with capital raised from the sale of fifteen hundred shares: only three hundred of which were reserved for sale in Great Britain.[13] The British government's earlier reluctance to allow a group of London-based merchants to establish a chain of banks in the Cape and New South Wales perhaps indicates their concern not to create any trans-colonial rival to the imperial government.[14] Certainly, the secretary of state advised Edward Barnard, one of the government-appointed joint colonial agents in London, that he could not also act as a director of the banking group.[15]

In the Australian colonies, the first private trading bank had been established in 1817; and several operated by the late 1820s.[16] The history of the Hobart-based Derwent Bank displays the close involvement of local officials in colonial financial structures. Several officials held important positions in this private bank, including William Swanston and W. H. Hamilton. John Montagu, the colonial secretary, undertook bank business while on home leave in London during 1839.[17] As with other early colonial banks, the Derwent was underwritten by a London bank, and employed London agents to honour bills and make metropolitan arrangements. As New South Wales experienced a brief boom in the 1830s, metropolitan groups became interested in investing in the colony through British-run banks. Imperial banks that started at this time all but overtook the smaller colonial enterprises, and indeed took over several, including the Cornwall Bank at Port Phillip. The vast majority of shares in these banks were reserved for metropolitan investors, and their structure gave only very limited control to the local colonial management.[18]

As most financial transactions were more secure if conducted in London, it was difficult for colonial residents to remain in control of their personal affairs. The requirement that colonial treasurers and other colonial financial officers provide personal security in London for government funds also created difficulties. Campbell Riddell, for example, appointed treasurer of New South Wales while en route to Ceylon, had to rely on his Edinburgh-based brother to cobble together his security. When another relative withdrew his financial support in 1831 Riddell was forced to contemplate returning to Britain: only extensive three way correspondence between the Riddell brothers and Robert Hay (their connection at the Colonial Office) meant this was avoided.[19] It was not uncommon for colonial officials to cite financial matters as a reason for their need to return to London on leave, especially where a family estate had to be divided up; Henry Somerset took leave from the Cape on this basis in 1832.

Colonial elites also believed that the business of marriage was best conducted in Britain. In this period, marriage settlements were often complex, and involved lengthy negotiations.[20] Official elites particularly were unimpressed by the marital opportunities available to them in the colonial sphere; they hoped for better prospects in Britain. When colonial officials did marry in New South Wales or the Cape Colony, the match was likely to be made with the daughter of another colonial official or army officer. Dudley Perceval, for example, fourth son of the assassinated prime minister, and clerk to the councils at the Cape, married Acting Governor Bourke's daughter, Mary Jane, in 1827; while Edward Deas Thomson, clerk to the councils in New South Wales (and later colonial secretary), married another Bourke daughter, Anne, in 1833. Alexander McLeay, the colonial secretary of New South Wales, married off his daughters to various colonial public servants; while John Montagu, colonial secretary in Van Diemen's Land, took the precaution of marrying the governor's niece before he left London. Colonial officials were more likely to marry the daughters of such settler families in the Cape Colony than in New South Wales; presumably because there were more well-established families, and there was less fear of the convict 'stain'.[21] Henry Dumaresq, Governor Darling's brother-in-law and private secretary, returned to England from New South Wales in 1829 to make a good marriage to Miss Sophy Butler Danvers. Although some of Danvers' connections were concerned at her consequent 'banishment' to New South Wales, they did what they could to make her life there comfortable, recommending to the metropolitan authorities the employment of her brother, Henry Butler Danvers, in the colony, and the promotion of Colonel Dumaresq.[22]

For those families who could afford it, and bear the separation, education was another tie between Britain and the colonies. John Montagu told Governor Franklin that he wanted to take metropolitan leave from Tasmania to arrange his sons' education.[23] The Macarthur family sent their sons back to Britain from New South Wales for years at a time. The son of Governor Bourke returned to London from New South Wales to read for the Bar in 1834. Other officials left their children behind in Britain when they left. A British education, as well as being regarded as superior to that available in the colonies, was also a sound means of networking, as is shown for the Macarthur family in chapter six.

Aside from the tangible links between colonial and metropolitan life described here, there was the equally important matter of perception. Both those inside and outside colonial government understood that influence operated in Britain, and in particular in London, with respect to almost all aspects of life. Scientific correspondence, for example, is littered with references to a desire to be in London over any provincial or colonial city, because it was so clearly believed to be the centre of intellectual activity, despite the considerable contributions made elsewhere. In politics the perception of metropolitan centrality was overwhelming, particularly for colonial elites, and especially when events and policies were not moving favourably. The small scale of politics in this period meant that a great deal of emphasis was placed on personal contact: even when complainants – officials or not – were unable to go to London to make their case, they hoped to, and felt the opportunity would make a positive difference to their cause.[24] Metropolitan patrons and friends were jealously guarded, for present or future use. When the parliamentary under-secretary, Robert Wilmot Horton, suggested to New South Wales judge, Francis Forbes, that it would be more appropriate to write to a different Colonial Office official on Australian affairs, Forbes assured him that 'officially, I will certainly',

> but in writing to you, it is as to a friend, in whose confidence I may trust, on whose liberal allowance I may always rely, who knows me personally, knows my manner of thinking and habit of expressing myself . . . and therefore I must continue to write to you, assuming that you will use your discretion as to any information and opinions I may convey to you.[25]

A decade later, when a relative of Glenelg, the secretary of state was given the position of sheriff in Van Diemen's Land, the governor quickly assessed how this relationship might be useful: 'he will if properly directed help us at home with Lord Glenelg and Mr Stephen [at the Colonial Office] as to our views'.[26]

Such perceptions of London as the fulcrum of imperial life, combined with the material connections described earlier, led to considerable traffic – both of letters and people – between London and the colonies. The mechanics of letter transmission are highlighted by a continual stream of official correspondence regarding postage, and the length of time it took for a letter to be answered. Colonial officials' use and abuse of the privilege of sending mail in government bags was the subject of numerous circulars and specific despatches over the period.[27] In Britain, the Colonial Office staff were often asked to send personal letters to colonial correspondents under the office stamp. Ordinary postage was calculated by weight, leading to letters on wafer thin paper cross-written in a tiny hand on both sides.

In terms of human traffic, apart from anecdotal evidence and the repeated appearance in London of colonial agitators encompassing all areas of policy, like Ebden from the Cape (financial), Lang from New South Wales (religious), and Robinson from Upper Canada (political), it is difficult to judge volume without detailed analysis of shipping records. Official correspondence about leave of absence provides some information about the frequency with which official elites visited Britain. While a small number of senior colonial officials managed to spend almost a greater proportion of their time in London on leave than in their colony, a much larger number made one or two extended trips back to Britain on personal business during their colonial tenure. Unsurprisingly, this was more frequent for those stationed in the Mediterranean and North American colonies than for those in southern Africa, or Australia.[28] Personal letters and official correspondence record that it was typical for an official on leave in Britain to undertake a wide variety of business: not uncommonly dealing with marriage; children's education; personal or corporate finance; the settlement of family legal affairs; waiting at the Colonial Office, or another government department in the hope of promotion or the satisfactory resolution of a dispute; or recuperation from ill health. Absenteeism remained a problem for colonial administrations which struggled to govern (under policies of retrenchment) even when all officials were available. However, with the passing of administrations such as Sir Robert Farquhar's in Mauritius in the early 1820s, it was increasingly unacceptable for an official to remain absent for long periods.[29]

Perhaps the single most important network for this study of colonial governance was the web of connections developed by Robert Hay, permanent under-secretary at the Colonial Office, between 1825 and 1836. Hay, a civil servant in the Admiralty during the French wars, drew on his existing political, administrative and social connections, and encouraged numerous colonial officials, governors and settlers to correspond with him on colonial affairs. The significance of his network is examined in subsequent chapters, while here three of the other most extensive and important networks – the Peninsular, the humanitarian and the scientific – are introduced. Other professional, family and political networks had a significant influence on colonial governance as well, and are considered (more superficially) during the rest of the book. Of the professional networks which are not examined in detail, the legal and ecclesiastical particularly deserve greater scholarly attention.

The Peninsular network

Established independently from concerns about colonial governance, the Peninsular network expanded through the entire British Empire with many links between and within colonies, as well as connections back to the heart of military power at Horse Guards Parade in London. As defined here, the network connected veterans of the campaigns in the Iberian Peninsula, the Battle of Waterloo, and those who enjoyed a personal association with the Duke of Wellington. While there were also important bonds between military veterans and personnel more broadly, the Peninsular network was particularly strong in the period 1815 to 1845. It connected a large number of colonial governors and senior officials to some of the most influential men in Britain, not only in the military command, but also in successive governments, parliament, the aristocracy and the royal court.[30] The network mediated patronage, transmitted information, influenced policy and maintained a sense of comradeship. There was a visible veterans' presence in British colonies, with frequent reunions and 'viceregal and mess dinners enlivened by a constant reliving of every moment and aspect of the campaign'.[31] Common bonds of military service could transcend even considerable political differences.[32] Contemporary perceptions of the network, especially those recorded by outsiders, accorded it considerable power. A senior colonial officer, educated at the Royal Military College, and a veteran of the Indian wars, but not the Peninsular campaign or Waterloo, expressed his frustration at lack of promotion in the following terms:

> I am unfortunately not one of those, coming under the happy circumstances of either being one of Lord Fitzroy's personal friends, or one of the still more fortunate soldiers of the Duke's Army. Still the duties of the service which deprived me either of the favor of the one, or the fame and honor of the other, ought surely not to be visited upon one as a crime.[33]

The Peninsular network was very hierarchical: those individuals important to the network who were based in London formed a military elite with access to the highest political and royal spheres; while those in the empire fell into two broad categories: an administrative and military elite – at the level of colonial commander-in-chief, governor and their immediate subordinates – and a lower level composed of career soldiers, or those who had transferred to more junior positions in colonial administrations or police forces. The elite are the subjects of this study, as it was this group, acting as both recipients and distributors of information and patronage, who most affected colonial governance.

In London, the Peninsular network extended most noticeably through the upper echelons of the military establishment, but also into political and royal circles. At the Horse Guards, where command of all army personnel (except the Royal Artillery and Royal Engineers) was exercised, almost every important individual was a Peninsular veteran, a situation which continued until the Crimean War. Wellington, without doubt the most influential military figure until 1850, was commander-in-chief in 1827–28, and again from 1842 to 1852. Lord Hill, commander-in-chief between 1828 and 1842, was described as a 'political naïf'. He frequently sought Wellington's advice; Wellington also exerted influence in this period through his former aide-de-camp, Lord Fitzroy Somerset, who stayed on as military secretary (dealing particularly with appointments and promotions) to Hill when Wellington became prime minister in 1828.[34] Other Peninsular veterans filled the remaining important positions at the Horse Guards and at the ordnance.[35] The master-general of the ordnance held a cabinet seat and thus exerted influence in both military and political affairs. Peninsular veterans who occupied this position included Wellington, Sir Hussey Vivian, Sir Henry Hardinge and Sir James Kempt.

Besides the master-general of the ordnance's cabinet position, it was not uncommon for high-ranking military personnel to be members of the government. While the most important example was Wellington himself, Hardinge, Sir George Murray, the Duke of Richmond and the Marquis of Conyngham all held cabinet positions in the 1820s and 1830s. While aristocrats like Richmond and Conyngham often acquired their military roles as a result of their social position, they nevertheless created connections important to this study. The Peninsular network extended to the royal family with links through Sir Herbert Taylor, an intimate of three kings, and Sir Andrew Barnard, George IV's equerry.[36] While parliament controlled the army's finances, the crown commanded the army more directly, thus giving the upper echelons of the army establishment direct and privileged access to the monarch.

In the metropolis, colonial networks provided not only a way of rewarding comrades, but also a means of exerting authority. For decades after the Napoleonic Wars, seventy-five per cent of the British infantry was stationed overseas.[37] The Horse guards wanted as much influence as possible over the colonies where troops were stationed, including, if possible, either a commander-in-chief who was also governor, or a governor with a military background. Historians have not examined the military's desire for imperial control sufficiently; as Hew Strachan has observed, although the empire was the 'most consistent and most continuous influence in shaping the army as an institution' it nevertheless 'gets forgotten' in most British military history.[38] While it is a commonplace that a succession of Cape governors were Peninsular veterans, the extent to which veterans were involved in the governance of other colonies and the close links they maintained among themselves are less well documented. By taking samples spread around the mid-century, historians have underestimated the proportion of earlier governors with a military background. A survey of eighty-two governors who served between 1820 and 1845 found that military or naval service played a significant role in their post-services career for fifty-seven men, a lesser role for twelve, while only thirteen had no military or naval background.[39]

At the level of the colonial elite, veterans often held military and administrative positions in a sequence of colonies (and sometimes domestic military bases) culminating perhaps in a governorship combining the positions of civil governor and commander-in-chief. It was most common to move, as Lieutenant-Colonel John Bell did in the Cape Colony, from the army to the civil administration, although there were others, like his superior, Major-General Sir Benjamin D'Urban, who finished a career which included the governorships of Antigua, British Guiana, and the Cape Colony, as commander of the forces in Canada. A majority of the smaller British colonies in the 1820s and 1830s had military governors and, even in larger colonies, it was thought expedient to combine the roles of governor and commander-in-chief. In this era of administrative amateurism, it was regarded as much more important for a governor to have military expertise and rank than civilian qualifications, even in the settler colonies. Struck hard by the reduction in employment after the Napoleonic Wars, and accustomed to the difficulties of life beyond Britain (particularly in terms of climate, isolation, and interaction with non-European peoples), soldiers were more likely both to seek and to accept colonial appointment. A typical early post would be in one of the West Indian crown colonies, the smaller Mediterranean islands or Mauritius; while success in these colonies, or a higher initial profile, might secure a governorship (or military command) in North America, India, Australia or southern Africa. A list of only those Peninsular veterans who governed the Cape Colony or New South Wales includes Thomas Brisbane, Ralph Darling, Richard Bourke, George Gipps, Rufane Donkin, Galbraith Lowry Cole, Benjamin D'Urban, George Napier, Peregrine Maitland, George Cathcart and Harry Smith.

A typical member of this cohort of senior colonial veterans was born between 1775 and 1785, served in the Iberian Peninsula as a young officer (probably in an infantry regiment with periods on loan to the central peninsular staff), received several rapid promotions and came into personal contact with the Duke of Wellington and others in the military elite. This contact took a variety of forms: the performance of a special task which required proficiency in Spanish or Portuguese; a particular instance of courage on the battlefield; or a period as aide-de-camp to Wellington, the Prince Regent or Sir John Moore. The type of contact did not matter much – as long as it was sufficient to fix a favourable impression in the minds of those who went on to wield power in the post-war army. Many of those who proceeded to significant colonial careers came from middle-class professional backgrounds, rather than from the landed gentry: they were the sons of career soldiers, clergymen and doctors.

Ralph Darling provides a good example. The son of a non-commissioned officer stationed in Grenada, Darling used the connections he made as military secretary to three successive commanders of the West Indies to build a military career that interspersed staff appointments in London (giving him administrative experience and connections) with periods of active service in India and the Iberian Peninsula under Sir John Moore. He became a protégé of the Duke of York while serving as deputy adjutant-general of the

Horse Guards between 1810 and 1818, and cemented connections with Sir Henry Torrens (York's private secretary), Sir Henry Calvert and Sir John Macdonald.[40] Darling would go on to be acting governor of Mauritius and governor of New South Wales. Like many others, from unremarkable beginnings and with no military education (at this time compulsory only for engineers and artillery officers), he rose much higher than his father.

To those in colonial administrations, the Peninsular network was perceived as a considerable source of patronage and inside information, as well as a means of applying pressure to the metropolitan government. While colonial administrations suffered the same frustrations of time, distance, obfuscation and inconsistency whether dealing officially with the Horse Guards or the Colonial Office, Peninsular veterans nevertheless believed that their cases would be viewed more sympathetically at the Horse Guards than at the Colonial Office. Networks based on shared military experience also promised the chance to encounter others with similar experiences, mores and outlook.

Patronage, in the form of gaining offices and promotions, was the first and most unambiguous manifestation of the Peninsular network's power. While few civil colonial offices were in the gift of the Horse Guards, patrons of the standing of Wellington, for example, moved a protégé to the top of the Colonial Office's list – whether the incumbent government was Whig or Tory. There is considerable anecdotal evidence that Wellington and other powerful military figures secured colonial positions, including governorships, for their protégés.[41] It must be noted, however, that perceptions of influence were probably stronger than the employment of influence itself. A powerful patron like Wellington had to be careful not to dissipate the impact of his patronage by spreading his influence too thinly; or to waste influence which might later be employed for metropolitan political purposes. Nevertheless, many successful colonial candidates can be linked closely to Wellington, although they are often also linked to at least one other influential Horse Guards figure.

Benjamin D'Urban was one officer who benefited from Wellington's favour. Having entered the army as a cornet at the start of the Peninsular campaign he achieved rapid promotion through a number of staff appointments. He was Lord Beresford's quartermaster-general, and through that role had contact with not only Wellington, but also other figures of post-war importance. Sir Henry Hardinge, for example, was for a time D'Urban's immediate subordinate; while D'Urban also conducted a 'lengthy correspondence' with Sir Herbert Taylor, future secretary to the king.[42] After an appointment at the Horse Guards, D'Urban was appointed governor of Antigua in 1820. His appointment to the Cape Colony in 1833 had more to do with his experience administering a slave colony than his military connections, but during his controversial governorship he remained in private contact with Hardinge, Taylor and Sir Willoughby Gordon; all of whom, like Wellington, supported him in London.[43] Dismissed in 1837 by the Colonial Office, D'Urban was rehabilitated ten years later when Wellington appointed him to the command of the Canadian forces.[44]

But, as D'Urban would discover, while the network of Peninsular patronage was highly influential in securing advancement for senior colonial officials (in itself a considerable influence on colonial governance given the status of the individuals involved) its direct influence on colonial policy and action was less certain. This type of influence was manifested in several ways: first, the ability to change, or modify, the government position in response to calls from the network's colonial members; second, the manipulation of military policy emanating from the Horse Guards or the secretary of state for war; and finally, the provision and transmission of information between colony and metropole. While the mediation of patronage and the transmission of information were matters which fell comfortably within the remit of the links of friendship and loyalty forged between former comrades, the exertion of sustained and significant pressure on non-military matters, or even on military matters, put more at risk. In fact, the manipulation of the Peninsular network for such purposes by colonial elites was more illusory than concrete.

The D'Urban administration's attempts to place pressure on the Colonial Office through the Horse Guards in the mid-1830s demonstrated a strong faith in military links to London – to Wellington and Lord Fitzroy Somerset.[45] This faith, however, was based on earlier assistance in less awkward circumstances. During the period 1835 to 1837, Governor D'Urban struggled against the Colonial Office to be allocated more troops and to have his annexation of Xhosa territory ('Queen Adelaide Province') approved. As chapter four demonstrates, despite substantial private communications with London, and the despatch of two personal envoys, D'Urban's expectations of support from the Peninsular network exceeded reality. Any pressure that was applied by the metropolitan military authorities – and there is little evidence of it – failed to alter the cabinet and Colonial Office decision to abandon Queen Adelaide Province and to demand the immediate return of the extra regiment D'Urban had retained at the Cape. Indeed, the only opposition to the metropolitan government's policy came from the crown: the ailing William IV was lobbied by his private secretary, Sir Herbert Taylor, on D'Urban's behalf. But without support from the military establishment, even this royal support could only serve to make Colonial Office despatches ambiguous, delaying the renunciation of Queen Adelaide Province by a few months. In 1837, following a D'Urban despatch which even Taylor described as 'very violent and offensive', the governor was dismissed.[46]

The Horse Guards' failure to support D'Urban in practice, despite their apparent support in principle, can partly be explained by the character and actions of D'Urban and his envoys, and is examined in more detail in chapter four. Another factor which may have influenced the military administration was the concurrent Royal Commission run by Viscount Howick, the secretary of state at war, which was investigating the military bureaucracy and its administration.[47] Hoping to retain as much power as possible at Horse Guards Parade, the military hierarchy judged it not in its interest to stir up any controversy. The possibility that the Horse Guards did not support D'Urban because of metropolitan concerns, while difficult to gauge accurately, is important.

That the Peninsular network's greatest success lay in influencing patronage reflects its closed nature, and foundations separate from the empire. While gentlemen and officers would go to great lengths for one another, they were bound by the past rather than by hopes for the future, unlike the next network under consideration.

The humanitarian network

More than either the peninsular or the scientific networks, the broadly defined 'humanitarian' or 'philanthropic' network tended to operate outside metropolitan and colonial government. While the term 'humanitarian' is contested, and the motives of humanitarians questioned by historians, there is no question that networks of individuals were formed on the basis of connections made through religious movements and the anti-slavery campaign.[48] While individuals' motivations differed, the connections formed between them, and the way in which they were used, are more important for this investigation.

Including many individuals outside government and the traditional spheres influencing government, the humanitarian network was not particularly important in terms of patronage to government offices. (Although, that said, in every year between 1807 and 1830 either or both the chairman and deputy chairman of the East India Company's Board of Directors was an evangelical.[49]) Instead this network was more consciously operated by those in the metropolis in order to influence colonial governance. This manipulation is examined in detail in chapter six, while this chapter concentrates on the network's construction.

In London, the years of anti-slavery campaigning created an elite who were adept in the techniques of lobbying metropolitan government and manipulating the relatively new phenomenon (in its modern sense) of 'public opinion'. Within the House of Commons a clearly defined group of evangelical politicians, 'the Saints', emerged in the early nineteenth century. Although the Saints did not vote together on all, or even most, issues, historians have discovered important bonds between them on certain issues, and also that those beyond the group, both in and out of parliament, perceived them as an important and powerful lobby.

Thomas Fowell Buxton, brewer and graduate of Trinity College, Dublin, was the parliamentary leader of the anti-slavery movement and the 'Saints' after William Wilberforce. A well-connected evangelical Anglican, Buxton held the seat of Weymouth between 1818 and 1837, starting his public career as a philanthropist by advocating prison reform, education and relief for the distressed inhabitants of Spitalfields. In the early 1820s he became interested in the anti-slavery campaign and the progress of the colony of Sierra Leone. Wilberforce asked him to succeed to the parliamentary management of the anti-slavery lobby in 1823. During this decade Buxton also lobbied on the rights of indigenous inhabitants of the Cape Colony; in the 1830s he expanded his interests to include the civilisation and protection of indigenous people throughout the British Empire. This interest led to his part in the formation of the Aborigines Protection Society; his management of the 1835–37 Select Committee on Aborigines; and his promotion of the Niger expedition of 1841 via the African Civilization Society. The connections that Buxton formed in all these activities, combined with others arising from family, business and religion, made him a linchpin of the humanitarian network in this period. In his life beyond the sphere of parliamentary politics, Buxton was an avid supporter of both bible and missionary societies, and a director of the officially non-denominational, although essentially Congregationalist, London Missionary Society (LMS).

In the early 1830s, as Richard Brent has demonstrated, Buxton's parliamentary influence extended beyond his obvious allies and outweighed his lack of government office.[50] Both Whigs and Tories perceived that, although an Anglican, Buxton influenced a significant section of non-conformist opinion. He was also well-connected personally to a wide range of influential businessmen, politicians and church leaders. Having married Hannah Gurney in 1807, Buxton's brothers-in-law included the wealthy Quaker brothers Sam and Joseph John Gurney, and also Samuel Hoare; while one of his sisters-in-law was Elizabeth Fry. Dr Stephen Lushington (the eminent anti-slavery lawyer); Thomas Denman (a future chief justice); Lord Suffield; and Thomas Spring Rice (later Baron Monteagle) were others among Buxton's influential supporters.[51] As the 'heir to the Clapham Sect leadership', Buxton had important evangelical contacts including Zachary Macaulay, James Stephen senior, Charles Grant senior, Daniel Wilson (Bishop of Calcutta) and Wilberforce. Buxton's contact through this network with James Stephen junior and Charles Grant junior (who became Lord Glenelg in 1835) also gave him personal connections inside the 1830s' Colonial Office. Throughout the British colonies Buxton had correspondents and friends – clergy, missionaries, administrators and humanitarian settlers – who provided valuable information for his various metropolitan campaigns.

Missionary society headquarters were also based in Britain. Most British societies – the Church Missionary Society (CMS), the LMS, the Wesleyan

Methodist Missionary Society (WMMS) and the Baptist Missionary Society
– were centred in London by this period, although the Glasgow Missionary
Society was also influential in the Cape Colony. The missionary societies'
structures provided ready-made imperial networks. In London, each had a
director and a few full-time staff, usually at least a foreign and a home
secretary, who co-ordinated the society's efforts.[52] The religious press
surrounding the societies connected missionaries to their metropolitan
supporters, while the annual meetings at Exeter Hall generated camaraderie.
As well as individual societies' annual reports, the *Missionary Register*
reported on all Anglican missionary and bible societies.[53] The societies had
varying levels of contact with the metropolitan government: they lobbied
continually on matters of missionary access; but only periodically on issues
such as the treatment of indigenous people and the expansion of colonial
churches. Most were concerned to portray society activities as non-political
and non-partisan, meaning that sustained political campaigns were rare.
Such lobbying depended on either the passions of a particular mission staff
member in London, or a colonial issue achieving widespread metropolitan
attention, as with anti-slavery. The rivalry between missionary societies
also undermined their metropolitan political impact, although there were
counter-examples, such as the 1830s collaboration of the metropolitan-
based staff of the LMS, WMMS and CMS during the Select Committee on
Aborigines. Although their Cape-based missionaries disagreed, the
metropolitan secretaries gave joint evidence to the select committee.[54]

Depending on the size of their various colonial establishments, the
missionary societies sometimes employed colonial directors or
superintendents to oversee a colony's missionaries. Such individuals provided
an important colonial focus for the humanitarian network, connecting
almost all the members in a colony at only one or two removes. In the Cape
Colony, the Reverend Dr John Philip performed this role for the LMS from
1819. Aside from co-ordinating the efforts of LMS missionaries in southern
Africa, Philip also kept track of LMS funds, reported back to the London
authorities, and liaised with the colonial administration and influential
colonists. Philip took particular interest in cultivating useful contacts, such
as Governor Benjamin D'Urban; Eastern Cape administrator, Andries
Stockenström; and the commissioners of Eastern Inquiry, Colonel William
Colebrooke and J. T. Bigge.[55] When Philip's daughter married John Fairbairn,
the editor of the *South African Commercial Advertiser*, Philip cemented
an already strong relationship with a powerful although controversial Cape
figure. The LMS's missionaries were spread throughout the Cape Colony,
so Philip regularly travelled to the mission stations and kept up an extensive
correspondence with them at other times.[56] Through LMS missionaries
like James Read and James Kitchingman, and the Glasgow Missionary
Society's John Ross, Philip had access to the views of indigenous people.

These provided a powerful source for metropolitan humanitarians who used the 'indigenous voice' to considerable effect in metropolitan publicity campaigns. Philip also travelled back to London to lobby on behalf of the Cape's Khoi and Xhosa populations, there making contact with influential evangelicals and humanitarians he thought likely to support his campaigns. As the LMS authorities were extremely cautious about open interference in 'politics', Philip's link with Thomas Buxton, and the latter's belief in the effectiveness of political campaigning on humanitarian issues, proved critical to the network as it affected the Cape. During the 1830s, when the condition of indigenous peoples came to the fore in metropolitan politics, the Buxton connection enabled John Philip to feed useful information from his network of colonial contacts, missionaries and sympathisers to the heart of metropolitan politics.

Philip was also part of a much broader missionary and humanitarian network which extended across the world and particularly to America. Although this wider network was of less explicit relevance to colonial governance, it was important to the ending of slavery, while the consciousness of a large supportive movement provided individuals like Philip with confidence and purpose.[57] Unlike the other networks examined in this chapter, the humanitarian network included many women. John Philip's wife, Jane, for example, effectively ran the LMS in the Cape while Philip returned to London during 1836 and 1837, and she was always responsible for the accounts.[58] As missionaries were often married couples, this pattern was repeated across the globe. The women in the extended Buxton family were also great colonial correspondents, metropolitan collators of information, and co-ordinators of philanthropic campaigns.[59]

This network connected the far colonial extremities to the secretary of state in the Colonial Office. Unlike the Peninsular network, its currency was more frequently information than patronage. In this sphere it was sometimes pre-eminent, outshining government mechanisms for information transmission during the 1830s. The concern of religious members of the humanitarian network about the nature of their involvement in politics, and even whether they should be involved in political questions at all, also marks out the network from its contemporaries. This concern is particularly apparent in the records of the missionary societies, but also appears in private correspondence between individuals, and can be seen at a variety of levels – from discussions over the stage at which public opinion should be employed on an issue (rather than private connections with powerful individuals) to the need for truly 'religious' individuals to renounce the world completely. A great number of religious humanitarians did choose to engage with the world, and to pass on information on colonial matters, and they form the basis of the network examined here.

Scientific networks

While membership of a military or humanitarian network was based on vocation and experience, membership of the expanding scientific networks was both more accessible and more intangible. As scientific outlook and organisation developed in the nineteenth century, the empire became both a focus for scientific endeavour and a ground for scientific patronage. While the connections which emerged (often carefully cultivated) to form an imperial scientific network differed from the other networks considered here, they too affected colonial governance: through patronage; the transmission of information; and their impact on perceptions of empire and colonies.

Two late eighteenth- and early nineteenth-century trends in science formed a backdrop to the creation of these networks. First, the growth of interest in the taxonomic branches of botanical, zoological and geographical sciences both fuelled and was fuelled by exploration and imperial acquisition.[60] Scientists in Britain needed data from the empire, if only to establish their own scientific niche. While many of the big contemporary names – Joseph Hooker, Charles Darwin, Joseph Banks, John Herschel and Thomas Huxley, for example – had themselves collected early in their careers, they relied on others to collect for them as they became established. Thomas Mitchell, the New South Wales surveyor-general, was one colonist who routinely sent botanical, zoological and geological samples back to Britain. Mitchell sent his seed collections to his friend Professor John Lindley, professor of botany at University College, London and assistant secretary of the Horticultural Society; Lindley in turn forwarded samples to the professional and amateur scientific elites. During 1837 Lindley received thanks for Mitchell's seeds from John Henslow, professor of botany at Cambridge, who promised to place Mitchell's seeds in the hands of the curator of the Botanical Gardens 'immediately'; from the sixth Duke of Devonshire, who assured Lindley that he had never seen his gardener, Joseph Paxton, 'more interested and gratified' than on receiving Mitchell's 'most valuable' seeds; and from William Hooker, who offered his thanks both to 'Major Mitchell for an interesting collection of seeds from the interior of New Holland' and 'to Dr Lindley for his kindness in forwarding them'. Hooker's seeds were destined for the Glasgow Botanical Gardens.[61]

The second trend involved changes in the practice of science. Alongside the landed patrons of former times, government sponsorship and the professionalisation of science led to the increased importance of scientists themselves and the burgeoning scientific societies as patrons. The Royal Geographical Society (RGS), for example, the premier promoter of British scientific exploration for much of the century, was founded in 1830. Among the RGS's founders were John Barrow, second secretary at the Admiralty for forty years, and John Murray, the leading publisher of explorers' journals.

The practice of sending naturalists with naval survey ships provided one avenue of nineteenth-century patronage, another was the various imperial survey projects. Individuals like Sir William Hooker, director of Kew Gardens, possessed considerable patronage when it came to the appointment of government botanists and directors of the nascent colonial botanical gardens. In the colonies, as in Britain, many colonial administrators had an amateur interest in science, and some were members of metropolitan scientific societies. In New South Wales, for example, both Alexander McLeay, colonial secretary (1826–36) and his successor, Edward Deas Thomson, were members of the Linnean Society. McLeay had devoted a substantial portion of the eight years he spent in retirement before moving to New South Wales studying entomology, and counted William Hooker and Sir Edward James Smith, president of the Linnean Society, among his friends.[62]

The combination of the need for imperial empirical data and the metropolitan elevation and professionalisation of 'science' thus created pivotal metropolitan members of an imperial scientific network, who believed they co-ordinated an imperial project.[63] For finance and support they drew on government and the scientific societies; a task that was made easier by the overlap of personnel between government and scientific society.

Gentlemen scientists within government were a powerful aid to imperial science. Government support for the imperial endeavours required to collect scientific data – ranging from Admiralty sponsorship of hydrographic surveys to the Colonial Office's willingness to promote the collection policy of the British Museum – was fostered by the amateur scientific interest of senior civil servants. Barrow at the Admiralty, and Robert Hay at the Colonial Office (a well-known member of the Linnean and the Royal Geographical Society), provide good examples.[64] Their connections of friendship and interest, with professional scientists like William and Joseph Hooker, and Sir Joseph Banks, encouraged them to use their patronage and influence to extend scientific networks to the colonies, appointing both scientific professionals and administrators with scientific interests. Allan Cunningham and William Harvey were such beneficiaries. Cunningham, a protégé of Banks, was a Kew Gardens' collector, and joined several expeditions to New South Wales' interior. He was offered the directorship of Sydney's botanical gardens in 1832, but declined in favour of his brother Richard.[65] Harvey, an Irish botanist from a poor background, was appointed treasurer of the Cape Colony (1836–41) through Hooker's connections; there he collected and collated important data on the flora of the region.[66]

Scientific networks were extended by contact between amateur colonial naturalists and visiting scientific professionals – on naval survey ships or terrestrial expeditions. Charles Darwin, Joseph Hooker and Thomas Huxley continued to correspond with the colonial connections they made as members of naval survey crews for many years afterwards. Huxley, for example, was influenced by the ideas of the naturalist William Sharp McLeay, son of New South Wales' colonial secretary. While in Australia, Huxley gave a paper at McLeay's home, 'the best scientific salon in Sydney'.[67] The arctic explorer, Sir John Franklin, knew Philip Parker King, a member of the New South Wales legislative council, from their early careers as naval officers posted in Australian and Brazilian waters.[68] Colonial governors and administrators who were known to be sympathetic to scientific endeavours were frequently approached by letter or in person by metropolitan-based scientists eager for data.[69]

Military connections overlapped with and fostered the scientific networks. With their technical training, veterans of the Peninsula and engineering graduates of the Woolwich academy provided the backbone for colonial surveying and engineering. Both Thomas Mitchell and Charles Michell, surveyors-general of New South Wales and the Cape Colony respectively, were Peninsular veterans, and both had military patrons, scientific contacts and exploratory interests. Many nineteenth-century explorers were military or naval veterans, like Captain James Alexander, who was sponsored by the Colonial Office and the Royal Geographical Society during his mid-1830s' explorations in southern Africa.[70]

The employment of engineers and surveyors was one way in which the scientific network extended into colonial governance. Another was the number of explorers – both maritime and terrestrial – who were appointed as colonial governors. Between 1837 and 1843 Sir John Franklin, the famous (later infamous) naval explorer, was the lieutenant-governor of Van Diemen's Land. His presence there attracted the prolonged and profitable stay of his old colleague, John Ross, on his way to and from Antarctica with the *Erebus* and the *Terror* in 1841. Franklin equipped his colonial secretary, John Montagu, with instructions on scientific patronage, and letters of introduction to scientists (as well as to politicians), when the latter returned to London on leave in 1838. Montagu was to urge the appointment of Dr Hobson as colonial naturalist on the metropolitan government, with the assistance of 'Herschel, Sawinson, Murchison, Buckland, etc'.[71] In 1841, Franklin was able to appoint his nephew Lieutenant Henry Kay – who had been with Ross's expedition – to the Hobart observatory.[72] Apart from Franklin, Edward John Eyre (New Munster and Jamaica), Sir George Grey (South Australia, the Cape Colony and New Zealand), and Charles Joseph La Trobe (Port Phillip) are just some who went on to colonial governance after making their names in exploration. Thomas Mitchell, another explorer, unsuccessfully urged his own promotion to a colonial governorship on the basis of this acknowledged trend.[73]

For ambitious young men making their way in the colonial world, scientific contacts and metropolitan interest in scientific subjects were a means of progress, both scientifically and professionally. Colonial officials therefore consciously tapped into scientific networks. John Walpole Willis, for example, successively a puisne judge in Upper Canada, British Guiana, New South Wales and Port Phillip, attempted to cultivate a connection with Colonial Office under-secretary, Robert Hay; and secure an acquaintance with the Earl of Derby, by taking an interest in botany and zoology – well-known passions of both men. Although Willis admitted he knew 'virtually nothing' about plants, he knew Hay belonged to a 'medico-botanical society' (the Linnean) and he offered to send the permanent under-secretary as many seeds and plants from Georgetown in British Guiana as could be collected. In fact Willis went so far as to employ a German naturalist for the purpose.[74] In 1842 'a box of birdskins' for Derby, were the pretext for one of a sequence of letters from Willis to Derby's son, Lord Stanley, who was secretary of state for the colonies. These put Willis's side of a prolonged and bitter dispute with other Australian colonial officials.[75] Thomas Mitchell managed to combine his personal ambitions with his passion for science and exploration with marginally more subtlety: although it is certain that he revelled in the variety of titled and important individuals to whom his specimens and maps made their way. Apart from his contact with Lindley on horticultural specimens, Mitchell corresponded with Captain John Washington of the RGS and Hydrography division of the Admiralty; Richard Owen at the Royal College of Surgeons; and Ogilvy of the Zoological Society who sent him lists of birds that Lord Derby hoped to acquire.[76] In London in the late 1830s, Mitchell met with Charles Darwin to whom he lent a 'curious stone', and later made enquiries on behalf of Darwin's servant who was emigrating to Australia.[77] In November 1841, Mitchell urged his patron Sir George Murray to make sure the colonial secretary, Lord Stanley, knew that Mitchell's map of Australia was dedicated to him, as he felt that this would encourage Stanley to 'consider my claims favourably'.[78] Mitchell frequently pressed Murray, or his connections at the RGS, to lobby for his promotion, put his side in one of his frequent colonial disputes, or demand that his (already lengthy) periods of leave in London be extended, sometimes citing scientific demands for these claims.[79] Captain James Alexander, whose explorations of southern Africa were interspersed with periods as aide-de-camp to the governor and involvement in conflict in the Eastern Cape, was another who prevailed upon the RGS to help him have his leave (this time from the army) extended.[80]

The bonds between members of the scientific network were relatively loose, except where they involved patronage. Material items such as artefacts and specimens were transmitted across the empire – almost always back to London from the colonial periphery. Patronage, goodwill and money flowed back through the network in response. Other goods travelled both ways, as well as between colonies. Theories came back to the metropolis from the colonies (like William McLeay's influence on the young Huxley), while imperial patrons were able to test their theories through colonial connections. Gossip, as always, travelled in all directions. While the impact of this contact was varied, both scientific and other agendas were furthered. Friendships were fostered, and so too were numerous careers within both science and the colonial administrations.

Conclusion

The networks described in this chapter, and the traffic back and forth between Britain and the colonies, underlie chapters four, five and six, which focus on governance in the colonies of New South Wales and the Cape of Good Hope. By emphasising the importance of personal connections and the trouble to which nineteenth-century colonial residents went to establish them, new light is shed on the operation of imperial and colonial rule. Private correspondence demonstrates that issues of patronage, personal rancour, and financial and psychological insecurity motivated colonial elites to extend and employ their networks, while the information passed through such networks could be critical to colonial governance.

It is worth re-emphasising the extent to which the networks discussed in this book overlapped. Individuals enjoyed, and sought out, a wide range of personal connections during their lives. Sometimes overlaps reinforced networks' strength, making bonds stronger; on other occasions, competing interests, or differing attitudes, undermined networks' efficacy. But throughout the period under consideration, imperial networks remained, above all else, personal. Imperial networks connected people first, and places second. Work since the 1990s, by highlighting the liminal nature of, for example, colonial port cities, has served to obscure this distinction.[81] The final section of this book will return to the question of whether, in the 1840s, the displacement of such personal connections altered the structure of imperial networks.

Notes

1 BP, A1733, pp. 47–8, Richard to Dick Bourke, 26 October 1834.
2 Watts, *Small worlds*; Watts, *Six degrees*; Scott, *Social network analysis*.
3 Lester, *Imperial networks*, pp. 1–8, 197; Ballantyne, *Orientalism and race*, pp. 2–4, 9, 14–16.
4 Watts, *Small worlds*, pp. 4–33, 88, 142–6.
5 *Kitchingman papers*, pp. 136–7, James Read to Kitchingman, 27 May 1834; CO 48/165, fo. 88, James Read to Philip, 9 December 1834.
6 CO 201/251, fo. 529, Lt Gen. John S. Wood to Glenelg, and enclosures, 6 October 1835.
7 Ballantyne, *Orientalism and race*, pp. 1–3, 9.
8 Hamilton, 'Croker', 54.
9 Silberman, *Cages of reason*, p. 311.
10 CO 854/1, fo. 7, précis of circulars, 1 May 1828, 31 May 1828.

11 This also worked in reverse, with the metropolitan newspapers taking much of their colonial news from the settler press, and the colonial newspapers of one colony also picking up stories from other colonies: see Lester, 'British settler discourse', 30–2; McKenzie, *Scandal*, p. 7.

12 Keegan, *Colonial South Africa*, pp. 49–50.

13 Arndt, *Banking and currency*, pp. 197–238; Keegan, *Colonial South Africa*, pp. 163–4.

14 CO 48/163, Committee of Privy Council to Treasury, 16 April 1835, encl. in Treasury to Colonial Office, 20 June 1835, cited in Arndt, *Banking and currency*, p. 221.

15 CO 49/29, fos 180–2, Glenelg to Barnard, 18 March 1836.

16 Kociumbas, *Possessions*, p. 112.

17 Fitzpatrick, *Franklin*, pp. 250–7.

18 Butlin, *Foundations*.

19 CO 323/167, fos 30, 33, C. Riddell to Hay, 11 April 1831, 26 April 1831; *ibid.*, fo. 49, J. Riddell to Hay, 23 July 1831.

20 Vickery, *Gentleman's daughter*, pp. 39–41, 54–5. For a colonial example see Rhodes House Library (Bodleian Library), Afr/t/7/3, fos 36–7, 38, 40, Bourke to Spring Rice, 4 July 1827, 29 July 1827, 6 August 1827; *ibid.*, fos 1–2, Bourke to Coote, 28 April 1826.

21 On Cape fears of being tainted with the convict stain, see McKenzie, *Scandal*, pp. 176–8.

22 CO 323/136, fo. 56, H. Doyle [?] to Hay, 3 February 1829.

23 Fitzpatrick, *Franklin*, p. 207.

24 E.g., ML, A4301, p. 449, F. to W. McLeay, 11 November 1831; ML, A4302, p. 544, F. to W. McLeay, 19 May 1834.

25 ML, A1819, pp. 91–2, Forbes to Horton, private, 6 February 1827.

26 Franklin, *Private correspondence*, i, pp. 85–7, John to Jane Franklin, 17 May 1839, 22 May 1839.

27 E.g., CO 324/105, fos 69, 124, Hay circular, 28 February 1832, Glenelg circular, 15 September 1836.

28 One hundred and one instances of leave of absence are recorded in the précis of CO despatches in the 1830s from the Cape Colony, New South Wales, Ceylon, Van Diemen's Land and the Ionian Islands. Periods of absence were noticeably longer the further a colony was from Britain; and governors only very rarely applied for leave of absence from the Cape, never from Australia, but quite commonly from Canada or the Mediterranean. Colonial governors almost always supported leave for their subordinates, although they frequently discussed the difficulties of finding acting replacements, especially for judges and legal officers. Most correspondence gave no indication of the reason home leave was required, but the most common reason cited (fifteen cases) was ill health. Not infrequently, officers who intended to resign, but could not easily afford the long voyage back to Britain, applied for leave of absence and resigned in London: some governors colluded in this. CO 714/34–7; CO 714/41–2; CO 714/113–14; CO 714/148–9; CO 714/168–9.

29 Farquhar spent almost five years on leave. On the subject of leave, see also CO 201/309, fos 371–2, Stephen to Hope, 12 October 1841, on Gipps to Russell, 29 May 1841.

30 Strachan, *Politics of the British army*, p. 27; Harries-Jenkins, *Army in Victorian society*, ch. 8.

31 Mostert, *Frontiers*, p. 660.

32 E.g., the promotion of the Whig, Richard Bourke, for the position of governor of New South Wales, by Tory colonial secretary, Sir George Murray. See BP, A1738, pp. 55–6, Murray to Bourke, 15 May 1832.

33 BFC, MSS 403/9, pp. 136–8, Cloete to Bourke, 29 September 1837. See also CO 201/251, fo. 529, Wood to Glenelg, 6 October 1835.

34 Strachan, *Wellington's legacy*, pp. 6–7.

35 Sir John Macdonald was adjutant-general, 1830–50; Sir James Willoughby Gordon was quartermaster-general, 1812–51. Sir Rufane Donkin, also a former governor of the Cape Colony, was surveyor-general of the ordnance 1835–41.

36 Although Sir Herbert Taylor (1775–1839) fought in the Napoleonic Wars and had close Peninsular connections, he did not serve in the Iberian Peninsula.

37 Strachan, *Politics of the British army*, p. 75.

38 *Ibid.*, p. 74.
39 (Survey by the author.) Of the fifty-seven the army was important for forty-eight, the navy for nine. Of the thirty-two governors listed in Appendix two (which does not include those mentioned only because of their military background in this chapter), only five had neither a military or naval background. Cell found that only half of 262 traceable governors from the period 1830–80 were veterans, which led Francis to assert that 'colonial governors often lacked a military background' for the period 1820–50. The earlier period does seem to have been more dominated by military governors. Cell, *British colonial administration*, pp. 48–9; Francis, *Governors and settlers*, p. 2.
40 Fletcher, *Darling*, chs 1–2.
41 E.g., Wellington was involved in the appointment of Harry Smith to the Cape as governor in 1847 (Mostert, *Frontiers*, p. 930); of William Broughton, as archdeacon and then first bishop of Australia in 1828 (WO 80/2, Wellington to Sir George Murray, 29 October 1828); and of Sir Lionel Smith as governor (Taylor, *Autobiography*, i, pp. 243).
42 D'Urban, *Peninsular journal*, p. 186 and *passim*. Hardinge did D'Urban favours well into the 1840s: CA, A1415/77, pp. 82–3, Hardinge to Napier, 30 January 1843.
43 See, e.g., CO 323/173, fos 23, 30, Hardinge to Hay, private, 24 June 1834, 11 July 1834; DP, A519/7, pp. 73–80, Taylor to D'Urban, 16 August 1837; DP, A519/18, pp. 110–11, D'Urban to Gordon, 26 June 1835; DP, A519/2, p. 237, Beresford to D'Urban, 12 September 1835; DP, A519/8, pp. 10–12, Extract from Gladstone to Chase, 9 December 1837, encl. in Chase to D'Urban, private, 9 March 1838.
44 Lancaster, 'D'Urban', p. 327.
45 DP, A519/4, p. 199, Smith to D'Urban, very private, 30 May 1836; DP, A519/18, p. 111, D'Urban to Gordon, 26 June 1835.
46 DP, A519/7, p. 75, Taylor to D'Urban, 16 August 1837.
47 *PP 1837*, xxxiv (78), Royal Commission on Practicability and Expediency of consolidating Departments connected with the Civil Administration of the Army; *PP 1836*, xxii (59), Royal Commission for inquiring into the System of Military Punishments in the Army; Burroughs, 'An Unreformed Army?', pp. 168–78.
48 Hickford, 'Making "territorial rights"', pp. 1, 5–11. In the nineteenth century, the networks' members were more commonly referred to as 'philanthropists' than 'humanitarians', by both supporters and opponents. 'Humanitarian' was more uniformly applied in twentieth-century accounts. E.g., Porter, 'Trusteeship'.
49 Bradley, *Call to seriousness*, p. 76.
50 Brent, *Liberal Anglican politics*, pp. 252–87.
51 Madden, 'Attitude of the evangelicals', p. 13.
52 See Stanley, *Bible and flag*; Stanley, *Baptist Missionary Society*; Ward and Stanley, *Church Mission Society*; De Gruchy, *London Missionary Society*; Lovett, *London Missionary Society*.
53 Altholz, *Religious press*, pp. 16–25.
54 Coates, Beecham and Ellis, *Christianity*.
55 Ross, *Philip*, p. 101.
56 See, e.g., *Kitchingman papers*.
57 Ross, *Philip*, pp. 215–28.
58 SOAS, LMS archives, CWM, South Africa, 15/3/A, Jane Philip to Ellis, 14 February 1837, 10 March 1837.
59 Laidlaw, 'Aunt Anna's report'.
60 See Drayton, *Nature's government*, pp. 122, 126–7, 170–2, and *passim*.
61 TLM, A292, pp. 334, 336, 343, Henslow to [Lindley], 25 October 1837, Devonshire to Lindley, 30 October 1837, Hooker to Lindley, 11 November 1837.
62 King, 'Man in a trap', 39.
63 Drayton, *Nature's government*.
64 CO 324/87, fo. 31, Hay to Bourke, 6 December 1831.
65 Desmond, *Kew*, p. 140.
66 'W. H. Harvey', *DSAB*, i, pp. 352–4.
67 Desmond, *Huxley*, pp. 89–90, 92, 176.
68 Franklin, *Private correspondence*, i, p. 60, John to Jane Franklin, 19 April 1839.

69 E.g., correspondence between J. Barnard Davis and Governor Grey in New Zealand on Maori skulls. Auckland Public Library, Grey letters, 24 August 1852, D11(1); 27 August 1853, D11(2); 13 January 1854, D11(3); 17 May 1854, D11(4). I am indebted to Damon Salesa for these references.

70 DP, A519/2, pp. 60–1, Alexander to D'Urban, 10 June 1835; DP, A519/4, pp. 170–1, Alexander to D'Urban, 3 May 1836.

71 Franklin, *Private correspondence*, i, pp. 57–8, 91, John to Jane Franklin, 19 April 1839, Jane Franklin, 20 June 1839. Fitzpatrick, *Franklin*, p. 207.

72 Fitzpatrick, *Franklin*, p. 246.

73 LRO, 920 DER (14) 137/9, notes made by Derby of letter from Mitchell to Murray, 9 February 1844.

74 CO 323/175, fos 404, 413, 423, Willis to Hay, 18 February 1835, 27 July 1835, 1 November 1835.

75 LRO, 920 DER (14) 134/4, Willis to Stanley, private, 16 May 1842.

76 TLM, A292, pp. 337–9, Washington to Mitchell, 28 October 1837; TLM, A293, pp. 61, 120, Owen to Mitchell, 29 March 1840, Ogilvy to Mitchell, 25 July 1840.

77 TLM, A295, pp. 3–5, Darwin to Mitchell, 31 May [1839].

78 LRO, 920 DER (14) 137/9A, Mitchell to Murray, 1 November 1841.

79 TLM, A293, pp. 105–6, 142–5, 257–60, Murray to Mitchell, 30 June 1840, 11 August 1840, 11 May 1842; LRO, 920 DER (14) 137/9, Murray to Stanley, private, 13 April 1843, 24 July 1843; *ibid.*, 137/9A, Murray to Stanley, 13 April 1842.

80 DP, A519/4, pp. 170–1, Alexander to D'Urban, 3 May 1836.

81 McKenzie, *Scandal*, pp. 4–7, 17.

CHAPTER THREE

Asserting metropolitan control:
the Colonial Office, 1815–36

The history of the British colonies undoubtedly shows, that when colonists become numerous and opulent, it is very difficult to retain them in proper subjection to the parent state. It becomes then a question not very easily answered, how far they are entitled to the rights they had as inhabitants of the mother-country, or how far they are bound by its laws? ('Colony', *Encyclopaedia Britannica*, 1823)[1]

Between 1780 and 1815 Britain acquired extensive new colonial territories. Some were the spoils of victory, others had been taken for immediate or longer-term strategic purposes during the French wars, or, as in the Indian subcontinent, to secure the internal stability necessary to protect Britain's interests. As Bayly has argued, few were acquired with primarily an economic purpose in mind.[2] Some of the new colonies, such as Mauritius, Ceylon and the Cape, had been part of the French or Dutch empires, and brought with them a history of European law and tensions between settlers and indigenous peoples; others, like Malta and the Ionian Islands, were Mediterranean garrisons, with established European elites. The combination of the diverse histories, peoples and administrative systems of the new territories, their geographical distribution, unclear purpose, and the perceived Jacobin threat of unrest or insurrection, posed considerable challenges for the British in the post-war era.

Of course, British thoughts were not only of expansion. The loss of the thirteen colonies underlined the need to reassess the empire and its relationship to Britain, although no systematic plan for imperial control would emerge. As Marshall and others have argued, there was no revolution in colonial government, and changes to the metropolitan administration of the empire before 1801 hardly clarified the relationship between Britain and the colonies. Rather, the late eighteenth and early nineteenth centuries saw the emergence of attitudes towards empire which combined 'an insistence on due subordination to imperial authority . . . with an increasing willingness to use that authority in ways that were guided by rough concepts of utility'.[3]

This chapter examines the response of the metropolitan government to the challenges posed by the British Empire, and specifically to New South Wales and the Cape Colony, between 1815 and 1836. In this discussion, the networks of personal connection which emanated from the Colonial Office emerge as critical for imperial governance. Tracing the changes that occurred in the twenty years following Waterloo leads finally to a reconsideration of the Colonial Office in the later 1830s, when a change of guard among the senior civil servants has long been credited with inspiring a bureaucratic revolution. What role would imperial networks play in the modern Colonial Office?

Bayly has argued that the British coped with the imperial challenges of the late eighteenth century by establishing 'colonial despotisms . . . characterised by a form of aristocratic military government supporting a viceregal authority, by a well-developed imperial style which emphasised hierarchy and racial subordination, and by the patronage of indigenous landed elites'. Although 'never planned from the centre', the colonial despotisms were 'enforced by similar military despotisms, informed by similar autocratic ideals, and directed against widespread and interlinked manifestations of social crisis'. They endured from the 1780s until the 'triumph of liberalism' in the 1830s.[4] A degree of devolution to proconsuls was certainly one way of dealing with the difficulties of metropolitan control, and indeed across the empire – perhaps the single unifying theme to early nineteenth-century British rule – autocratic governors could be found, bolstered by military power and an emphasis on colonial hierarchies and their personal authority.[5] Colonial governors were typically drawn from a pool of aristocratic Britons, often with military experience. Their subordinates were expatriates who often shared a similar background. Both governors and senior officials were rewarded with large salaries, grants of colonial land and local patronage. The autocratic style of government was supported by the structural changes that the British made to Dutch, French and indigenous systems of government. While the British seemed to dissipate some of the harsher aspects of rule – ameliorating slaves' conditions; protecting Indian peasants from rapacious tax collectors; and intervening between Boer settlers and their Khoi labourers – the very changes they made allowed greater (if more regulated) state intervention in the lives of colonial residents. The collection of information was increased; garrisons of soldiers and police were established; expatriate Britons replaced indigenes and settlers in colonial administrations; and racial hierarchies were more clearly defined.[6]

But Bayly's argument that the colonial despotisms were the characteristic form of British imperial governance up to the 1830s requires some modification, at least for the settler colonies. There was no leap from despotism to responsible government as his chronology implies, but a gradual, and often haphazard, transition.[7] Certainly developments were more organic than programmatic, reflecting attitudes much tempered by uncertainty and pragmatism. Nevertheless metropolitan conceptions of imperial power – and how it should be exercised – were different in 1835 from those of 1815. Two main objectives were kept in mind during this transition: the empire had to be run more efficiently and cheaply; while the authority of the metropolitan government – over governors and settlers – had to be asserted.

The governor 'should be assisted (if not rather controul'd)'

In 1801 a third secretary of state was appointed for war and the colonies, supplanting the Board of War and the Colonies and providing a central agency to deal with the empire beyond Ireland and British India. Under Earl Bathurst, colonial secretary from 1812 to 1827, the Colonial Office's permanent establishment gradually expanded. Henry Goulburn was appointed in 1812 as parliamentary under-secretary (that is, a junior minister) and Bathurst withstood calls in 1816 for the third secretaryship to be abolished on grounds of economy.[8] In December 1821, Robert Wilmot Horton replaced Goulburn as parliamentary under-secretary, heralding a period of expansion and change. A senior clerk was assigned to each of seven geographical regions from 1822, taking considerable responsibility by the end of the decade.[9] In 1823 the department's legal counsel, James Stephen, was made permanent on a half-time basis, while the first permanent under-secretary from the civil service, Robert Hay, was appointed in 1825.[10] Despite the enlargement of the permanent staff the Colonial Office establishment was tiny when compared to the expanding empire's overseas servants. By one estimate, more than one thousand new colonial positions were created during the French wars, while the number of staff in the Colonial Office who 'executed some responsible duties' grew to about ten by 1830.[11]

As the metropolitan government could not hope to exercise close control over the colonies, the idea of an empire run by proconsular despots had its attractions, as long as the metropolitan government was able to endorse the governors' actions and afford their services. But in the years immediately following Waterloo, both of these conditions were challenged. Domestically, the government faced difficult times. While popular agitation in 1816–17 and again in 1819 led to the suspension of civil liberties, and an authoritarian stance compatible with that of the colonial despotisms, it was the government's fiscal problems and the opposition's attacks on 'Old Corruption' which encouraged the Colonial Office to take a greater interest in the colonies' administration. The Tory government, forced in 1816 to abolish income tax, struggled to support the expanded government created during the war. Opposition attacks on sinecures and irregular emoluments had increased since 1806, and became particularly pointed after 1815.[12] In

1817 a select committee was appointed to inquire into colonial sinecures, and from 1821 Joseph Hume 'relentlessly' attacked 'Old Corruption' throughout the empire via the scrutiny of returns and accounts and demands for inquiries.[13] While the number of metropolitan civil servants did not dramatically decline, the rate of increase in government expenditure was slashed, and it was expected that cuts would be passed on through the Colonial Office to the empire.[14] Military and naval estimates were reduced through the early 1820s, pensions revised and salaries cut, as the Tories made an effort 'to project an image of probity'.[15]

The climate of hostility towards corruption and the need to reduce ostentatious expenditure encouraged a move away from the appointment of aristocratic governors in the 1820s. The decade saw substantial reductions in salaries, sinecures, absenteeism and other colonial perks. As aristocratic governors expected high salaries, long periods of leave and colonial offices for their relatives and dependents, the disadvantages and responsibilities of colonial life began to outweigh its benefits for the most elite sections of British society.[16] Apart from considerations of expense, the Colonial Office had experienced problems with demanding aristocrats like Lord Charles Somerset, younger son of a duke and governor of the Cape from 1814 to 1826, so the appointment of governors from a less elevated and more dependent position had some appeal.[17] Even so, the military or naval backgrounds possessed by most governors in New South Wales and the Cape Colony often indicated a predisposition to rigidity and autocracy quite independent of inherited social status.

Less financially and socially secure than Somerset, the many soldiers put on half-pay after 1815 were ready to take up colonial appointments. Although disappointed and bitter about colonial retrenchment, and often expressing a preference for a metropolitan or Irish office, these ex-soldiers could not afford to be put off by the prospect of life thousands of miles from Britain and London society.[18] They bore continuing downward pressure on salaries, tightened restrictions on land grants, and metropolitan incursions into governors' patronage.[19] While some of the new governors were landed gentry, as many came from a humbler background, rising usually through professional military success. In New South Wales, this was particularly apparent: between 1820 and 1840, the governors were Lachlan Macquarie (son of a tenant farmer on the Hebridean island of Ulva, who made his fortune as a soldier in India); Sir Thomas Brisbane (landed gentry from the Scottish borders); Ralph Darling (son of a non-commissioned officer, a career soldier); Richard Bourke (Anglo-Irish landed gentry, another military careerist); and Sir George Gipps (son of an Anglican clergyman, a military engineer). They were supported by lieutenant-governors in Van Diemen's Land such as William Sorrell, George Arthur and Sir John Franklin, none of whom possessed even a landed background. At the Cape, the governors' social backgrounds were more elevated, although not uniformly so: Lord Charles Somerset was followed by Richard Bourke, Sir Galbraith Lowry Cole (Anglo-Irish gentry, previously governor of Mauritius); Sir Benjamin D'Urban (the only son of a doctor); and Sir George Napier (grandson of the second Duke of Richmond, through his mother). Aside from Napier (the rather less talented brother of William and Charles) each was appointed with capability or experience firmly in mind. In a handful of prestigious colonies – Jamaica, Canada and the Indian empire – aristocratic appointments continued for longer; but in the rest of the empire, a definite diminution of governors' social status can be seen.

But whether governors were aristocrats or army officers on the make, they, and their subordinates spent an inordinate amount of time bickering and competing among themselves: sometimes over matters of policy, but often over perceived personal affronts, such as precedence lists, or a colleague's promotion. Robert Hay, the senior Colonial Office civil servant, lamented the proportion of the Colonial Office's time spent resolving or mediating disputes between members of colonial administrations.[20] The time lost prompted the metropolitan civil servants, and sometimes their political masters, to work out, and attempt to implement, a series of pan-colonial reforms which would simplify procedures, increasing efficiency and raising standards of good governance.

While the Colonial Office's view of colonial officials' disputes was often unsympathetic, the metropolitan government's view of settlers was more profoundly negative. Throughout this period, when the devolution of government – not to despotic proconsuls, but to democratic-leaning settlers – was a real, if often unspoken, possibility, metropolitan attitudes towards colonists were almost uniformly paternalistic and limiting.[21] Even when settlers were deemed to have a valid grievance, as over governors' zealous suppression of a free press, or the limitations on their access to colonial offices, the metropolitan government's response was extremely cautious.[22] While not averse to citing settler agitation or complaints in order to restrain governors, or justify legal or administrative changes, the metropolitan government remained convinced that the lack of social hierarchies, or any long-standing ruling class in the settler colonies, could only lead to some sort of undesirable democratic system. Thus, while the 1820s would see governors' authority reduced, the Colonial Office was careful not to let settlers exploit any vacuum of power. The metropolitan government must take up the slack.

The reforming 1820s?

Even in the 1830s, when the great reforming events encouraged public and parliamentary scrutiny of colonial affairs at unprecedented level, their treatment by the Colonial Office was often fragmented and inconsistent.

Interest groups like the Wakefieldian systematic colonisers, or the anti-transportation lobby, could generate intense public interest and force the establishment of parliamentary inquiries and even legislation, but the Colonial Office dealt with many such issues reactively, case by case. As James Stephen wrote in 1832, consideration of all subjects 'to which attention was not awakened by some external stimulus' had been postponed indefinitely.[23] Most political members of the Colonial Office – the secretaries of state and the parliamentary under-secretaries – were busy dealing with specific issues which came under parliamentary or public notice. Much of Goderich's period as secretary of state (1830–33) was taken up with the agitation to end slavery; Glenelg grappled with warfare at the Cape in 1835; and from 1836 political attention was focused on Canada. For political members of the department, the combination of a high turnover, the demands of parliament and the administration of patronage, made it difficult to gain either an overarching or a profound sense of the colonies.[24] The image of political staff lurching from crisis to crisis and from colonial mail to colonial mail, if clichéd, is also accurate.[25]

Few of the politicians responsible for colonial affairs left any impression of great engagement with the empire; nor were contemporary judgements of Sir George Murray, Viscount Goderich, Lord Glenelg, or Viscount Normanby, particularly flattering. Some, like Sir George Grey, who went on to have a successful and important metropolitan-orientated career, or Lord John Russell, certainly gave the impression of competence and insight during their periods in the Colonial Office, as well as being forceful parliamentary performers.[26] Historians, however, have decided that as a group the political staff at the Colonial Office were not of high quality. Beaglehole argued that the rapidity of change combined with 'so much merely affable mediocrity' gave the permanent staff of the department more influence than they would have had under more impressive political leaders; while Williams noted that the unimportance of the Colonial Office to domestic politics meant that either its political staff were not first-rate minds or they were early in their political careers.[27] Ignorance and lack of interest were probably as important as mediocrity, but it certainly did not help that the cabinet as a whole were interested only in colonial crises, and even then were woefully uninformed.[28] There were, of course, exceptions. The parliamentary under-secretaries Robert Wilmot Horton (1821–27) and Viscount Howick (1830–33[29]) both took an active interest in trans-colonial issues such as emigration, law reform, slavery and transportation; and maintained these interests beyond their periods as under-secretary. They were, nevertheless, exceptions. It was very unusual for the political staff to display an understanding of how the empire functioned (or did not function) as a whole, or might be made to. More usually, it was the permanent staff who engaged with such questions.

This is not to suggest that the Colonial Office's permanent officials were either particularly omniscient or systematic in their approach to the governance of empire especially before the arrival of the political economist and colonial theorist Herman Merivale in 1846. But, because they were faced daily with the problems of administration, management and bureaucracy, senior civil servants developed a number of schemes to improve imperial governance. As suggested above, political developments were often viewed with weary resignation: there was little the civil servants could do to prevent lobbyists from creating unwelcome publicity or to deflect parliamentary interest from a particular colonial crisis. They could try to limit the fallout, to control information, and to influence the outcome of parliamentary inquiries, the shape of legislation, and cabinet decisions. Minutes reveal scepticism of politicians' knowledge or understanding of the empire and about colonists' ability to run their own affairs. This was mixed with pessimism about the possibility of effective imperial control, given problems both in London and in the empire.[30]

The Colonial Office's response to the contemporary enthusiasm for good government can be seen in a number of projects mooted or implemented in the 1820s and early 1830s. Several of these focused on making imperial administration more uniform and efficient, and were fostered particularly by the permanent staff, especially Robert Hay and James Stephen. Hay put forward the idea of an imperial civil service in 1826, writing to senior colonial administrators to collect their responses to a plan (discussed in chapter five) for centralised training, uniform salaries and guaranteed pensions. In 1832 he and Howick considered the possibilities of a pan-imperial budget, and the dissemination of colonial information from the Colonial Office to other metropolitan departments for this purpose.[31] Hay argued that the introduction of colonial constitutions, and governors' instructions that were both clearer and more uniform across the empire would reduce the time the Colonial Office spent on resolving intra-colonial squabbles.[32] James Stephen similarly hoped to improve governance by standardising practice across the colonies. As he wrote in an 1830 departmental minute, he had always advocated 'some unity of system in the internal Government of these [crown] colonies'. He had in mind identical legislative authorities and standard procedures for the creation of colonial laws, as well as 'one common system for regulating the expenditure of the public revenue'.[33]

Despite their recognition that the plethora of forms and laws operating across Britain's colonial possessions caused many of the problems of governance, Hay and Stephen could not easily overcome the diversity of needs and situations which the colonies encompassed. When Hay asked for governors' opinions on the idea of a colonial civil service all the responses conflicted, each geared to the colonial situation in which it was written.

Private correspondence received from colonial officials reinforced the picture of difference. In one colony it was the judiciary that needed immediate attention, in another the military establishment, in a third the customs department was corrupt, or land surveying had fallen so far behind demand that property rights were being called into question. With the style of colonial acquisition ranging from conquest to cession to the settlement of 'uninhabited lands', the British had no tabula rasa, rather a patchwork of Dutch, Roman, French and Spanish law and indigenous custom. As Stephen wrote by way of illustration, it was difficult to imagine 'any two civil societies more remote from each other in character and circumstances than those of St Lucia and the Cape of Good Hope'.[34]

Thus despite their enthusiasm for uniformity Hay and Stephen were cautious about instituting policies which too closely prescribed arrangements for colonial institutions and administrators. They recognised that explicit instructions from London, especially where they attempted to create blanket conditions for even a subset of colonies, could be more damaging than helpful.[35] When the parliamentary under-secretary, Horace Twiss, rather naively drafted a six-page constitution which he hoped to introduce to all the crown colonies, Stephen responded coolly:

> A perfect identity is, I suspect impracticable and I think that in attempting it you probably aim at too much . . . Much surely should be left on a question so delicate as this to the decision and management of your agents on the spot. Though not perhaps men of very large capacity, their proximity to the scene of action is an advantage which in this case would more than compensate for any other incompetency.[36]

A constitution which did not adequately cover every eventuality could create a vacuum of law and precedent potentially leading to the destruction of colonial society.

The concern for efficient and rational good government, combined with the political need to respond to public and parliamentary interest, led to the appointment of a series of commissions of inquiry into colonial affairs in the early nineteenth century. Thus metropolitan commissioners travelled to the colonies both to investigate specific complaints and to assess colonial government more broadly. While demonstrating the power and inclination of the metropolitan executive to investigate and expose colonial malpractice, the commissions also recommended reforms which would anglicise colonial government and limit the power of governors. A wide range of witnesses were called, from governors and senior officials to settlers and missionaries, and the inquiries were lengthy, in some cases lasting several years. By no means uncontroversial or unbiased, these commissions initiated some reforms, and provided a justification for others which encapsulated pre-existing Colonial Office ideas.

The Bigge Commission was sent to New South Wales in 1819. As Woods has demonstrated, while Commissioner Bigge was appointed officially to inquire into settler complaints about Governor Macquarie's administration of the convict system, Bathurst gave Bigge a wider brief which included the administration of justice, the colonial establishment, prospects for economic development and the state of New South Wales' society in general.[37] The Bigge Commission was followed in 1822 by the Commission of Eastern Inquiry which examined the establishment in the Cape Colony, Mauritius and Ceylon; a commission of inquiry into the administration of civil and criminal justice in the West Indies; and an 1828 select committee on civil government in Canada.[38]

The commissions ushered in substantial changes in the relationship between London and the governors of crown colonies, intended to clarify and shore up imperial authority. The introduction of colonial councils of advice and supreme courts, combined with changes in governors' backgrounds, and the increased collection of colonial information, substantially changed the balance of power between metropolis and governor. Historians have disagreed about the timing of such changes. Eddy places the transformation in the mid-1820s; while Bayly denies that the end of proconsular despotisms was foreshadowed by the rise of economic liberalism or other factors before 1830 (as he puts it for anti-slavery, the period 1790–1838 should not be seen as 'emancipation in waiting'). In fact, while the introduction of councils of advice and supreme courts began in 1823, other changes can be seen from 1819.[39]

The commissions themselves reflected one of the first changes: the exertion of control through the increased return of colonial information. Foreshadowed by the West Indian slave registry acts (which meant that by 1820 all the British colonies in the Caribbean were submitting annual returns to a central registry in London), the appointment of commissions marked a recognition by the Colonial Office that the collection of information could provide a check, of sorts, on colonial activity.[40] In response to parliamentary demands for assurances that colonial sinecures and absenteeism were being reduced, annual colonial returns listing appointments and salaries had been introduced already in the years leading up to 1820. These were prepared by each colonial government, until by 1835 the number of absentee office-holders and sinecures had fallen to virtually none in the crown colonies.[41] Although the Colonial Office did little with these returns apart from present them to parliament, their collection demonstrated to governors and official elites both metropolitan interest and their own accountability. Over the 1820s the number and size of returns expanded. Centrally produced forms made returns more uniform, and compliance with modes of presentation and prompt return were enforced, underlining the impact of the Colonial Office's exertion of power.[42]

Councils of advice in the crown colonies were introduced and strengthened by the Colonial Office from the early 1820s. Bathurst appointed a New South Wales legislative council in 1823, and an executive council in 1826; while at the Cape, a council of advice of nominated officials, before which the governor was 'obliged to lay all matters of importance', was appointed in 1825.[43] Discussions of the councils' role emphasised that they would simultaneously take pressure off the governor, and act as a check against gubernatorial irresponsibility. As the councils were wholly nominated, and initially composed entirely of officials (three settlers were nominated to the New South Wales legislative council in 1826, and three to the Cape council of advice in 1828), their increased power represented a metropolitan check on the governor rather than a genuine concession to settlers. James Stephen, in an 1825 paper reviewing governors' instructions, understood Bathurst's intention to be that 'in many acts of mere Executive Government, the Governor should be assisted (if not rather controul'd) by the advice of an Executive Council'.[44] Governors found themselves obliged to consult their councils more frequently, and, while not compelled to follow their recommendations, to report dissenting views and council minutes to the Colonial Office. Thus, if a decision taken against the advice of the council should later prove injudicious, the governor was left exposed to metropolitan censure.[45] Governor Darling of New South Wales tried to assert his dominance over the executive council, but was reprimanded by the secretary of state, Sir George Murray, for taking advice from outside the council. While McMartin argues that the councils did not limit governors' executive powers in New South Wales, the evidence from London and Sydney suggests this was their perceived intention.[46]

Another check on governors' power was the introduction of supreme courts in Sydney, Hobart and Cape Town, on the advice of the commissioners of inquiry.[47] An anglicising force which carried the prospect of helping to unify different colonies' laws, the supreme courts also assessed legislation which originated in the colonies. The chief justice, second in importance only to the governor in the colony, was to determine the validity of new legislation. If rejected by the chief justice, a law was suspended pending a metropolitan decision. The chief justice was also to assess existing colonial legislation for repugnancy to British law, although if it was found wanting, no action was taken until the Colonial Office had given advice. Although Bathurst told Governor Brisbane that it was 'confidently hoped' this arrangement would 'prevent any collision of opinion between the Governor and the Chief Justice', it led to such delays and disharmony in both the Cape and New South Wales that it was abandoned by the early 1830s.[48] Nonetheless, the increasing independence of the judiciary from the colonial executive marked a further reduction in governors' powers.[49] The substantial body of educated (and opinionated) judges, barristers and court officials from England, Ireland and Scotland, who arrived with the supreme courts, also helped to dissipate the autocratic power of the colonial governor.

Finally, the Colonial Office complemented its power over the new cohort of non-aristocratic governors by building up networks of unofficial links with them, other colonial officials and settlers. Key political and permanent members of the Colonial Office were central to the establishment of a culture of private correspondence. McLachlan attributes the genesis of unofficial networks to Earl Bathurst, secretary of state between 1812 and 1827: he developed 'what amounted to a dual system of administration' consisting of despatches announcing official decisions and 'ostensible reasons for them', while 'private letters went to the heart of the matter'. But the parliamentary under-secretary, Robert Wilmot Horton, was also a great private correspondent, and the practice increased after Robert Hay's appointment in 1825.[50] Hay explicitly encouraged colonists – particularly officials – to write to him privately about colonial affairs.[51] The creation of such links with governors built up their trust and confidence, allowing the Colonial Office to explain the rationale for delicate decisions, to solicit extra support for particular policies and to boost morale. Unofficial links with colonial officials and settlers allowed the Colonial Office to gather a variety of opinions and views of the colonies, creating a more complete and nuanced picture through this affective, often gossipy, information.

The changes to the structure of colonial government signalled a concerted attempt to exert greater control over the crown colonies. Although some changes – like the chief justice's role in certifying the validity of colonial legislation – did not last, the combined package both served to increase the Anglicisation of colonial establishments and to make governors aware of the limitations on their power through the 1820s and 1830s. This concern to limit the power of governors, while asserting gubernatorial and metropolitan authority, would last until settler self-government became the more pressing problem – in effect until governors had their powers diminished structurally. In October 1839, the metropolitan government attempted to strengthen governors against their advisers, and then from 1840 advocated a modest increase in governors' salaries, and sometimes the granting of a title.[52] But this was in recognition of the governor's anomalous position in colonial society: expected to live in considerable style, but, as the 'only Office to which no Colonist expects to attain', subjected to 'parsimonious' salaries by colonial assemblies.[53]

A revolution in colonial governance?

For much of the twentieth century, imperial historians were concerned primarily with the roots of imperial humanitarianism and responsible self-government. They correctly identified the 1830s as a decade of considerable change and reform in imperial affairs, with significant policy shifts brought to fruition by the Whig government such as the emancipation of slaves and the Durham Report, and major parliamentary inquiries like the select committees on convict transportation, apprenticeship, aborigines, and waste lands. But they portrayed the Colonial Office too as undergoing significant reform, with the appointment of James Stephen as permanent under-secretary in 1836. On the whole, the preceding fifteen years were written off as a period of stagnation in colonial governance, marked by Colonial Office inefficiency, confusion and corruption. For them Stephen ended this spectacularly in a rational and bureaucratic revolution.[54] Henry Hall, for example, started his account of the Colonial Office in 1836, because the absence of minutes on documents before then made any 'detailed' study of an earlier period 'useless'.[55] Paul Knaplund, John Cell, D. M. Young and Brian Blakeley all similarly stressed how Stephen's appointment as permanent under-secretary marked the onset of bureaucratic modernity.[56] But, in the light of the changes of the 1820s unacknowledged in earlier accounts – the metropolitan efforts to limit the power of despotic governors, and to link the new cadre of governors to the Colonial Office via networks of personal connection – is the strength of this claim diminished? And what were the causes of developments within the metropolitan government of empire in the 1830s?

The most important legacy with which Stephen has been credited is the creation of an institutional archive. Stephen recognised that a permanent member of the Colonial Office staff had to 'be placed in full possession of all that knowledge without which it is impossible that we should persevere from year to year, or even from day to day, in any fixed plans, or upon any settled principles'. He continued:

> Any man may read the correspondence and learn what has been done. But to know the motives of past measures, and the motives why particular measures were *not* taken, the student must look much further than to our Despatches and Entry Books.[57]

Stephen encouraged the practice of keeping drafts of outgoing correspondence and minutes on incoming correspondence; and introduced a system (best described by John Cell) whereby official incoming and outgoing despatches travelled up and down the Colonial Office bureaucracy, annotated with dated minutes and 'a forwarding stamp'.[58]

This was important, but it was not revolutionary. Wilmot Horton had started the practice of having a précis made of all official letters on their arrival at the Colonial Office in 1822, and had encouraged the secretaries of state, Bathurst, and then Huskisson, to keep more helpful minutes on departmental business.[59] Hay had acknowledged the need to maintain better records in 1832, but believed that there was not the political will to put reform into practice.[60] The filing of his own private correspondence on Colonial Office affairs was particularly chaotic: from 1825 to 1830 it was catalogued according to a different geographical arrangement every year; for each of the next four years it was arranged alphabetically by author, with no reference to colony. Given the volume of correspondence involved (over fourteen hundred incoming pages in 1831, for example), such a system presumably made it as difficult for Hay's contemporaries as for historians to follow a particular issue, colony or individual over time. The arrangement of outgoing correspondence also fluctuated, according to the distribution of colonies between the two under-secretaries, inclination and perceived relevance to colonial affairs.

Thus, although perhaps overstating the novelty of Stephen's conception of a more accessible Colonial Office archive, historians have been right to emphasise the importance of the changes he managed to implement, particularly as they mark an important transition in metropolitan government practice towards the late nineteenth-century style of civil service. Stephen's thoughts on recruitment and bureaucracy, for example, were cited as late as the Trevelyan-North report in the 1850s.[61] But it is also worth noting that Stephen's changes made the permanent under-secretary – that is, Stephen himself – even more critical to Colonial Office operations. Combined with his reluctance to delegate, this burden would counteract much of the efficiency Stephen hoped to achieve.[62]

The lionisation of Stephen by the imperial historians Hall and Knaplund, keen to present the British empire as a force for rational, humanitarian good, entailed a dismissal of Stephen's predecessor, Hay.[63] Generally this was done quickly on the basis of a quotation from the autobiography of Hay's subordinate (and admitted enemy), Henry Taylor. Taylor, the Colonial Office's senior West Indian clerk, condemned Hay as 'certainly not equal to the office he held'.[64] While Hall merely repeated this assessment, Young and Knaplund also described Hay's love of 'gossip' and encouragement of private correspondence as signs that he was not 'paying much attention to the real business of the office entrusted to his care'.[65] Only Cell attempted to explain changes within the Colonial Office with reference to something other than Hay and Stephen's personalities, citing, but not analysing, the combined forces of utilitarianism, humanitarianism, economic understanding, industrialisation, the 1832 Reform Act and a recognition of the difficulties of communicating with distant colonies.[66]

The combination of historians' dismissal of Hay and celebration of Stephen has meant that they have overlooked, or underestimated, another, equally profound, change in Colonial Office practice in the mid-1830s. This was the effective abolition of the Colonial Office's reliance for information gathering on networks of private correspondence. Given the ramifications of this change, both structurally and for the short-term governance of the colonies, Stephen's role in it undermines his status as a disinterested force for rationality and modernisation.

As we have seen, Hay and Stephen shared an appreciation of the problems of the Colonial Office, a broader metropolitan preoccupation with centralising government, and a desire to collect information from (and therefore to control) the colonial empire. Nevertheless, their relationship became increasingly strained from the advent of the Whig government in 1830. Hay was very firmly a Tory, while Stephen, with his legal and anti-slavery background, found himself attracted both to the Whigs' programme and, particularly, to the potential for promotion they provided.[67]

From 1823 Stephen divided his time between the Board of Trade and the Colonial Office as legal counsel. Although he worked phenomenally hard, and was openly relied upon by senior Colonial Office staff for advice well beyond narrow legal issues, he made considerably less money than he had as a barrister in private practice.[68] When the Whigs came to power in 1830, Stephen began to press his claims for appointment as an additional permanent under-secretary, or failing that for some other office under the Whig government.[69] Hay interpreted Stephen's attempts to gain promotion – including plans for Colonial Office reform he otherwise agreed with – as a threat to his own position. Increasingly, it seemed to Hay, the independence of civil servants was undermined by attacks on (specifically his) tenure. Similarly, Stephen's conviction grew that Hay was a perfect example of venal 'Old Corruption'. The relationship between the two was particularly soured by the brief interlude of Tory government between November 1834 and March 1835, when the Tories managed to reduce the possibility of Hay's dismissal by granting him a substantial retiring pension. Stephen felt his advance had been permanently barred. The best that the new secretary of state, Glenelg, could offer Stephen was the 'distinct assurance' that he would be Hay's 'immediate successor' – if he was still a fit member of the department when the under-secretary eventually retired.[70]

Despite this uncertain assurance, Stephen was, nevertheless, the Whigs' preferred senior civil servant within the Colonial Office, and from April 1835 he took over many of Hay's responsibilities while the permanent under-secretary was increasingly excluded.[71] Stephen's case for promotion was particularly championed by Viscount Howick, the department's former parliamentary under-secretary. Howick had intervened on Stephen's behalf as early as mid-1834, but from November 1835 he was intimately involved in the attempt to remove Hay from office, meeting with Glenelg, Sir George Grey, Charles Poulett Thomson (president of the Board of Trade) and Lord Melbourne.[72] Howick used the lessons of the brief Tory administration to persuade Melbourne that the Whigs should secure their friends in the civil service before they lost office again, or they would never overcome the legacy of their fifty years of political opposition. Hay was Howick's major target, condemned as 'unfit for the situation he holds', his tenure branded illegal, and he was even blamed – breathtakingly unfairly – for the 1834–35 war in the Cape Colony.[73]

In an attempt to isolate Hay further – and because the departmental divisions meant the political staff no longer derived much benefit from them – Glenelg banned colonial officials from corresponding privately with any member of the metropolitan government apart from the secretary of state in October 1835.[74] As Hay maintained the most useful and influential networks of colonial correspondence, this was devastating not only for Hay's colonial correspondents, but also in terms of information flow to the Colonial Office. Most immediately, Governor D'Urban's private correspondence with Hay about the war at the Cape was lost from Colonial Office view. As D'Urban failed to keep the department officially informed, this was to have serious consequences.[75]

In January 1836 Glenelg wavered over Hay's position 'in great tribulation' under pressure from Howick, Grey, Thomson and Melbourne. Providing an insight into the personal considerations which accompanied any broader political aims, Howick suggested that Glenelg could not 'possibly get on' without Stephen, but neither could he dismiss Hay 'for fear that when the Tories come in they w[oul]d dismiss his brother-in-law, Philips, of the Home Office'.[76] Eventually Glenelg agreed to act, and by 28 January Hay had learnt of his dismissal.[77] Henry Taylor recorded that Hay had complained to Lord Melbourne of Stephen's behaviour, but was 'probably unaware to what extent the Government was a party to what was going on'.[78] Melbourne reported that Hay took the news 'very much amiss and complains of having been very ill used'; Howick, although his plans had been realised, had to admit Hay's feelings were not unjustified.[79] Hay saw his dismissal as the result of Stephen's personal vendetta, implemented by the Whigs. It was, for him, a depressing sign of the times: 'Party runs very high and the race for popularity is conducted in a most perilous manner', he told his old correspondent and friend, Henry Dumaresq. He had 'made the best fight in my power for my office, and in so doing, for the offices of all those who hold similar situations', before being compelled to give way.[80]

It is perhaps ironic that James Stephen – the man credited with creating the Colonial Office archive – managed effectively to destroy the department's existing (if poorly organised) institutional memory in 1835. And, having made much of Hay's venality, nepotism and links with Old Corruption, it was now politically impossible for the Colonial Office to re-establish his private networks. In fact, Stephen would turn to alternative means of acquiring information and asserting imperial control: the ever more active official regulation of colonial officials' behaviour and a greater emphasis on the collection of statistical data. The reasons for choosing these methods and their impact are discussed in chapter seven.

This chapter has emphasised the Colonial Office's concern simultaneously to control the governors of crown colonies, to limit their power, while maintaining their authority. This was a difficult line to maintain, and one which the changes of personnel, priorities and external pressures (from London and the colonies) did nothing to alleviate. During the 1820s the Colonial Office did manage to limit governors' power, but – as the history of the supreme courts and nominated councils demonstrates – often at the expense of their authority. The Colonial Office's response to this, its reliance on personal communications and patronage, was one of the few available to its staff, but belonged to an era fast being challenged in domestic discourses on government. The crisis in the Colonial Office during late 1835 would largely destroy the delicate, but critical, networks of communication on which crown colony governance relied, without leaving an obvious alternative.

Notes

1 *Encyclopaedia Britannica*, 6th edn (Edinburgh, 1823), vi, pp. 271.
2 Bayly, *Imperial meridian*, pp. 100–7, 198–202.
3 Marshall, 'Empire and authority', 116–20; Marshall, 'Britain without America', pp. 588–90. Gould, *Persistence of empire*, pp. 213–14.
4 Bayly, *Imperial meridian*, pp. 8–10, 209.
5 Francis, *Governors and settlers*, pp. 30–70.
6 Bayly, *Imperial meridian*, pp. 196–216; Carroll-Burke, *Colonial discipline*, pp. 43–9; Murray, *West Indies*, pp. 94–7.
7 Ward, *Colonial self-government*.
8 *Hansard*, 1st ser., 1816, xxxiii, 892; xxxiv, 1094; 1817, xxxvi, 51.
9 Young, *Colonial Office*, pp. 121–3. James Stephen claimed that the clerks took more than their proper share of responsibility: CO 537/22, fos 5, 13–14, Stephen memo, 30 March 1832, private and confidential. On the lower level workings of the Colonial Office, see Ray, 'Administering emigration', pp. 103–9, 198–205, 212.
10 Stephen's services were shared with the Board of Trade. Young, *Colonial Office*, pp. 54–83; Cell, *British colonial administration*, pp. 1–43; Eddy, *Britain and Australian colonies*, pp. 1–20.
11 Bayly, *Imperial meridian*, p. 136; Young, *Colonial Office*, p. 123.
12 Harling, *Old Corruption*, pp. 69–77, 107, 136–90.
13 *PP 1817*, xvii (129), pp. 231–42, An Account of All Offices, Civil and Military, held under the Crown, either in possession or reversion, in the Colonies and other Foreign Settlements; Harling, *Old Corruption*, pp. 145, 172–3.
14 Eddy, *Britain and Australian colonies*, pp. 8–10.
15 Harling, *Old Corruption*, pp. 136, 152–60, 177.
16 The desirability of particular colonies in terms of climate, salary, society and remoteness varied wildly. By the late 1840s only ten of forty-five governors and lieutenant-governors (outside British India) were paid £5,000 per annum or more. None received more than £7,000. Twenty-four governors were paid £2,000 or less. *PP 1849*, xxxiv (3), pp. 573–6. Earlier governors' salaries were much higher. Somerset was appointed to the Cape on £10,000 p.a. in 1814; in 1823 Lowry Cole was appointed to Mauritius on the same salary. However, this was soon reduced to £9,000, and his appointment to the Cape in 1828 was at only £7,000 per annum.
17 *Hansard*, NS, 1825, xiii, 903, 1166, 1274, 1483; 1826, xv, 961; 1826–27, xvi, 303, 320; 1827, xvii, 883, 1168, 1427. *PP 1826–27*, xxi (444), Communications between Colonial Department and Sir Rufane Donkin; *PP 1826–27*, xxi (454), Correspondence between Lord Charles Somerset and the Colonial Department.

18 Richard Bourke hoped for an Irish office, or the command of a regiment, in preference to another colonial governorship: BP, A1736, pp. 68–9, 77–8, 87–9, Bourke to Spring Rice, 22 November 1830, 9 December 1830, 6 March 1831.
19 McMartin, *Public servants*, pp. 109–10, 202–3; Eddy, *Britain and Australian colonies*, pp. 223–32; and Duly, *Land policy*, pp. 95–8, 116–17, 141–4. In 1826 Bathurst fixed schedules for salaries, significantly limiting governors' informal exercise of patronage; in 1838, Lord Glenelg formally specified who could make appointments in various salary ranges. These rules appeared in the second edition of the Colonial Office's *Rules and regulations for Her Majesty's colonial service*, pp. 16–20. HRA, I, xii, pp. 483–93, Bathurst to Darling, 11 August 1826.
20 E.g., CO 324/78, p. 133, Hay to Ponsonby, 3 April 1827; CO 324/80, pp. 77–8, Hay to Lowry Cole, private and confidential, 19 June 1828.
21 E.g., see Elliot minute on Second Report of Lower Canada Commissioners, 16 May 1836, Bell and Morrell, *Select documents*, pp. 18–20.
22 Keegan, *Colonial South Africa*, pp. 97–8; Peires, 'British and the Cape', p. 479; Fletcher, *Darling*, pp. 58, 233, 248–51; Eddy, *Britain and Australian colonies*, pp. 107–17.
23 CO 537/22, fos 11–12, Stephen memo on Colonial Office, 30 March 1832.
24 *Ibid.*, fos 17–18, Hay memo, 2 April 1832.
25 Cell, *British colonial administration*, pp. 32, 41–2.
26 It should be noted that this Sir George Grey, first cousin of Viscount Howick, was not the George Grey who became governor of South Australia, New Zealand and the Cape Colony.
27 Beaglehole, 'Colonial Office', 186; Williams, 'Colonial Office in the thirties', 151.
28 E.g., on the Canadian crisis: GRE/V/C3/2, Howick Journal, 20 April 1836; GRE/V/C3/4, 2 February 1839. On the NSW Bill, see GRE/V/C3/2, Howick Journal, 27 June 1836.
29 As the third Earl Grey, Howick was also secretary of state for the colonies, 1846–52.
30 MacDonagh, *Government growth*, pp. 146–7.
31 GRE/B109/5B, fos 9–10, Hay to Howick, 10 January 1832.
32 CO 324/79, pp. 324–5, Hay to Taylor, private, 19 April 1828.
33 CO 111/98, fo. 122, Stephen to Twiss, 25 August 1830. On crown colonies, see also Ward, *Colonial self-government*, ch. 4.
34 CO 111/98, fo. 122, Stephen to Twiss, 25 August 1830.
35 E.g. CO 324/83, p. 240, Hay to Bell, private, 27 October 1831.
36 CO 111/98, fos 122–5, Stephen to Twiss, 25 August 1830.
37 Woods, 'Bathurst's policy', pp. 236–47.
38 Bigge was in New South Wales 1819–21, the Commission of Eastern Inquiry in the Cape 1823–26, Mauritius 1826–29, and Ceylon, 1829–31, while the West Indian commissioners reported between 1825 and 1829.
39 Eddy, *Britain and Australian colonies*, p. 27; Bayly, *Imperial meridian*, pp. 5, 8–10, 109–12, 117, 162, 194.
40 Murray, *West Indies*, p. 178.
41 PP 1817, xvii (129), pp. 231–42, An Account of All Offices; PP 1835, xviii (507), p. 445, Report of the Select Committee on Sinecure Offices.
42 See chapter seven for a full discussion of metropolitan demands for colonial returns of information.
43 Peires, 'British and the Cape', p. 495; Donaldson, 'Council of Advice'; Ward, *Colonial self-government*, pp. 136–7. The Eastern commissioners also recommended councils for Mauritius (introduced 1825) and Ceylon (introduced 1833).
44 HRA, I, iv, p. 594, Stephen to Horton, 27 March 1825.
45 Lancaster, 'D'Urban', pp. 49–56.
46 ML, Arthur Papers, A2167, Darling to Arthur, private, 15 January 1826; HRA, I, xiv, p. 366, Murray to Darling, 30 August 1828. McMartin, *Public servants*, p. 145. Ward, *Colonial self-government*, pp. 108–11, 139–44; Neal, *Rule of law*, p. 104.
47 During 1823 in Sydney and Hobart and 1828 in the Cape Colony, where the commissioners followed Judge Ottley's 1823 plan for Ceylon. See HRA, IV, i, pp. 509–20, Charter Establishing Courts of Judicature in New South Wales; McMartin, *Public servants*, p. 85; Keegan, *Colonial South Africa*, p. 101.

48 *HRA*, I, xi, pp. 67–9, Bathurst to Brisbane, 31 March 1823. *Records of the Cape Colony*, xxviii, pp. 1–111, Report of J. T. Bigge to Earl Bathurst upon Courts of Justice, 6 September 1826. Knaplund, *Stephen*, p. 230.

49 *HRA*, IV, i, pp. 595–8, Stephen to Horton, 27 March 1825. Neal, *Rule of law*, pp. 108–13.

50 McLachlan, 'Bathurst', 500; Eddy acknowledges that Wilmot Horton really initiated the practice of private correspondence, although Hay extended it: *Britain and Australian colonies*, pp. 32–3. Young, in contrast, argues that Wilmot Horton attempted to rein in Hay's private correspondence: *Colonial Office*, pp. 86–7.

51 E.g., CO 324/81, pp. 161–4, Hay to Adam, private, 7 May 1829; CO 323/149, fos 472–3, Burnett to Hay, 18 March 1827.

52 CO 854/2, fos 300–1, circular, 16 October 1839. Stephen's comments on CO 217/175, 2 November 1840, fo. 480; CO 201/308, 23 July 1841; both cited in Knaplund, *Stephen*, pp. 52–4.

53 CO 217/193, Stephen minute, cited in Knaplund, *Stephen*, pp. 52–4.

54 Eddy is one historian who has suggested that the Colonial Office in the 1820s was more complicated. *Britain and Australian colonies*, p. 27.

55 Hall, *Colonial Office*, p. 6.

56 Knaplund, *Stephen*; Cell, *British colonial administration*, p. 10; Young, *Colonial Office*, pp. 86–7; Blakeley, *Colonial Office*, pp. vii–viii.

57 CO 537/22, fo. 14, Stephen memo, 30 March 1832.

58 Cell, *British colonial administration*, pp. 9–12.

59 For Horton's reforms see Young, *Colonial Office*, pp. 48–57, 82–3. Young's explicit disagreement with Beaglehole's assertion that Horton '(to put it mildly) adorned little that he touched' is convincing. Beaglehole, 'Colonial Office', 181.

60 CO 537/22, fos 25–7, Hay memo on Colonial Office, 2 April 1832.

61 Fry, *Statesmen in disguise*, p. 44.

62 The deficiencies, as well as advantages, of Stephen's tenure at the Colonial Office were recognised by Pugh, 'Colonial Office', pp. 721–4; Young, *Colonial Office*, p. 94; and Cell, *British colonial administration*, pp. 10–12, chs 7–8.

63 Knaplund turned Stephen into the father of the modern Commonwealth: *Stephen*, pp. 5, 41–3.

64 Taylor admitted that Hay was 'almost the only man I have served under who was disagreeable to me'. Taylor, *Autobiography*, i, pp. 231–2, see also pp. 117–18; Hall, *Colonial Office*, p. 70.

65 Knaplund, *Stephen*, p. 40; Young, *Colonial Office*, pp. 86–7.

66 Cell, *British colonial administration*, pp. 10, 40.

67 Hay, the son of an Anglican clergyman and grandson of the archbishop of York, was educated at Christchurch, Oxford. Before joining the Colonial Office, he had been private secretary to Lord Melville, first lord of the Admiralty, and then a commissioner at the Victualling Office. *Alumni Oxoniensis, 1715–1886*, ii, p. 632; Young, *Colonial Office*, pp. 85–6. Stephen toyed with being apolitical, 'a looker-on', although by 1838 he admitted to being a Whig. CUL, Add 7888/II/118, Stephen to Macvey Napier, 22 March 1838.

68 Beaglehole, 'Colonial Office', 184; Knaplund, *Stephen*.

69 GRE/B126/11, Stephen to Howick, 10 February 1832, 7 January 1836; LRO, 920 DER (14) 131/8, Stephen to Stanley, 1 April 1833, 2 April 1833; CUL, Add 7888/II/2, Howick to Stephen, private, 19 June 1834; CUL, Add 7888/II/73, Stephen to Grant, 24 April 1835.

70 CUL, Add 7888/II/55, Glenelg to Stephen, [after 6] May 1835. See also CUL, Add 7888/II/73, Stephen to Grant, 24 April 1835; CUL, Add 7888/II/54, Glenelg to Stephen, 27 April 1835.

71 CUL, Add 7888/II/76, Stephen to Glenelg, copy, 11 November 1835; GRE/V/C3/1B, Howick Journal, 11 November 1835.

72 CUL, Add 7888/II/2–3, Howick to Stephen, 19 June 1834, 7 January 1836; GRE/B126/11, Stephen to Howick, 26 October 1835, 7 January 1836; CUL, Add 7888/II/62, Glenelg to Stephen, 14 January [1836]; GRE/V/C3/1B, Howick Journal, 11 November 1835–12 January 1836.

73 Viscount Melbourne Papers, microfilm 1076/4, Royal Archives 7/46 (Bodleian Library), Howick to Melbourne, 22 December 1835. See also Mandler, *Aristocratic government*, pp. 115, 125, on Howick and concerns about 'whig jobbery'.
74 CO 854/1, fo. 427, circular, 27 October 1835.
75 Stephen wrote to Howick on 26 October 1835, the day before private correspondence was banned: 'The Caffre War, is a subject on which we are, again, left in almost total darkness by our Governor.' GRE/B126/11.
76 GRE/V/C3/1B, Howick Journal, 20 January 1836; CUL Add 7888/II/62, 63, 65–6, Glenelg to Stephen, 14 January [1836], 23 January 1836, confidential, and two further undated letters.
77 Howick heard from Spring Rice on 27 January, but Glenelg had not then had the courage to tell Hay of his decision. GRE/V/C3/1B, Howick Journal, 27 January 1836.
78 Taylor, *Autobiography*, i, pp. 232–3.
79 GRE/V/C3/1B, Howick Journal, 28 January 1836.
80 CO 324/87, fos 132–3, Hay to Dumaresq, 17 February 1836.

PART II

Colonial struggles

CHAPTER FOUR

The isolation of governors

My dear La Trobe,

The *Bangalore* arrived this morning with the Govr. of New Zealand – & though she sailed early in July she picked up news at the Cape to the 24 Augt.

No news as yet of Major Childs.

No chance of the end of the Session of the Leg. Council –

No chance of my assenting to the Pfandbriefe Bill though it has passed a second reading.

No chance (I fear) of amendment of any sort –

No chance of People's becoming honester than they are,

As little of their becoming richer.

No chance (or very little) of Salaries for any officers of Govt. three months hence.

No chance (as I know of) of my being relieved – from my troubles –

Some chance of 5000 Emigrants.

Some chance (and a good one) of a War with France.

Some chance of Parker's, being sorry for himself.

No chance of my ever having time to write a Long letter.

Yrs

G.G.[1]

Gipps's tongue-in-cheek letter identifies some of the difficulties that a colonial governor faced: isolation from metropole and colonists; constant financial pressure; professional uncertainty; and grinding hard work. Gipps was lucky to have a confidant like Superintendent La Trobe separated by only the week's travel between Sydney and Melbourne. Many other governors were far more isolated, mediators between centre and periphery who fitted in neither sphere. Such a situation, exacerbated by distance from Britain, led governors to modify their actions according to not only their instructions, inclinations and the colonial situation, but also their perceptions of how decisions would be received by the (frequently changing) imperial administration. Apart from isolation, governors struggled with the contradictions inherent in their role before the advent of colonial self-government;

a governor was at once an independent colonial autocrat and the metropolitan government's puppet. This apparent paradox was heightened by ongoing debates about the suitability of military men (autocratic martinets) or civilians (ineffectual administrators) as governors.[2] To operate – to govern not only more effectively and confidently, but to govern at all – governors relied on the support and information available through the networks described in chapter two.

Governors inspired much of the colonial history written in the middle decades of the twentieth century, but the effect on colonial governance of their uncomfortable and lonely position has not yet been considered adequately by historians. Too often, the role of governor has been either ignored or sketchily caricatured, sometimes used to delineate eras, rather than to inspire an assessment of an individual's impact on a colony. While, in general, biographies of Cape governors have been hagiographic (and historically inadequate), Australian biographies – of Bourke, Franklin, Arthur and Darling – are more rewarding. These sensitively marshal private correspondence alongside official evidence to reveal governors as individuals firmly situated in a context which frustrated, exhilarated and constrained them. Although the Australian biographies incorporate unofficial sources, they have sometimes lacked a broader imperial and metropolitan perspective. A consideration of the importance of the demands of patronage and metropolitan politics – revealed via networks – and a comparison between colonies which breaks down any false exceptionalism, adds significantly to these worthy accounts.

Little comparative work on governors between colonies has been completed; Mark Francis's *Governors and settlers* is a notable exception. Francis identifies the problems that flow from a lack of comparison across colonies; an over-reliance on official documents; a nationalist-inspired desire to present the history of former colonies as progressive and teleological; and an ahistorical approach to governors' intellectual contexts. He takes care to examine governors' motivations: considering not only their rationally held beliefs about governance ('mentalities'); but also their unstated, subconscious 'mores'. Unfortunately, Francis does not repeat this careful analysis for settlers, the other colonial inhabitants he addresses. *Governors and settlers* too readily accepts the highly politicised and partial views of settlers as neutral and omniscient, whether endorsing William Wentworth's impeachment of Governor Darling; or exonerating Upper Canada's attorney-general on the evidence of his best friend.[3] Determined to expose the languages within which colonial societies operated, Francis is himself led into ahistorical assessments. His claim that freedom of the press and political representation were not radical and contested issues, because they were consistent with the British constitution, overlooks evidence of viciously fought battles from London, the Cape Colony, Mauritius, New

South Wales, Van Diemen's Land and several of the British North American colonies.[4]

The flaws in Francis's work detract from a useful project. This chapter, having identified many of the same problems with the existing colonial historiography, attempts to overcome them more successfully. The following discussion draws on the private and official papers relating to several governors' administrations to chart the development of governors' relationships with the metropolitan government in the period 1815 to 1845. In the process, the importance of frequent and honest private correspondence with networks of trusted and powerful individuals in Britain is revealed. First, however, it is important to address the relationship between governors' official and unofficial communications.

The nature of official correspondence put certain constraints upon those who used it. Official communications between governors and the Colonial Office took the form of despatches which met certain formal requirements as to style and content. By the late 1820s, each colony's despatches were numbered and classified under different subject headings, and regulation of the style and content of despatches increased through the 1830s, especially under the influence of James Stephen from 1836. Stephen's first edition of the *Rules and regulations* for colonial officials included an entire chapter regulating correspondence.[5] Despatches were public documents and, although they were not generally published, parliament could – and did – require the disclosure of some official correspondence and records, even if marked 'confidential' or 'private'. Back-bench campaigners on the slave trade, aborigines, convicts, and colonial representation, demanded Colonial Office documents during this period.[6] Coupled with parliamentary demands was a recognition by government that an increased level of disclosure could be politically expedient. Only controversial colonial issues came before parliament: in that highly politicised atmosphere releasing 'private' and 'confidential' despatches was one way of generating an air of openness. However, while this sometimes relieved the Colonial Office in the short term, it did little for governors' confidence or reputations.[7]

In official correspondence, therefore, governors were constrained by regulation and audience: unable to comment honestly where any ambiguity or controversy existed. Governors were also hampered by the knowledge that from a distant colony there was no quick remedy for any misinterpretation of their official communications. In these circumstances governors neither wanted to be understood nor misunderstood. The rapid turnover of secretaries of state after Bathurst's departure (with the exception of Glenelg's four-year tenure) increased the chances that a governor and his metropolitan superior had no pre-existing relationship, encouraging further the opaqueness and excessive formality of official despatches.

Unofficial correspondence with senior Colonial Office staff allowed governors to circumvent the constraints imposed by official communications, and until 1835 was recognised as a necessary complement to official correspondence by both governors and the Colonial Office. Governors sent unofficial communications, at least intermittently, because they allowed the discussion of ambiguous or sensitive situations with the imperial government in ways otherwise impossible. Entrance into the circle of private correspondents of a senior Colonial Office official also strengthened governors' relationships with the metropolitan department, a benefit of significant, if incalculable, value. Equally, the benefits of unofficial communications applied to the Colonial Office (as discussed in chapter three): private correspondence allowed the department to add to its influence over governors and colonial officials and to canvass colonial opinion on sensitive matters.

Unofficial – that is, truly private – correspondence was needed for a variety of sensitive personnel and policy matters. Three examples, drawn from 1834 when the influence of unofficial communications was well-developed, indicate the range of topics for which unofficial correspondence was necessary. Governor D'Urban of the Cape Colony corresponded unofficially with Robert Hay every six to eight weeks early in the year, discussing, among other things, the delicate case of a sacked public notary in Cape Town. Via Hay, the secretary of state let D'Urban know that the metropolitan government did not want to take further action, and the reasons for this decision, without fear of potential exposure.[8] In September George Arthur, lieutenant-governor of Van Diemen's Land, took the opportunity to convey privately his opposition to Archbishop Whately's position on convict transportation to Hay. While Arthur did not want to inflame an existing controversy, he knew that his unofficial correspondence with Hay would allow his arguments to be placed 'before influential persons in a clear light . . . to remove any prejudices that may have arisen from misapprehension'.[9] In the same month, the Colonial Office unofficially informed Sir Colin Campbell, governor of New Brunswick, that London would pay the colony's civil list arrears if Campbell could not resolve his deadlock with the colonial assembly. Such information was clearly vital to Campbell, but not something the Colonial Office wanted leaked to the colonists.[10]

During the 1820s governors were explicitly encouraged to report confidentially to Colonial Office under-secretaries or to the secretary of state.[11] As Eddy has observed, by the end of the decade the role of unofficial correspondence was formalised: it was in fact 'demi-official', kept on record and thus playing an important part in policy discussions.[12]

The limitations on governor's power of the 1820s – the strengthening of colonial judiciaries, the introduction of councils of advice, the reduction in gubernatorial salaries and metropolitan status – added to the attraction for governors of unofficial communications with the Colonial Office. By this route, the governor could receive privileged metropolitan information which potentially could make governing easier, or more palatable. Unofficial correspondence made governors feel more like insiders than isolated subordinates. Poulett Thomson, governor-general of Canada, and a former cabinet minister, had an exceptionally privileged relationship with the secretary of state, Lord John Russell. Nevertheless, Thomson's description of the importance of his correspondence with Russell highlights the more general experience that unofficial correspondence reassured a governor that he had the confidence of his distant masters. 'Whatever success I have been able to obtain here', Thomson wrote to Russell in November 1840:

> I owe to my perfect reliance upon your friendship and your public character. Without a friend to consult, and obliged to rely entirely on my own judgement on all occasions, I have gone steadily forward with confidence because I have felt throughout that I could rely on your firm support and defence as a minister and my Chief. But I should no longer feel the same confidence in any other, and my powers of being useful here would cease when any hesitation arose.

Were there a less sympathetic Tory administration in London, Thomson concluded, he could be 'of little service'.[13]

The bonds forged were equally valuable to the Colonial Office. When one of the periodic reallocations of the colonies between permanent and parliamentary under-secretaries occurred in 1827, moving New South Wales out of Robert Hay's portfolio, Hay urged the colony's governor to 'continue to let me hear from you on all matters upon which you are unwilling to write officially'.[14] Hay immediately informed the next governor, appointed in 1831, that New South Wales had reverted to his care, 'in case you should be desirous of addressing any private communications to me, and to assure that I shall at all times receive them with much satisfaction'.[15]

The practical ramifications of unofficial correspondence went beyond sensitive policy discussions. Private, unofficial communications between the Colonial Office (and other metropolitan figures) and governors were a major means of mediating imperial patronage throughout this period. While London's oversight of the most valuable colonial appointments helped to reduce the incidence of gubernatorial nepotism, metropolitan nepotism was promoted. Hostility to 'Old Corruption' ensured that most discussions of patronage were conducted unofficially. Even the morally upright Glenelg placed a number of his less responsible relatives in colonial positions.[16] Sir George Murray was even less inhibited. In an otherwise coy 1832 application to Governor Bourke for support for a Mr Moncrieff, Murray explicitly reminded Bourke that he had recommended his appointment as governor.[17]

Unofficial correspondence had some drawbacks. Although it was finally banned (except to the secretary of state) in October 1835 because of the breakdown inside the Colonial Office, governors also had reservations about the use of unofficial communications. Their main difficulty was that a range of colonial officials corresponded unofficially with the Colonial Office: from the early 1820s governors' frustration with Earl Bathurst's tolerance of unofficial communications from their colonial subordinates was reported.[18] Through patronage and connection some colonial officials enjoyed greater claims on senior members of the Colonial Office than did the governors they served. Merely within New South Wales during the administrations of Darling and Bourke, Robert Hay conducted unofficial correspondence with the surveyor-general, treasurer, archdeacon, chief justice and colonial secretary, each of whom had a serious conflict with one or other of the governors. The October 1835 despatch that ended the era of 'demi-official' correspondence did not completely prevent unofficial communications between governors and the Colonial Office.[19] Nonetheless, such correspondence became notably less oriented towards public affairs and was no longer kept at the Colonial Office.

Governors had never relied solely on private communications with the Colonial Office in any case. Through networks of the type examined in chapter two, most governors had a variety of other metropolitan connections whom they used as sounding boards, informants and representatives to the imperial government on both public and personal matters. Given the insecurity which dogged most governors, the employment of a range of connections was not at all surprising. The private correspondence of governors with their immediate subordinates within the colonies demonstrates the continual assessment and re-assessment of metropolitan politics, imperial policies, and the reception of colonial lobbyists, which provided the context for colonial governance.[20]

These networks grew from a wide variety of relationships. The first, and generally the most useful, connection available to a governor was his patron. Many, if not most, governors were the protégés of powerful men within British politics or government. A governor might also have well-connected friends. Richard Bourke, during his African and Australian administrations, for example, kept up a regular correspondence with his Irish neighbour and political ally Thomas Spring Rice. Spring Rice was a Whig politician, chancellor of the Exchequer, and even, for a short period during Bourke's New South Wales tenure, colonial secretary. The Peninsular network and the army more broadly were good sources of both comrades and patrons. As discussed earlier, the military experience of the generation which came of age in the Napoleonic wars was particularly useful in providing contacts at the Horse Guards. Relatives and in-laws provided another category of potential correspondents. Family networks, while small and personal, fostered probably the strongest links between individuals. The useful liaisons of Bourke's daughter with the son of a Tory prime minister and Ralph

Darling's in-laws (discussed in chapter two) were by no means unusual. Governors, like others, exploited any connection available to them.

Networks like Bourke's which connected a governor to influence on both sides of politics were especially useful during periods of metropolitan turbulence. As we shall see, governors could otherwise be left exposed. Lancaster has argued that the administration of Governor D'Urban was profoundly weakened by his unwise gamble on 'a Tory ministry with a Tory Secretary of State' in 1835.[21] D'Urban wrote for a Tory audience, and despatched envoys with exclusively Tory connections, mimicking his own which were concentrated within the Peninsular network. But D'Urban's obsequious attempts to link himself with the Tory hierarchy fell flat. The compliment, for example, of naming 'one of the most beautiful glens imaginable', after the Tory colonial secretary, Lord Aberdeen, was probably wasted on the Whig minister who received D'Urban's despatches.[22]

The right metropolitan connections could put pressure on the government or members of parliament, pass on information, provide assessments of the metropolitan political scene, or publicise a colonial situation. Very few British residents, however, were well enough informed or motivated to act as advocates for governors on political issues. On personal matters – when the question was of salary, honour or promotion – relatives and friends could be counted on to continue lobbying almost indefinitely. But on colonial policy or particularly sensitive issues, constraints of knowledge, and probity, intervened. Governor Bourke acknowledged that even his influential friend Thomas Spring Rice would have trouble understanding the intricacies of colonial affairs. 'Australian politics' was

> a crooked subject which I should despair of prevailing on you to look into, did I not represent that I am personally interested in your understanding something of the matters to enable you to bother to support your absent friend if you sh[oul]d find it necessary.[23]

Some governors found it a more effective solution to send an envoy with recent colonial experience to London, someone who could act as a 'man on the spot' drawing on their first-hand experience of the colony. Usually these representatives were either on the private staff of governors – typically an aide-de-camp or a private secretary – or were members of the official colonial establishment visiting London on leave.

Although the Colonial Office's *Rules and regulations* made no reference to gubernatorial envoys – except to note that allowance for travelling expenses would not normally be made to 'any officer or other person bringing dispatches' to the Colonial Office – there is considerable evidence that their use was common. Envoys were employed by Lord Charles Somerset and Benjamin D'Urban at the Cape, Peregrine Maitland and George Arthur in Upper Canada, and Ralph Darling, Richard Bourke and John Franklin in

Australia in the 1820s and 1830s, and the Colonial Office's reaction to envoys generally suggests that they formed an accepted part of colonial governance. As Hay wrote to Darling, who had despatched his private secretary (and brother-in-law) to London, 'I am glad to have had the opportunity of talking over New South Wales matters with Colonel Dumaresq, from whom we have obtained much useful information with respect to the Colony.'[24] None of the envoys mentioned found it difficult to gain access to the upper echelons of the Colonial Office (although by no means all were successful in convincing the government of their case); indeed they were viewed in their own right as a valuable source of information as well as the bearers of despatches and advocates of a governor's views.

The advantages to a governor of using such an envoy were several. A personal representative could be instructed to explain the colonial situation to the imperial government in greater detail and with less reserve than even an unofficial letter demanded. Properly managed, an envoy in London could keep a particular colony, or area of policy, at the forefront of Colonial Office attention – no minor matter. A skilful and assiduous envoy would not only inform, but also persuade the metropolitan government of the governor's case, and would additionally lobby members of parliament and other powerful figures. In this way the governor's views could be represented in parliamentary debates and on committees. Having the advantage and status which first-hand experience brought, a colonial envoy could respond quickly and authoritatively to misleading or damaging press reports or private publications, while at times envoys might feed information to the press, or publish pamphlets independently. As importantly, a representative in the capital would send the governor frank and relevant information on metropolitan events as they happened. This was explicitly acknowledged by the Colonial Office.[25] By sending an envoy to London a governor could build on his existing personal relationships with powerful networks in Britain; the Colonial Office, and indeed the whole government, was at this time sufficiently small for a few enhanced contacts to make a considerable difference.

In using envoys, governors were not alone. An added incentive to having a representative in London was the frequency with which colonial lobby groups – whether of missionary, settler or political origin – also used metropolitan agents. Colonial lobbyists – who might be opposed to the governor – often had powerful and well-connected friends of their own, and ready access to the Colonial Office. Increasingly during the 1820s and 1830s, they too would appear before select committees, lobby parliamentarians and write letters to the press. A colonial governor who could not provide his own representative to make his case was thus at a considerable disadvantage. While governors' envoys often enjoyed privileged access to official communications, and more immediate access to the metropolitan government, similar tactics and connections were employed by all lobbyists who could manage it, as discussed in chapter six.

Given the obvious advantages of well-informed colonial representatives in the metropolitan capital, and the increasing emphasis in the metropolis on the need for accurate and centralised empirical information, it might appear odd that such individuals were not maintained officially. During the eighteenth century, this had indeed been the case with agents from the American and West Indian colonies, but following the War of Independence the Colonial Office ceased to recognise officially the agents of colonial governments, although some of the older chartered colonies maintained paid representatives of their assemblies in London.[26] Until the early 1830s, each of the crown colonies also had a colonial agent, although they performed a largely financial role – transmitting money to and from the colony and paying metropolitan bills – for which they received a generous retainer. The metropolitan government, which usually held the patronage for these agencies, typically distributed them among the Colonial Office clerks as a reward for good or long service. During the early 1830s attempts to remove any appearance of corruption, economise, and address the commissioners of Eastern Inquiry's finding that the agents were not particularly useful, led to the amalgamation of the old agencies. The Joint Colonial Agency was created in 1833, with Edward Barnard and T. P. Courtenay dividing the crown colonies between them. Barnard had been agent for the Australian colonies since 1822, and was recognised by the New South Wales colonists as 'the surest channel for the complaints of the colony . . . to Lord Bathurst'.[27] However, as Barnard took on more colonies, this route was less frequently utilised. The lack of first-hand colonial experience of the joint colonial agents, the number of colonies they represented, and their previous employment within the metropolitan government (Barnard had originally been a Colonial Office clerk) may have been factors which counted against them, when compared to an envoy who had recent colonial experience, one colony only to represent, and no conflict of interest.

The need for colonial agents or representatives with a broader political remit was debated during this period, both in parliament and in the growing number of pamphlets and books on colonial governance. In 1831 Joseph Hume argued in the House of Commons that colonial misgovernment was due to metropolitan ignorance, both in and out of doors.[28] He suggested that some form of colonial representation – preferably in the imperial parliament – would provide a remedy. Henry Labouchere agreed about the cause of the problem, but suggested that metropolitan ignorance might be reduced by revitalising the languishing colonial agency.[29] This suggestion was repeated by R. M. Martin in 1837 and G. C. Lewis in 1841, but did not attract much serious government attention.[30] Partly, this may have stemmed from a sense that agents had been part of the American problem during the

1770s – independent and powerful figures who on occasion manipulated both their colonial masters and the metropolitan government.[31] In 1835, when the Australian Patriotic Association (APA) applied to Governor Bourke for two thousand pounds to pay Lytton Bulwer as the official New South Wales parliamentary advocate, Bourke refused.[32] The governor's decision was supported by the Colonial Office, although mainly because the metropolitan government did not want to support agents for 'any other association of private persons who might have demanded it'. Further, the government would not agree to pay MPs to act as colonial agents in parliament. 'Such a measure would be alien from the spirit and principles of the British Constitution.' The possibility of a future (representative) colonial council appointing an agent in Britain for the purposes of correspondence was not ruled out, subject to proper regulation.[33] In fact, the perceived need for official colonial agents was weakened by the reorganisation of the metropolitan administration in the later 1830s; and, from the 1840s, by the anticipation of greater self-government in the settler colonies.

The limitations of officially maintained colonial agents did not deter governors from using personal envoys, or from charging colonial officials visiting Britain on leave with tasks to fulfil in the metropolis. Practicality and expense meant that the practice of asking colonial officials already in London on leave to lobby the Colonial Office was more frequent than the employment of explicitly assigned envoys. George Arthur used this approach from Upper Canada, corresponding with the chief justice, John Beverley Robinson, during the compilation of the Durham report. Robinson, officially in England for his health, concertedly lobbied the Colonial Office, other parliamentarians and Lord Durham over the period October 1838 to April 1840.[34] Governor Bourke used Chief Justice Sir Francis Forbes to inform and persuade the Colonial Office of the utility of his proposed New South Wales Act during 1836 and 1837. Forbes used his London leave also to communicate with the Criminal Law commissioners, and appear before the Transportation Select Committee.[35] In 1839 John Montagu, the duplicitous colonial secretary of Van Diemen's Land, was entrusted with delivering confidential despatches by Lieutenant-Governor Sir John Franklin. The instance of Montagu, who betrayed Franklin personally and politically at the Colonial Office, seriously damaging his administration, indicates that the employment of an agent was not without risk. Montagu had applied for leave ostensibly to organise his sons' education. Actually he intended to lobby for a new colonial position. To this end he was prepared to undermine Franklin's administration, telling the Colonial Office that Franklin was a terrible administrator, and advocating policies which directly contradicted Franklin's instructions.[36] Although Montagu was an extreme example, all agents had personal motivations which could interfere with the conduct of the governors' business. Governors, aware of the ambitions of their subordinate officials, preferred to employ an envoy whose loyalty could be guaranteed.

Governors needed personal envoys who would not only faithfully advocate the governor's interests, but also anticipate correctly his response to situations which arose in the imperial capital. Envoys who were junior officers or members of a governor's private staff could be expected both to travel cheaply and to be sufficiently dependent on the governor to pursue his case in London accurately and passionately. Sometimes these men were well-connected, as with D'Urban's envoy Captain Beresford, the grandson of a marquess; or Darling's envoy, Henry Dumaresq, who was seen walking 'arm in arm conversing' on colonial matters with the Duke of Wellington when in London on Darling's business.[37]

The next section of this chapter examines more closely governors' use of personal envoys during the 1830s, when pressure from colonial lobbyists and the Colonial Office's changing attitude to unofficial correspondence made attention to good communications particularly vital. Although many governors had such representatives, this discussion draws primarily on two: Richard Bourke, governor of New South Wales; and Benjamin D'Urban, governor of the Cape Colony. Bourke sent his son (also Richard, but known as Dick) to London in 1834 where he worked on behalf of his father on a variety of political and personnel issues until 1837. D'Urban used the services of two men, Captain George Beresford and Major Abraham Cloete, to present his version of events and policy to London about the frontier war of 1834–35. Beresford and Cloete were each in London for less than a year, and devoted most of their attention to their main objective. These two examples are chosen both because of the richness of the documentary records, and because – despite similarities in the tasks and tactics of the envoys – they illustrate quite different experiences and outcomes.

As most governors' envoys had no official status, very little official documentary record of their dealings at the Colonial Office is available. Letters from individuals were entered in departmental records, but much of an envoy's activity was done in person, and records of interviews were not generally kept. Consequently the impact of governors' envoys must be assessed mainly from the letters between envoys and governors. A further difficulty arises as the letters from governors to envoys are less likely to have survived, unless copied into letter books, than the letters from envoys to governors. Nevertheless, most envoys sent extremely detailed reports of their activities in London, and enough commentary from governors and others is available for some conclusions to be drawn about their service.[38] The envoys' correspondence – although tending to place their efforts in a positive light – provides a rich source of evidence which details metropolitan networks of power and connection, assumptions about colonial and imperial governance, and the tactics of lobbyists and envoys in London.

Evidence about the relationship between Richard Bourke and his son is found both in the series of letters between them, and in their private correspondence to others. There is no record of Dick Bourke's actions or visits to the Colonial Office in the official files; so it must be assumed that most of his considerable contact with the Office, and its staff, was carried out on a direct personal level. Thirty-three letters from Bourke to Dick between mid-1834 and mid-1837 have been located, and thirty-eight from Dick to Bourke in the same period. Dick numbered his letters, indicating that those extant cover the great majority of the pair's correspondence. The extent and intact nature of the letters allow a more confident analysis to be made than the more usual one-sided record of envoys' letters to governors. The Bourkes' letters are long and detailed, routinely running to fifteen pages, and rarely devoting much space to matters unrelated to government. For the most part they convey a sense of considerable honesty. Bourke used Dick as a confidant, highlighting the isolation of his position in New South Wales: it is clear that he felt the necessity of remaining somewhat removed from the colonists; and that he was alienated politically and personally from most of the officials in whom he might have been able to confide. His letters are littered with praise for Dick's exertions, and suggestions about whom Dick might approach to resolve particular matters. Dick's letters express alternately his satisfaction and frustration with the proceedings of the Colonial Office. They also grow in confidence. Over the three years he acted as his father's representative, Dick emerged as independent and confident, a man who held more radical opinions than his father.

Unfortunately, the extant record of Beresford and Cloete's correspondence with D'Urban during 1835 and 1836 is not as complete as that between the Bourkes. None of D'Urban's letters to either Beresford or Cloete survive, although their correspondence makes it clear that D'Urban did write to them, if rather infrequently. Nor do all the letters from Beresford and Cloete back to D'Urban remain, although it seems judging from context that the great majority are available. In all, eight letters from Cloete to D'Urban survive regarding his experiences as an envoy, and eleven from Beresford. In this case, the extensive correspondence between D'Urban and his subordinates John Bell and Harry Smith, helps to indicate the status of the reports of Beresford and Cloete and their impact on colonial affairs.

Richard and Dick Bourke

Governor Richard Bourke sent a personal envoy to London because his government was being undermined by his colonial subordinates. Politically liberal, with experience as acting-governor of the Cape Colony (1826–28) and as an Irish landlord, Bourke had progressive and contentious views on the direction in which New South Wales should head.[39] He wanted to replace military with civilian juries; and to introduce a legislative assembly with a majority of elected members. The franchise, he thought, should be extended to men who met financial criteria, regardless of their status as emancipated convicts or free emigrants. Bourke was also opposed to the continuation of transportation to New South Wales. Although personally a pious Anglican, he opposed the establishment of the church in New South Wales, and the Church of England's desire to be the major stakeholder in public education.

Arriving in New South Wales in 1831, Bourke was greeted by a firmly entrenched cadre of Tory officials. The reforms of the 1828 New South Wales Act meant that Bourke required not only the advice, but also the consent, of his legislative council to pass legislation: if all the officials on the council voted with him, this consent was automatic, but Bourke found he could not rely on their support. The governor soon became convinced that the 'Tory incubus' had to be removed, if he was 'to carry on an administration upon quiet and impartial principles'.[40] Thus, although Bourke had powerful Whig friends in the imperial government, he was effectively hamstrung in New South Wales until he could install a more sympathetic set of colonial subordinates. Additionally, his metropolitan connections – such as Thomas Spring Rice, Bourke's Irish neighbour and colonial secretary and then chancellor of the Exchequer during the 1830s – were poorly informed about the colonial situation.[41] Bourke's frustrations were brought to a head by the departure for London of Archdeacon William Broughton in 1834. Broughton was a protégé of Wellington, and well-connected in Tory political and ecclesiastical circles. He returned to the metropolis to lobby against Bourke's non-sectarian proposals for the funding of the colonial church and schools.

Until 1834, Bourke had relied on official and unofficial correspondence with members of the Colonial Office, and on a series of personal letters to his other connections in Britain – especially Spring Rice – to gather support for his colonial policies. But the thought of Broughton making good personal use of his connections in London encouraged Bourke to establish his own informed and reliable representative in the metropolis. Bourke wanted someone who could act as his voice on issues of personnel and policy.

There were several reasons for Bourke's choice of his son, Dick, as envoy. Between 1831 and 1834, Dick Bourke had worked as his father's private secretary in New South Wales and therefore had a comprehensive grasp of both New South Wales affairs and his father's position on most colonial matters. Bourke had originally taken Dick to New South Wales because he was afraid that his son, aged in his early twenties, did not have 'sufficient application to make good use of his time if left alone'.[42] But by 1834 Dick wanted to study law in London, and Bourke was mindful not only of his need for a representative in the capital, but also of the advantages of introducing his son to metropolitan political and social circles. The close family relationship meant that Bourke could place more than ordinary trust in Dick, and also that Dick's access to Bourke's friends and relations was guaranteed. One of Bourke's daughters had married the son of former prime minister, Spencer Perceval; another the nephew of the bishop of Limerick; a third, the son of a Tory appointee to the Admiralty. These gave Dick access to some Tory and ecclesiastical circles to add to his Whig connections. There were few other candidates in New South Wales as well qualified. Bourke would also use colonial officials on leave in London as personal representatives – for example, Sir Francis Forbes, the chief justice during 1836 and 1837[43] – but colonial officials could not be as flexibly despatched.

Bourke told Dick that, with Spring Rice's assistance, he would give 'much useful information' to the Colonial Office and remove 'any unfavourable impressions' created by Archdeacon Broughton.[44] Thus Dick was regarded by the governor not merely as a messenger, but also as an informed, articulate and reliable representative who would draw on special knowledge, good connections, and the ability to use Bourke's established networks.

Dick's first task was to gain access to the Colonial Office, which he did very successfully. When he first arrived in London in August 1834, Spring Rice had been appointed colonial secretary, which made Dick's initial contact with the Colonial Office particularly easy. From early September to mid-November, Dick enjoyed a series of meetings with Spring Rice, both at his home and in the Colonial Office. They discussed 'colonial politics', the Cape surcharge and judicial affairs; while Dick was convinced that Broughton's views on the church and education had 'failed in impressing Spring Rice or the cabinet'.[45] But the Whigs lost office in November for several months, restricting Dick's access to the Colonial Office, although he managed to maintain contact with assistant under-secretary, James Stephen, who advised him on Colonial Office instructions sent to New South Wales.[46]

This rapid change of fortune emphasises how vulnerable even the best laid connections were. Regardless of the effort put into reinforcing and extending networks, chance and good fortune always played an important role. The winter of 1834–35 was a period of considerable political uncertainty in London. Archdeacon Broughton, whose departure for London had precipitated Dick's despatch, hoped for an enduring Tory administration. Well-connected to Tories through high Anglican circles, and from his earlier employment as the Duchess of Wellington's preferred chaplain, Broughton attempted to make the most of the Tories during their stint in power. However, their government was so brief that, although it enabled Broughton to gain access to the Colonial Office for the first time, he was 'quite uncertain' what was going on and 'annoyed at the impossibility of doing business'.[47] Although the Tories offered Broughton the chance to become the first bishop of Australia, they were in fact hostile to his plans on the colonial church lands; he returned to Sydney in 1836.[48]

The return of the Whigs to office, however, favoured the Bourkes: they were lucky, and their assiduous cultivation of connections in London was repaid. From Lord Glenelg's appointment to the Colonial Office in April 1835, Dick Bourke gained both access and confidence, becoming more likely to take the initiative in dealing with the government. Letters to his father described 'long conversations' with Glenelg, and his subordinates Sir George Grey, James Stephen and Robert Hay, perhaps the four most influential men in colonial affairs at the time. In these meetings Dick expanded on his father's plans for education, the judiciary, the church and the New South Wales constitution, using the information and supporting evidence – such as newspaper articles – which Richard Bourke sent him. Not all contact was initiated by Dick; members of the Colonial Office also asked him for advice and information on a range of colonial matters.[49]

Not everything was easy, nonetheless. Dick struggled valiantly to keep New South Wales' issues at the forefront of Colonial Office attention. This difficulty was common to other governors' envoys. Dick found it 'very hard to prevent' anything requiring detailed examination from 'being *shirked*'.[50] Crises in Canada and the West Indies drew attention away from the relatively stable situation in New South Wales, while in general, Dick found that 'all Colonial subjects are deferred, and made to yield to the many important matters at home that are constantly pressing on the Government'.[51] On issues such as Bourke's attempts to replace the colonial secretary, Alexander McLeay, with his own candidate, too much direct discussion between Glenelg and Dick would have been indelicate. Less direct approaches involved Spring Rice lobbying Glenelg, or Dick lobbying James Stephen.[52] Spring Rice, who as chancellor of the Exchequer could speak to Glenelg as an equal, was employed particularly in the period leading up to Bourke's resignation, when the Bourkes wanted a frank response from Glenelg about the various rumours which were circulating.[53]

Quantities of information on the colonial issues Bourke identified as important, potential lines of argument to pursue, and also a sense of the anxiety Bourke felt, and which he expected to be conveyed to the Colonial Office, were provided for Dick. 'Do not fail to urge the measures I have proposed for this country and for my own relief', was a familiar sentiment.[54] Bourke identified various officials within the Colonial Office for Dick to target. As it became apparent that James Stephen was 'now a *very leading* man in the Colonial Office', Bourke instructed Dick to gain his attention particularly on matters involving personnel, in the hope that he could expedite their resolution, while Glenelg prevaricated – a state for which he was famous.[55] Bourke regularly gave Dick confidential official and 'inside' information to enable him to lobby more successfully. Both knew that

Dick, if he were to be useful, must have as full a knowledge as possible of his father's plans and any changes in policy.[56] This was perhaps the most critical aspect of managing an agent, and, as will be seen, this was an area in which Governor D'Urban's envoys from the Cape Colony were disastrously undermined. D'Urban kept his envoys so poorly informed that long after the governor had changed his policies, with the explicit hope that this would make his actions more acceptable to the Colonial Office, he had failed to tell his London lobbyists of the change. When Bourke made decisions which were, or might become, controversial, he was on the whole quick to inform his son.

Information flowed both ways: Dick pressed for information from the Colonial Office officials, just as he made sure his father's views were well represented. During 1836 and 1837, for example, he conferred successfully with Sir George Grey on the in camera sessions of the Transportation Select Committee. Not only did Dick find out what was going on, but he was even able to alter evidence he regarded as incorrect or damaging to his father's reputation and plans.[57] Dick's recognition of the importance of conveying information as rapidly as possible was highlighted by his early report of the fall of the Whig ministry in mid-November 1834. He learnt of the change from Spring Rice as it occurred (they were at church together) and immediately wrote to his father to advise him. As Dick put it: 'I thought no [other] person might so soon write to you about it.'[58] Bourke's letters indicate that rumours arrived in Sydney long before official or reliable confirmation; such reports came via Hobart, or from private correspondence, and had to be accounted for, even when they could not be relied upon.[59] Dick's letters were not only frequent and up to date, but increasingly provided an insider's view of domestic politics gained from his contact with the Colonial Office. 'Many thanks for writing so regularly,' wrote Bourke appreciatively in January 1836. 'Your letters are a great comfort and I sh[oul]d be very unreasonable if I were not fully satisfied with the manner in which you execute my English commission.'[60]

Dick extended the Bourke networks in the Colonial Office, establishing strong and useful connections with Lord Glenelg and James Stephen, neither of them close acquaintances of his father. Glenelg invited Dick to dinner more than once, and sought out and valued his opinion.[61] Part of this success must have been due to Dick's recognisable social position, as the son of an established and well-connected Anglo-Irish family. But in 1835 Bourke had told Dick that he 'did not expect that you could execute any part of the Commission I gave you unless a friend were in possession of the seal' at the Colonial Office.[62] By this Bourke meant a personal connection, not just a Whig. Nevertheless, Dick performed above expectations, largely because of the new relationships he established.[63]

Apart from his liaisons with the Colonial Office, Dick was instructed to lobby members of parliament with information and arguments suggested by his father and to insert useful stories into the metropolitan press.[64] If the New South Wales Act came before the Commons, he was to see which parliamentarians were interested in, or might support Bourke's vision, and to 'see some of the Ministers on the subject . . . guarding them against any adoption of [false] principles – or of compromising in any way'.[65] In September 1834 Bourke sent to London a copy of a potentially damaging petition raised against him in the colony. To undermine the petition's impact, Bourke had published it in Sydney accompanied by his own commentary. He sent some copies to Spring Rice, and others to the Colonial Office; Dick and his brother-in-law Dudley Perceval were also to 'distribute them where you may think it would be useful to do so'.[66]

Dick met with other Australian representatives in London, including the Joint Colonial Agent, Edward Barnard. In late 1836 he secured an introduction to the Australian Patriotic Association's parliamentary agent, Henry Lytton Bulwer, in order to ensure that he was 'well informed on New South Wales matters'.[67] Dick also worked to undermine the agents of Bourke's opponents in the capital. Apart from Archdeacon Broughton, Dick was instructed to make sure that the Colonial Office knew the cultivated James Macarthur was merely 'a Botany Bay Tory'. Dick did this, while maintaining outwardly friendly contact with the Macarthur brothers – also at his father's request.[68]

Matters relating to other individuals employed in the colonial government required delicate handling by Dick and his father. Some were quite straightforward, such as Bourke's instruction to 'undeceive James Stephen' over a slander cast on the New South Wales solicitor-general; or to advocate the promotion of a colonial official; or even Bourke's half-joking remark that '[g]ood Whigs are scarce. Send me over a few liberals to look the Tories in the face.' In 1836 Bourke asked Dick to mention to James Stephen his desire that Francis Forbes, the chief justice of New South Wales should be knighted. Bourke had written to Glenelg on the matter, but recognised that a combination of official and unofficial communications would be most successful. The knighthood was duly granted.[69]

In 1835, Governor Bourke decided that the metropolitan government should demand that the officials of New South Wales publicly support all his actions as governor. Apart from Archdeacon Broughton's, Bourke had faced persistent opposition from his colonial secretary, Alexander McLeay, the colonial treasurer, Campbell Riddell, and the surveyor-general, Thomas Mitchell, all official members of the legislative council.[70] The manner in which Bourke pursued this objective provides a good example of the range of ways in which communications between colony and metropole were managed and manipulated. Bourke recognised that it would be presumptuous of him to tell the Colonial Office what to do in an official despatch. Instead, he prepared the ground by sending a series of official complaints to London about individual cases of insubordination.[71] A 'separate and confidential' despatch sent to Glenelg in November, for example, was bluntly critical of the colonial treasurer, 'the open mouth-piece and . . . the willing tool, of the small, but active Party, who are in declared hostility to my administration', but stopped short of indicating the action which should be taken by the Colonial Office.[72] It was Dick's responsibility to intimate to Lord Glenelg in person the need for a more general reprimand to all of the colony's officials. The combination of official despatch and unofficial explanation – although more usually delivered by letter than in person – was quite common. Decisions could be reached based on unofficial intelligence and argument, but they could only be announced and implemented on the basis of official despatches. This, obviously, made both forms of communication crucial.

The increasingly frequent and serious conflicts between his father and various colonial public servants made Dick's job more demanding. These conflicts led Dick to negotiate his way skilfully through rumour, contingency, bluff and ever more frequent threats of resignation from the governor. In June 1835 Bourke told Dick and the Colonial Office that one of his most difficult opponents, colonial secretary Alexander McLeay, had announced his intention to resign within a year. This (questionable) claim precipitated a bid by Bourke to have his son-in-law, Edward Deas Thomson, appointed to this critical position.[73] Previously Bourke had recommended another man as the best successor to McLeay, but he now urged Dick to back Thomson. 'If my own friends be in office', he wrote,

> and near connexion shd be urged against such an appointment, I wd promise *them* to resign on [Thomson's] nomination – but I would not do so if the opposite Party be in power for my [colonial] Enemies wd take occasion to say I was removed.

This threat was repeated over the coming months as the Bourkes pressed the Colonial Office, officially and unofficially, for Thomson's appointment.[74] Dick had to tread carefully as James Stephen had identified the appointment as unacceptably nepotistic, but his confidence was such by this time that he carried on open debates with both Glenelg and Stephen, managing finally to persuade them to accept his point of view.[75] Dick's brother-in-law, Dudley Perceval, told Bourke that 'Dick's judicious management of your proposal to resign' was crucial to winning the day.[76]

When Bourke did resign, over yet another conflict with the colonial treasurer, matters were complicated by his uncharacteristic failure to keep Dick informed. Dick knew his father was considering resignation, but believed this had not been communicated to the Colonial Office.[77] In fact, Bourke had told the Colonial Office that he would resign if the treasurer was not appropriately disciplined. The metropolitan government, used to dealing with a well-informed Bourke representative, seems to have taken Dick's failure to mention his father's threat as a means of discounting it.[78] It was a tragicomic episode: each of the parties was misinformed about all the others' desires, knowledge and intentions; Dick, frustrated by the slow pace of the Colonial Office during the London summer of 1836, escaped to the continent for a critical three months; and, ultimately, even a series of poignant communications between father, son and secretary of state could not repair the damage. Bourke's threatened resignation was accepted in mid-1837, in large part because Bourke was too proud to accept tentative Colonial Office overtures for a rapprochement. Bourke's resignation, to his contemporaries, as well as to historians, signalled a rare failure in communications between the governor and his envoy.[79] The Bourkes' successes up to this point in covering a range of eventualities, made their failure on this occasion all the more devastating.

Bourke's resignation did not signal the end of Dick's role as personal envoy. He continued to lobby the imperial administration throughout 1837, at some points operating quite independently of any explicit or even implicit instructions from his father. When Sir Francis Forbes resigned, for example, Dick urged the Colonial Office to appoint Judge William Burton as chief justice instead of Sir James Dowling.[80] Bourke knew nothing of this. It was also during this period that Dick lobbied Sir George Grey on the Transportation Select Committee.[81] Dick continued too to be consulted by the Colonial Office, both on colonial affairs and regarding Bourke's career. In consultation with Perceval and Spring Rice, Dick rejected on his father's behalf the governorship of the Cape Colony, where D'Urban's inability to maintain a working relationship with London had led to his recall.[82] At a private dinner held by Glenelg, Dick was introduced to Sir George Gipps before his appointment as Bourke's successor was made public; he met with Gipps subsequently to discuss New South Wales' affairs.[83]

Between 1834 and 1837, the relationship between Richard Bourke and his son was extremely important for Bourke's administration. On many matters of significance Dick's presence in London smoothed the passage of Bourke's plans, regarding both personnel and policy. On occasion, as with the appointment of Edward Deas Thomson, he was able to reverse a strongly held Colonial Office position. Initially despatched to supplement Bourke's unofficial correspondence with Robert Hay, Dick was able to note and respond to changes within the Colonial Office which sidelined both Hay and much unofficial correspondence during 1835. Dick's presence increased the profile of New South Wales and he was called upon by the Colonial Office to provide intelligence, but he had also to battle with metropolitan bureaucracy and the demands of other, more desperately situated colonies. Dick's utility depended largely on the nature and extent of the information provided to him by his father. When this communication broke down, problems emerged.

The nature of Dick's role developed over his period as London representative. While the presence of Whig friends in government contributed significantly to Dick's early success, he built on his father's friendships and created new and equally important ones. Dick became more useful as he grew in confidence and began to operate independently of direct instructions from his father. Given the long delay between sending a report to New South Wales and receiving a response – it took from five to seven months to travel in one direction – this was critical.

The extent to which Dick increased his father's confidence is hard to quantify. Dick's letters were full of assurances of Bourke's good standing with the Colonial Office, and both men became more confident with respect to the metropolitan government as the correspondence progressed. Did the governor perhaps become overconfident? Would he have acted more slowly, and perhaps from better foundations, in battling his colonial opponents if he had had a slightly more modest view of the esteem in which he was held in Downing Street? It is impossible to tell conclusively, but the extent to which confidence was built by gubernatorial envoys is also of relevance to the next case study, that of Governor Benjamin D'Urban in the Cape Colony.

Benjamin D'Urban – a network's failure?

At the Cape Colony, Governor Benjamin D'Urban also faced difficulties which pushed him to despatch personal envoys to Britain. Unlike Bourke, D'Urban was not disadvantaged by implacably opposed senior colonial officials (although he would complain about the incompetence of some of his military commanders), and he enjoyed the support of the majority of settlers. In many respects, in fact, D'Urban was a conscientious governor, who drew on his earlier experiences in the West Indies to oversee the transition from slavery to apprenticeship and the introduction of municipal government.[84] But despite D'Urban's successes and the colonial support his administration enjoyed, his term ended in an acrimonious recall in 1838. Its cause, broadly speaking, was a prolonged failure of communications between the governor and the Colonial Office regarding the conduct of the 1835 Xhosa–settler war. The war (known colloquially as 'the sixth frontier war' or 'the war of Hintsa's head') lasted from December 1834 to September 1835 and was fought by the British army and colonial regiments of settlers and Khoi soldiers against some of the Xhosa tribes beyond the Cape's eastern frontier. Critics of the colonial government's policy claimed that the conflict had quickly become an act of vengeance and greed on the part of frontier settlers and the military establishment, as defence became aggression and Xhosa crops, dwellings and stock were destroyed and captured.[85] A number of climatic moments off the field of battle became focal points for the government's opponents. On 10 May 1835 D'Urban prematurely announced victory, banishing the defeated Xhosa in a proclamation which labelled them 'irreclaimable savages', and annexing a large tract of land ('Queen Adelaide Province') to the colony. On 12 May Hintsa, a Gcaleka Xhosa chief, was killed and his body mutilated while in British custody; while at the end of May D'Urban 'emancipated' the Mfengu (to D'Urban the 'Fingoes'), the Xhosa's 'slaves'. The war's end was marked by a further proclamation from D'Urban on 17 September 1835 which announced that the defeated Xhosa would be made British subjects.

D'Urban's initial instructions had warned him against extending British territory in southern Africa. Consequently, the annexation of Queen Adelaide Province was a momentous decision, which would have to be defended to the metropolitan government. D'Urban based his justification on military grounds: the colony's new boundary along the Kei river was more easily and economically defensible than the old. He additionally argued that the Xhosa invasion had been unprovoked, and as such demanded substantial 'chastisement' from the colony; D'Urban's rhetoric made his support of substantial retribution against the 'irreclaimable savages' clear.[86] D'Urban knew that the 'philanthropists' who opposed the war and the annexation of Queen Adelaide Province were vociferous, well organised and well-connected in London. It did not matter that D'Urban's colonial critics, centred around the London Missionary Society's Cape director, the Reverend Dr John Philip, were marginalised in the colony, because their excellent connections to humanitarian networks allowed them to bombard the capital, and the Colonial Office, with vehement criticisms of D'Urban's conduct, the annexation of Xhosa territory and Hintsa's dramatic death. As early as 23 January 1835, D'Urban's colonial secretary, John Bell, had warned Robert Hay of the philanthropists' likely opposition, guarding against alternative accounts of the war which might reach London.[87] Bell and D'Urban were particularly suspicious of James Stephen's influence in the Colonial Office because of his evangelical connections.[88]

To strengthen his position, D'Urban increased private correspondence to his networks, drawing especially on military contacts such as Willoughby Gordon at the Horse Guards and Sir Herbert Taylor in the Royal Household.[89] He also entrusted the delivery of the 19 June 1835 despatch which defended and justified his actions during the war to his aide-de-camp, Captain Beresford. D'Urban had already despatched a personal envoy, Major Cloete, in late May 1835; Beresford left at the end of June.

Governor D'Urban did not spend a great deal of time selecting his envoys. Major Abraham Cloete was not chosen at all; rather he offered his services. He had applied for leave before the war broke out, intending to personally seek promotion at the Horse Guards in London. Shortly before his departure from Cape Town, he wrote to D'Urban (who had already provided him with a reference for the military authorities) to ask whether he could be 'made the bearer, or charged with *any* communications, on the public service'. Cloete's letter implied that being selected for the role of the governor's envoy would enhance his chances of promotion, both by disguising his primary motivation for travelling to London, and because of the inherent honour of selection for such an important task. An additional attraction was the hope that some of his travelling expenses would be met if he acted as D'Urban's envoy.[90] Cloete had good reason to believe that he would benefit personally from being selected as D'Urban's envoy: in 1822 he had travelled to London as a 'special emissary' for Governor Lord Charles Somerset and had been promoted to brevet major there.[91]

While Cloete's motivations were clear, his usefulness to D'Urban was less so. Although an officer in the regular British army, educated at the Royal Military College, Marlow, who had served commendably in India and commanded an expedition to Tristan da Cunha, Cloete was a Cape colonist of Dutch background. He had not fought in the Peninsular campaign; his connections in Britain were limited; and he had no first-hand experience of the war in progress.[92] Essentially, D'Urban was doing Cloete a favour by allowing him to carry despatches to London. Nonetheless, Cloete arrived in London several weeks before Beresford and was able to put D'Urban's position to the Colonial Office earlier: a task he carried out conscientiously. His military background gave him access to the Horse Guards as well as to the Colonial Office, and enabled him to present the strategic justifications for the extension of the frontier competently.

Captain George de la Poer Beresford, despite being Cloete's junior in rank and age, represented a far more natural choice as envoy for Governor D'Urban. The eldest son of Admiral Sir John Poo Beresford (himself the illegitimate son of the first Marquess of Waterford) and nephew of D'Urban's commander and friend from the Peninsula, General William Carr Beresford (later first Viscount Beresford), Captain Beresford had come to the Cape with D'Urban as his aide-de-camp. Beresford had left England with his already 'poor' reputation 'threadbare', probably as a result of gambling debts.[93] D'Urban gave Beresford the opportunity of redemption, which he took: on the basis of their acquaintance at the Cape, Harry Smith described him as 'a shrewd, sensible fellow'.[94] Beresford's selection as the governor's envoy put his star in the 'ascendant' leading to a reconciliation with his family in Britain. He regarded his appointment as a public expression of D'Urban's 'kindness', and (unsuccessfully) pursued promotion in London on its basis.[95] Thus, the personal debt which Beresford owed to the governor, combined perhaps with his friendship with D'Urban's sons, secured his loyalty.[96] Unlike Cloete, Beresford possessed first-hand experience of the frontier during the war; he had also been allowed to read D'Urban's despatches to the Colonial Office before he left Cape Town.[97] Beresford's connections, rehabilitated status and experience made him an obvious choice to communicate with D'Urban's natural allies, the military establishment.

Despite contravening his official instructions by acquiring more territory, D'Urban delayed justifying his actions to the imperial authorities: the formal annexation of Queen Adelaide Province took place on 10 May 1835; Hintsa was killed on 12 May; but D'Urban's despatch was not written until 19 June; and would not reach the Colonial Office until 30 September. No explanation for D'Urban's procrastination is sufficient: he may have been carried away by the support he received from Eastern Cape settlers; or by the confidence of his immediate subordinates; certainly, he seems to have believed that a sympathetic Tory administration in London would remain in office long enough to receive his despatch and absolve his actions. D'Urban's delay allowed opponents of the war to seize the opportunity to act as both providers and interpreters of colonial intelligence, as discussed in chapter six.

Despite their lack of Whig connections, the presence of a Whig government in London made D'Urban's envoys much more important. Whig networks could not be instantly created, nor private letters effectively redirected, but Cloete and Beresford could put the governor's case directly to the new government. Thus, like Dick Bourke, D'Urban's envoys had greater importance as spokesmen than as bearers of written communications. In London, they lobbied the Colonial Office and Horse Guards, justifying D'Urban's annexation of Queen Adelaide Province in both military and moral terms. In addition, both envoys appeared before the Select Committee on Aborigines in 1836 and sent back detailed accounts of metropolitan events and circumstances to D'Urban.

The unexpected political importance of the envoys left them in an awkward position. Both were military officers, best suited to describing the strategic justifications for D'Urban's actions. Instead, they had to compete with impassioned, informed and organised opponents who framed their arguments in historical, religious and legal terms, and drew on the considerable resources of humanitarian networks. Their first-hand colonial experience was countered by the humanitarians' use of other Cape colonists in London, most notably Andries Stockenström and John Philip. Before the Aborigines Select Committee – a de facto inquiry into the Cape which the 'Saint', Thomas Fowell Buxton, controlled – former Cape administrators, like Colonel Wade, and Sir Rufane Donkin, who might have supported D'Urban's position, were too concerned with protecting their own reputations to be useful.

Both envoys had bursts of activity followed by periods of Colonial Office inactivity – when parliament was out of session, key personnel were away, or more pressing colonial business arose. In the slow periods, Beresford and Cloete took the opportunity to travel beyond London, meeting with family and pursuing private business. The majority of Cloete's work as an envoy was done in the period between his arrival in London on 17 August 1835 and Beresford's arrival on 11 September. Within a few days, Cloete had separate meetings with Lord Fitzroy Somerset and Lord Hill at the Horse Guards; and with Robert Hay, Robert Grant (Glenelg's private secretary and brother) and Lord Glenelg at the Colonial Office. He initiated a meeting with Sir Herbert Taylor, and attended some of the hearings of the Aborigines Select Committee, suggesting pertinent questions to some of its members, although with little success.[98] After Beresford arrived in mid-September, Cloete's role became subsidiary; he reported in November that he had passed on private letters from D'Urban to Aberdeen, Taylor and Hay.[99]

Beresford arrived at Dartmouth on 9 September, and, on arrival in London two days later, went straight to the Colonial Office to deliver D'Urban's despatch. He met with Sir Herbert Taylor who told him 'that all had been well and ably done' and received a lengthy audience with the king 'who enquired minutely into all details'. He reported a 'long conversation' with Robert Grant, and met twice with Glenelg in quick succession, taking the opportunity to present an address from the inhabitants of the Cape. At the Horse Guards, D'Urban's actions received a positive off-the-record response.[100] Beresford met again with Glenelg on 16 September, and reported to D'Urban that he had also been in contact with 'the Commercial people connected with the Cape' – the Cape of Good Hope Trade Society – who were also lobbying the Colonial Office.[101] During October Beresford continued to appear at the Colonial Office, although he was 'constantly put off', told that 'other matters (the W. Indies Colony and St Helena) were so urgent' that the Cape had not yet received 'that grave consideration it required'. Beresford found Hay the most accessible of the Colonial Office staff – perhaps because Hay had been effectively excluded from departmental business by this time – and pressed him to read D'Urban's recent despatches. Beresford continued to keep in touch with the Trade Society and with Somerset at the Horse Guards.[102] When he learnt that the Aborigines Select Committee was likely to be revived in 1836, Beresford urged the Colonial Office that he might remain in England to give evidence before it, 'as the only officer in England who had been on the spot'.[103] In late December Beresford was summoned to London by Glenelg, who was drafting his infamous 26 December despatch, questioning D'Urban's moral, legal and military judgements and effectively revoking Britain's claim to Queen Adelaide Province. Beresford had two interviews with Glenelg and a further three with Sir George Grey. 'I have been very much questioned as to the nature of the ground comprising the two Frontiers and their respective defensibility', he reported to D'Urban, 'but I cannot make out what are their ultimate intentions.' At this time Glenelg and Grey told Beresford he would be required to appear before the Aborigines Select Committee.[104]

Beresford gave evidence to the select committee on 11 and 14 March 1836, attempting to undermine the credibility of John Philip. The style and content of the questions put to Beresford by the committee suggest that they found Beresford's account of Philip's role in the lead up to the frontier conflict rather flimsy, receiving it with considerable scepticism.[105] Over the next month Beresford attended the committee hearings regularly.[106] Cloete also appeared before the committee, on 20 April 1836, although, following his statement that he could add nothing to the evidence already given, he was quickly dismissed.[107]

This catalogue of appointments demonstrates the extent to which Cloete and Beresford went to deliver D'Urban's message to the Colonial Office. From their first letters back to the governor, both men made a point of detailing their perceptions of metropolitan views of D'Urban's actions, the strength of his opponents, and the counter-measures that D'Urban could take. In August Cloete reassured D'Urban of Glenelg's support. 'If I could infer anything,' he wrote of his first interview with the colonial secretary, 'it is that he saw the reasonableness of the plans proposed by you thoroughly, and I feel convinced that he will give them every support in principle.'[108] But Cloete also reported on the aims and influence of D'Urban's opponents,[109] and Beresford, too, was careful to report the range of metropolitan reactions. William IV, he told D'Urban, was 'highly satisfied and pleased with *all* you had done, and . . . said more than once, "I see the necessity of that" '.[110] Beresford's conversation with Robert Grant suggested that 'the only little stumbling block' to the endorsement of D'Urban's policy was 'the question of abstract justice, as to retaining the conquered territory'. Buoyed by his royal reception, however, Beresford was confident: the 'King's Secretaries and all *call it* the New *Province*, and as far as I can judge they will retain it'. Beresford thought that the official view was that the murdered Hintsa had received his just deserts, and that the 'release of the Fingoes' had been favourably received, a perception confirmed by Cloete: 'the release of 15,000 Fingoes will go far in silencing the outcry raised by the Saints'.[111] This humanitarian act, combined with the imperial authorities' general confidence in D'Urban's judgement, was vital to the Colonial Office position, as far as Beresford could judge. He thought that the Horse Guards also favoured D'Urban, although less warmly than the Colonial Office. Wellington's reaction was apparently that D'Urban 'would soon put all to rights'.[112]

When no definite endorsement of D'Urban's policies emerged, Beresford became frustrated. He reported that the Colonial Office were 'feeling the pulse of the Saint Party'; they would 'wait till as late a period as possible . . . to see what ulterior measures you may take . . . in order that you may bear as much responsibility and they as little as possible'.[113] After the revelation of the contents of the 26 December 1835 despatch sent to D'Urban, and his experience of the Aborigines Select Committee, Beresford was harsher in his judgement of the Colonial Office in May 1836. Glenelg was 'much given to vacillation, and fluctuated between what is just and right and what those whose hands the *real* power is in [the humanitarians], are continually driving at'. Beresford still believed that the Colonial Office would accept D'Urban's plan as the only possible solution to the frontier crisis, but reiterated that the ministry wanted to avoid any responsibility. Without doubt, he reported, the views of the Colonial Office staff had 'changed very much' between the previous September and the end of December, and it was likely that there had been a 'new change' since then.[114]

The envoys' active lobbying of the various political, military and royal authorities in London indicates that they understood that it was not enough to act as mere conduits of information. Cloete reported of his first meeting with Hay: 'I *think* I made the subject clear to him. He seemed to go along with me.'[115] Both envoys' correspondence contained repeated references to their 'urging', 'explaining', and 'arguing'. While Cloete tried to influence members of the Aborigines Select Committee, Beresford advised the Colonial Office about sources of false reports on the Cape – primarily identifying (and attempting to undermine) John Philip.[116] In March 1836, for example, Beresford corrected the Colonial Office on the identity of two colonists: D'Urban had commended settler Richard Southey, causing a metropolitan outcry when he was confused with his brother George, who had fatally wounded the Xhosa chief, Hintsa.[117] As noted earlier, Beresford liaised with the merchants interested in Cape trade, and he placed an address from the colonists supporting D'Urban in the metropolitan newspapers. He also provided information and advice to the Colonial Office and the Horse Guards on other Cape matters, including the emancipation of Cape slaves, military promotions, and the need to increase the number of troops in the colony.[118]

Although Beresford and Cloete received a good hearing at the Colonial Office and the Horse Guards, and passed information between the metropolitan authorities and Governor D'Urban, they did not convince the government to accept D'Urban's extension of the colony. The reasons for this failure lie not only in economic arguments, as Galbraith has argued, nor in humanitarian concerns, as others have suggested.[119] Communications, namely the provision, presentation and exploitation of colonial information and metropolitan opinion, were also central. First, D'Urban's failure to provide sufficient official or unofficial explanation to the Colonial Office after the 19 June despatch was exceptionally damaging. Because of Hay's exclusion from Colonial Office decision-making, D'Urban's private correspondence with the under-secretary was not as useful during 1835 as it had been in 1834. Stephen was unsympathetic to D'Urban's aims, and used the divide between unofficial and official correspondence to undermine the governor's position, noting that it was 'convenient to be able to leave . . . unnoticed' expressions of support for D'Urban enclosed in unofficial letters.[120] Not only did the breach in communications provide an opportunity for D'Urban's opponents; but, as both envoys noted, it gave the Colonial Office an excuse for prevarication. Cloete reported to D'Urban in August 1835 that the Colonial Office was unwilling to make any judgements on the governor's actions on the basis 'of having nothing official . . . from you, upon the various points I was pressing'.[121] Beresford told D'Urban on 8 December that 'till they hear from you again they will not decide, I mean officially'.[122] At the end of the month, Beresford reiterated the point, and was still 'most anxious for your answer to Lord Glenelg's dispatch of the 2 December' on 10 May 1836, because 'upon that answer something final will depend'.[123] As with the Bourkes, while the transmission of unofficial explanation from the colonies was critical, so were official despatches.

Exacerbating his envoys' difficulties, D'Urban failed to keep them informed of the changes he made in his frontier policy. The September 1835 treaty, which incorporated the Xhosa into the Cape as British subjects, making them subject to British law, demanded a new justification from D'Urban and his envoys. While the 26 December 1835 despatch was being composed in London, a private letter from D'Urban to Hay arrived at the Colonial Office outlining the new treaty, although no official statement arrived until the end of January.[124] The division with Hay allowed the unofficial communication to remain unacknowledged by the Colonial Office. D'Urban sent nothing to either Beresford or Cloete, who can only have appeared uninformed, and therefore unimportant, except as sources of background information.

Although D'Urban's letters to his envoys have not survived (not that they appear to have been either frequent or particularly useful), there is considerable evidence that he used the correspondence he received from both Beresford and Cloete to shape his responses to London. While he was in Grahamstown during 1835, D'Urban forwarded the letters to the colonial secretary, John Bell, who was administering the Cape Town government, and when he returned to Cape Town in 1836 he sent them on to his military commander, Harry Smith, who remained on the eastern frontier.[125] Consequently the letters and their contents became a major topic of discussion between the men, and from this evidence the effect of D'Urban's understanding of metropolitan politics can be seen.

Much of the men's correspondence was devoted to assessing the likelihood of various outcomes.[126] D'Urban and Smith attempted to reconstruct the mood in London, drawing on not only the reports of Cloete and Beresford, but also their background knowledge and information from third parties such as Smith's sister in London.[127] On the basis of Beresford's reports, Smith remained confident up to early December 1835. While he thought the Whig ministry weak, 'ultimately they will approve all you have done'.[128] D'Urban, however, was disturbed by Beresford's account of Glenelg's prevarication, which contributed to his conviction that the Colonial Office and the Whig government were under the 'overwhelming' influence of the Buxton party.[129] D'Urban believed that the ministry would attempt to throw all the responsibility for the war on him.[130] Gradually Smith also accepted this view of the ministry's tactics. By May 1836 he thought Glenelg's 'game' was 'very evident', and began to deploy his own metropolitan connections – within the Peninsular network – on D'Urban's, and his own, behalf.[131]

The information provided by Beresford may actually have undermined D'Urban's position. The strongly, yet ambiguously, worded Colonial Office despatch of 26 December 1835 seemed to offer D'Urban an alternative to relinquishing Queen Adelaide Province. In fact, only William IV's intervention prevented a total condemnation of the governor's actions; the Colonial Office had no desire to retain the new province.[132] Beresford's assessments, reflecting the changing and confusing reception he received at the Colonial Office, may only have made things worse. D'Urban had no unofficial correspondence with anyone at the Colonial Office by this time. Hay had left, and Stephen disapproved of private communications. Like Bourke, D'Urban had to rely on his envoys and his military connections, urging them to put his case before the king.[133] But the balance of power in London was shifting away from the monarchy towards ministerial government.

Beresford's and Cloete's actions in London during 1835 and 1836 highlighted D'Urban's problems of communication: officially and unofficially with the Colonial Office; and with his envoys. These problems were exacerbated by D'Urban's lack of connections within the Whig administration. The philanthropic opposition which D'Urban faced in London, despite its relative weakness at the Cape, managed the metropolitan flow and interpretation of information skilfully. D'Urban, in receipt of conflicting and ambiguous reports, lost his confidence in the metropolitan government and descended to the rashness of his December 1836 despatches which accused Glenelg of endangering the security of the colony by advertising the government's intention to renounce Queen Adelaide Province, and of undermining all colonial governors by publishing one of D'Urban's official despatches marked 'confidential'. 'Governors of colonies will henceforth be deterred from communicating to His Majesty's Government any confidential opinion upon the affairs of their respective governments', he wrote.[134] It was the tone of these irretrievable official despatches that led to his recall.

Conclusion

The experiences of Governors Bourke and D'Urban demonstrate the importance of personal communications and metropolitan representatives to colonial governance, especially in the era before self-government. Bourke's case demonstrates that as metropolitan decisions on many colonial matters were driven more by personal and pragmatic concerns than any coherent 'imperial' policy, unofficial agents could have a significant influence in London; while D'Urban's experience indicates that governors who failed to have a well-informed 'man on the metropolitan spot' risked their colonial opponents stealing a march on them. Both studies highlight the significance of confidence: governors needed to believe that they had the support of the metropolitan government.

Although D'Urban and Bourke communicated with London on very different issues, this chapter has shown that problems of communication and information, and the nature of the relationship between colony and metropole, were perceived in similar ways in both colonies. Both men attempted to utilise their metropolitan connections to affect government policy; both used unofficial communications and personal agents, who not only carried despatches, but lobbied the Colonial Office and other bodies and individuals. The governors' actions indicate the continuing importance of respectability, personal connections and patronage into the 1830s. Governors, although clearly unrepresentative of colonial society, had more cause than most to reflect on those societies' relationship with the metropole. Their concern, as displayed through the framing of requests to the imperial government, and the maintenance of imperial networks, illuminates the complex and contingent connections between metropole and colony.

Maintaining representatives in London was one way for governors to increase the flexibility of their response to metropolitan change, a potential that grew after the Colonial Office placed restrictions on private letters from late 1835. But the different experiences of D'Urban and Bourke also underline the importance of luck: networking assiduously, and keeping up good communications with an envoy, were critical, but could take a governor only so far. The political climate of the later 1830s suited Bourke; while D'Urban's reliance on the Peninsular network exposed him as being on the wrong side of the political spectrum for the times.

Notes

1 *Gipps–La Trobe correspondence*, pp. 238–9, 25 November 1843.
2 On this debate see, Taylor, *Statesman*, pp. 172–8; Molesworth, *Selected speeches*, pp. 204–5; Martin, *Colonial policy*, pp. 73–8; Buller, *Responsible government*, pp. 36–7, 68.
3 Francis, *Governors and settlers*, pp. 88, 91, 132.
4 *Ibid.*, p. 80.

5 Colonial Office, *Rules and regulations for the information and guidance of the principal officers and others in His Majesty's colonial possessions* (London, 1837), ch. 12.
6 Chester, *English administrative system*, pp. 120–1; Eastwood, 'Social legislation', 204.
7 See CO 48/167, fo. 352, D'Urban to Lord Glenelg, 5 December 1836.
8 CO 324/84, fos 102, 107, Hay to D'Urban, 14 May 1834, 4 July 1834. Hay acknowledged D'Urban's private letters of 1 February, 29 March and 7 April 1834.
9 CO 323/172, fos 51–4, Arthur to Hay, 24 September 1834.
10 *Ibid.*, fo. 213, Hay to Campbell, 6 September 1834.
11 E.g., CO 324/83, pp. 79–80, Hay to Adam, 5 February 1831; DP, A519/20, p. 54, D'Urban to Hay, 12 May 1834.
12 Eddy, *Britain and Australian colonies*, pp. 32–4.
13 *Letters from Lord Sydenham*, pp. 104–5, Poulett Thomson to Russell, 24 November 1840.
14 CO 324/86, fo. 11, Hay to Darling, 27 December 1827.
15 CO 324/87, fo. 31, Hay to Bourke, 6 December 1831.
16 NSW Archives, 4/1305, Glenelg to Gipps, 31 July 1838; *ibid.*, 4/1307, Glenelg to Gipps, 4 February 1839.
17 BP, A1738, p. 55, Murray to Bourke, 15 May 1832. See also BP, A1737, pp. 67, 143, Hill to Bourke, 22 March 1833, Taylor to Bourke, 1 October 1833.
18 McLachlan, 'Bathurst', 498–500.
19 Governor Arthur, for example, continued to correspond privately with Stephen and Glenelg, although he knew Stephen disapproved. Glenelg, on the other hand, explicitly approved of Arthur's private communications. *Arthur papers*, i, p. 91, Glenelg to Arthur, 27 April 1838; iii, p. 37, Arthur to Stephen, 16 April 1840.
20 See, e.g., not only the correspondence of Governor D'Urban with his subordinates Harry Smith and John Bell, which is used in this chapter, but also that between D'Urban's successor Governor Napier and Lieutenant-Governor Hare, or between Governor Gipps and Superintendent La Trobe in New South Wales.
21 Lancaster, 'D'Urban', p. 203.
22 CO 48/161, fo. 367, D'Urban to Aberdeen, 19 June 1835, private.
23 BP, A1736, pp. 209–13, Bourke to Spring Rice, 12 March 1834.
24 CO 324/86, fo. 11, Hay to Darling, 27 September 1827.
25 *Ibid.*, fo. 59, Hay to Darling, private, 3 September 1828.
26 Kammen, *Rope of sand*.
27 ML, A1992, fo. 413, Barron Field to Marsden, 18 June 1824, cited in Eddy, *Britain and Australian colonies*, p. 30.
28 *Hansard*, 3rd ser., 1831, vi, 112.
29 *Ibid.*, 125. See also Taylor, 'Empire and parliamentary reform'.
30 Martin, *Colonial policy*, pp. 50–7. Lewis, *Government of dependencies*, p. 301.
31 See Olson, *Making the empire work*; Kammen, *Rope of sand*.
32 CO 201/246, fos 356, 363, Bourke to Aberdeen, 25 July 1835, and encl. 1, Jamison to Bourke, 26 June 1835.
33 *Ibid.*, fos 358–60, CO minute, on Bourke to Aberdeen, 25 July 1835.
34 *Arthur papers*.
35 See, e.g., BP, A1738, pp. 543–5, 593–6, 603–6, Forbes to Bourke, 6 September 1836, 25 February 1837, 1 May 1837.
36 Franklin, *Private correspondence*, ii, pp. 20–1, Lady Franklin to Mrs Simpkinson, 18 July 1841. Fitzpatrick, *Franklin*, pp. 147, 207, 234–5, 250–8.
37 Fletcher, *Darling*, p. 233.
38 E.g., see Franklin, *Private correspondence*, i, pp. 115–16, Sir John to Lady Franklin, 20 March 1841.
39 Ridden, 'Making good citizens'.
40 BP, A1733, p. 18, Richard to Dick Bourke, 24 November 1834; BP, A1736, pp. 204, 215, Bourke to Spring Rice, 11 August 1833, 12 March 1834; BP, A1738, p. 238, Forbes to Bourke, 19 September 1834.
41 BP, A1736, pp. 209–13, Bourke to Spring Rice, 12 March 1834.
42 *Ibid.*, p. 117, Bourke to Spring Rice, 5 April 1831.

43 BP, A1738, pp. 543–5, 593–6, 603–6, Forbes to Bourke, 6 September 1836, 25 February 1837, 1 May 1837.
44 BP, A1736, pp. 209–13, Bourke to Spring Rice, 12 March 1834.
45 BP, A1739, pp. 16–27, 91–98, Dick to Richard Bourke, 1 September 1834, 20 September 1834, 15 November 1834.
46 *Ibid.*, p. 40, Dick to Richard Bourke, 18 January 1835.
47 *Ibid.*, pp. 42–7, Dick to Richard Bourke, 8 April 1835.
48 Shaw, *Patriarch*, pp. 87–97.
49 BP, A1739, pp. 68–70, 91–3, 173, Dick to Richard Bourke, 24 June 1835, 15 November 1834, 29 December 1836; BFC, MSS 403/2, pp. 156–7, Dick to Richard Bourke, 15 June 1837.
50 BP, A1739, p. 71, Dick to Richard Bourke, 24 June 1835.
51 *Ibid.*, p. 73, Dick to Richard Bourke, 11 July 1835. See also *ibid.*, pp. 71, 84, 104, 153–4, 209–10, Dick to Richard Bourke, 24 June 1835, 22 August 1835, 26 November 1835, 9 July 1836, 27 May 1837.
52 BP, A1739, p. 115, Dick to Richard Bourke, 19 January 1836.
53 BFC, MSS 403/2, pp. 153–4, Dick to Richard Bourke, 15 June 1837; BP, A1733, p. 168, Richard to Dick Bourke, 29 April 1836.
54 BP, A1733, p. 49, Richard to Dick Bourke, 26 October 1834.
55 BP, A1739, p. 52, Dick to Richard Bourke, 15 April 1835; BP, A1733, pp. 108–9, 127–31, 153–8, Richard to Dick Bourke, 30 November 1835, 1 January 1836, 2 April 1836.
56 E.g., BP, A1733, pp. 77, 103–8, 133, Richard to Dick Bourke, 1 August 1835, 30 November 1835, 17 January 1836.
57 BP, A1739, pp. 210–12, Dick to Richard Bourke, 27 May 1837.
58 *Ibid.*, p. 32, Dick to Richard Bourke, 16 November 1834.
59 BP, A1733, pp. 42, 48, Richard to Dick Bourke, 18 October 1834, 26 October 1834.
60 *Ibid.*, p. 134, Richard to Dick Bourke, 17 January 1836.
61 E.g., BP A1739, pp. 128–9, Dick to Richard Bourke, 29 March 1836; BFC, MSS 403/2, pp. 171–2, Dick to Richard Bourke, 21 July 1837.
62 BP, A1733, p. 81, Richard to Dick Bourke, 13 August 1835.
63 *Ibid.*, p. 134, Richard to Dick Bourke, 17 January 1836.
64 *Ibid.*, p. 206, Richard to Dick Bourke, 3 December 1836.
65 *Ibid.*, pp. 154–5, Richard to Dick Bourke, 2 April 1836.
66 *Ibid.*, p. 39, Richard to Dick Bourke, 26 September 1834; BP, A1739, p. 71, Dick to Richard Bourke, 24 June 1835.
67 BP, A1739, pp. 89, 174–5, 202, Dick to Richard Bourke, 25 August 1835, 29 December 1836, 13 April 1837.
68 BP, A1733, p. 180, Richard to Dick Bourke, 21 July 1836; BP, A1739, pp. 71, 74, Dick to Richard Bourke, 24 June 1835, 11 July 1835. Bourke maliciously suggested Glenelg should be referred to the 'Records of this Colony' to see evidence of the Macarthur family's 'former delinquency', a reference to John Macarthur's involvement in the 1808 Rum Rebellion. BP, A1733, p. 171, Richard to Dick Bourke, 15 May 1836.
69 *Ibid.*, pp. 138–9, 156–8, Richard to Dick Bourke, 28 January 1836, 2 April 1836.
70 On the antagonism between Bourke and his civil servants, see King, *Bourke*, pp. 232–9.
71 BP, A1733, p. 99, Richard to Dick Bourke, 7 November 1835.
72 CO 201/248, fos 216–17, Bourke to Glenelg, separate and confidential, 2 December 1835. See also *ibid.*, fos 180–2, Bourke to Glenelg, 2 December 1835.
73 McLeay maintained that he had not resigned, and the evidence of others at the critical meeting suggests that it was more likely that McLeay was expressing frustration with the processes of government. See BP, A1739, p. 163, Dick to Richard Bourke, 9 November 1836; CO 201/247, fo. 3, Bourke to Aberdeen, separate, 1 August 1835. Foster, 'Sharp practice?'
74 BP, A1733, pp. 67, 77, Richard to Dick Bourke, 6 June 1835, 1 August 1835.
75 BP, A1739, pp. 115–16, Dick to Richard Bourke, 19 January 1836.
76 BFC, MSS 403/4, p. 197, Perceval to Richard Bourke, 26 February 1836.
77 BP, A1739, pp. 159–60, Dick to Richard Bourke, 9 November 1836.

78 BFC, MSS 403/3, pp. 69–71, Glenelg to Richard Bourke, private, 5 July 1837.
79 BP, A1739, pp. 142, 154–5, 159–60, Dick to Richard Bourke, 2 June 1836, 9 July 1836, 9 November 1836; BFC, MSS 403/2, pp. 151–3, Dick to Richard Bourke, 15 June 1837.
80 BP, A1739, pp. 214–15, Dick to Richard Bourke, 27 May 1837.
81 BFC, MSS 403/2, pp. 156–7, Dick to Richard Bourke, 15 June 1837; also BP, A1739, pp. 210–12, Dick to Richard Bourke, 27 May 1837.
82 BP, A1739, p. 217–18, Dick to Richard Bourke, 22 June 1837.
83 BFC, MSS 403/2, pp. 172–3, 183, Dick to Richard Bourke, 21 July 1837, [August 1837].
84 Lancaster, 'D'Urban', pp. 10, 21, ch. 8.
85 Peires, House of Phalo; Mostert, Frontiers; and Galbraith, Reluctant empire.
86 CO 48/161, p. 367, D'Urban to Aberdeen, 19 June 1835; CO 48/167, fo. 47, D'Urban to Glenelg, 9 June 1836.
87 CO 48/161, fos 159–60, Bell to Hay, 23 January 1835.
88 DP, A519/2, p. 94, Bell to D'Urban, 26 June 1835.
89 E.g., see DP, A519/18, pp. 110–11, D'Urban to Gordon, 26 June 1835; NLSA, MSB 142, p. 596, D'Urban to Taylor, 7 May 1836.
90 DP, A519/1, pp. 94, 193–4, 266–9, Cloete to D'Urban, 22 February 1835, 24 April 1835, 15 May 1835.
91 Millar, Plantagenet, p. 266; DSAB, i, pp. 170–1.
92 Ibid.
93 Galbraith, Reluctant empire, p. 125.
94 NLSA, MSB 142, p. 662, Smith to D'Urban, 16 June 1836.
95 DP, A519/2, pp. 43–5, 96–100, G. Beresford to D'Urban, 31 May 1835, 26 June 1835; CO 323/174, fos 26, 119–20, Vice-Admiral Beresford to Hay, 1835, G. Beresford to Hay, 27 November 1835.
96 DP, A519/2, pp. 238, 268–70, Beresford to D'Urban, 12 September 1835, 22 September 1835; DP, A519/3, pp. 110, 202–3, 223, Beresford to D'Urban, 3 November 1835, 8 December 1835, 29 December 1835.
97 DP, A519/2, p. 96, Beresford to D'Urban, 26 June 1835.
98 Ibid., pp. 191–4, 199–201, Cloete to D'Urban, 23 August 1835, 29 August 1835; DP, A519/3, p. 146, Cloete to D'Urban, 12 November 1835.
99 DP, A519/3, pp. 146–7, Cloete to D'Urban, 12 November 1835; DP, A519/2, p. 270, Beresford to D'Urban, 22 September 1835.
100 DP, A519/2, pp. 231–9, Beresford to D'Urban, 12 September 1835; ibid., pp. 243–4, Cloete to D'Urban, 13 September 1835.
101 Ibid., pp. 239–40, 265–71, Beresford to D'Urban, 15 September 1835, 22 September 1835.
102 DP, A519/3, pp. 107–12, Beresford to D'Urban, 3 November 1835.
103 Ibid., pp. 198–9, Beresford to D'Urban, 8 December 1835.
104 Ibid., pp. 220–3, Beresford to D'Urban, 29 December 1835.
105 See Beresford's testimony to the Aborigines Select Committee: PP 1836, vii (538), pp. 252–75, especially pp. 267–71 regarding Philip acting as D'Urban's authorised agent.
106 DP, A519/4, pp. 102, 105–8, 183–4, Beresford to D'Urban, 17 March 1836, 10 May 1836.
107 PP 1836, vii (538), p. 355, Report of the Select Committee on Aborigines.
108 DP, A519/2, pp. 193–4, Cloete to D'Urban, 23 August 1835.
109 Ibid., pp. 200–2, Cloete to D'Urban, 29 August 1835.
110 Ibid., pp. 231–2, Beresford to D'Urban, 12 September 1835.
111 Ibid., pp. 231–6, 266, Beresford to D'Urban, 12 September 1835, 22 September 1835; ibid., p. 245, Cloete to D'Urban, 13 September 1835.
112 Ibid., p. 236–7, Beresford to D'Urban, 12 September 1835.
113 DP, A519/3, pp. 107, 200–1, Beresford to D'Urban, 3 November 1835, 8 December 1835.
114 DP, A519/4, pp. 184–6, Beresford to D'Urban, 10 May 1836.
115 DP, A519/2, p. 192, Cloete to D'Urban, 23 August 1835.

116 *Ibid.*, pp. 200–1, Cloete to D'Urban, 29 August 1835; *ibid.*, pp. 235–6, Beresford to D'Urban, 12 September 1835; *PP 1836*, vii (538), pp. 265–71, Beresford, 14 March 1836.
117 DP, A519/4, pp. 103–4, Beresford to D'Urban, 17 March 1836.
118 DP, A519/2, pp. 237–8, 241, 266, Beresford to D'Urban, 12 September 1835, 22 September 1835; DP, A519/3, pp. 111–12, Beresford to D'Urban, 3 November 1835.
119 Galbraith, *Reluctant empire*, pp. 26–7, 62, 132; Peires, *House of Phalo*, p. 115.
120 CO 48/162, fo. 197, Stephen, minute on D'Urban to Hay, private, 12 November 1835.
121 DP, A519/2, p. 193, Cloete to D'Urban, 23 August 1835.
122 DP, A519/3, p. 202, Beresford to D'Urban, 8 December 1835.
123 *Ibid.*, p. 221, Beresford to D'Urban, 29 December 1835; DP, A519/4, p. 187, Beresford to D'Urban, 10 May 1836.
124 CO 48/162, p. 29, D'Urban to Hay, 4 September 1835. See also *ibid.*, pp. 51–2, 54, Bell to Hay, 14 September 1835, 24 September 1835.
125 See, e.g., DP, A519/3, p. 218, Bell to D'Urban, 24 December 1835; NLSA, MSB 142, p. 307, Smith to D'Urban, 17 January 1836.
126 See, e.g., DP, A519/1, pp. 70–4, 84–6, 115–18, Bell to D'Urban, 22 January, 30 January, 13 March 1835; DP A519/2, pp. 36–8, 92–4, 139–41, 184–9, Bell to D'Urban, 29 May, 25 June, 7 August, 21 August 1835; NLSA, MSB 142, pp. 48–9, 117–20, 285–7, 491–2, D'Urban to Smith, 9 October, 3 November 1835, 8 January, 8 April 1836; *ibid.*, pp. 307, 415–16, 424–6, 486–9, 533–5, 544–50, Smith to D'Urban, 17 January, 28 February, 5 March, 3 April, 17 April, 28 April 1836.
127 NLSA, MSB 142, p. 424, Smith to D'Urban, 5 March 1836.
128 *Ibid.*, pp. 425, 449, Smith to D'Urban, 5 March 1836, 20 March 1836.
129 E.g., *ibid.*, p. 612, D'Urban to Smith, 3 June 1836; Macmillan, *Bantu, Boer and Briton*, pp. 154–5.
130 NLSA, MSB 142, pp. 570, 599–600, D'Urban to Smith, 6 May 1836, 27 May 1836.
131 *Ibid.*, p. 585, Smith to D'Urban, 16 May 1836. See also *ibid.*, pp. 424–6, 486–7, Smith to D'Urban, 5 March 1836, 3 April 1836; *ibid.*, pp. 570–1, D'Urban to Smith, 6 May 1836.
132 See the king's annotations on Glenelg's draft, CO 537/145, fos 1–72, especially fos 49, 52, 54, 68.
133 NLSA, MSB 142, pp. 572–5, 612, 644, D'Urban to Taylor, 7 May 1836, D'Urban to Smith, 3 June 1836, Bird to D'Urban, 9 June 1836; CO 48/164, fo. 43, Bird to Glenelg, 3 December 1835.
134 CO 48/167, fos 350–1, 352, 364–6, D'Urban to Glenelg, 2 December 1836, 5 December 1836, 21 December 1836.

CHAPTER FIVE

Traffic: the unofficial correspondence of colonial officials

I have no doubt, Sir, that Major Mitchell, however unwarranted, has presumed in his being known to you, to assume a tone of independence and adopt a course of proceeding, which he would not have attempted under other circumstances. He has repeatedly threatened . . . to refer an appeal to you . . . he desires that when the Governor sets aside or does not adopt his plans, that the correspondence may be referred to His Majesty's Government, as though the local Government had no power to control or interfere with him. (Governor Darling to Colonial Secretary, Sir George Murray)[1]

Despite Ralph Darling's stinging condemnation of his surveyor-general, and his warning that metropolitan failure to support the local government could only lead to disaster, Mitchell outlasted Darling in New South Wales by almost twenty-five years. The antipathy between the two men, which contributed to Darling's recall, was based on the strength of their parallel relationships with the senior staff in the Colonial Office. Mitchell, a Peninsular veteran, was a protégé of Sir George Murray (colonial secretary, 1828–30) and also communicated copiously and unofficially with permanent under-secretary Robert Hay. Ambitious and self-centred, Mitchell was quick to find fault with his peers and superiors in the colony, and as quick to report them, unofficially, to the metropolitan government. While Darling was by no means easy to work with (described as a 'martinet' who was quick to take offence), Mitchell undoubtedly presumed on his close, personal relationship with members of the metropolitan government to undermine the governor. Mitchell believed his first loyalty was to variously the 'public' or the 'Crown', not to the governor.[2] The relationship between Mitchell and Darling demonstrates how, in an atmosphere of uncertainty about officials' responsibility, networks of patronage and information not only sustained the empire, but also encouraged webs of gossip, deceit and intrigue. While intended to serve personal ambition, these connections resulted in a loss of confidence both in London and the colonial governments. In this chapter, the motivations, mechanisms and effects of private correspondence

[94]

between colonial officials and the metropolitan government are examined more closely.[3]

Britain's colonial civil servants operated in a context of confusion over the nature and responsibilities of public service and uncertainty about the potential of colonial societies.[4] They enjoyed no strong sense of colonial coherence, loyalty or government support, and were faced with intense social and financial pressure. After examining contemporary perceptions and pressures of office, this chapter demonstrates how colonial civil servants resorted to their personal metropolitan connections – via their professional, familial, political and interest-based networks – to gain promotion, security, prestige or vindication. Networks were utilised and expanded by the provision of information and colonial patronage, often with scant regard for the side effects of such potentially damaging traffic.

Primarily, this discussion focuses on the elites of colonial governance; considering those who ended their careers as one of the most important colonial officials: the lieutenant-governor; senior military commander; colonial secretary; treasurer; attorney-general; solicitor-general; auditor-general; chief justice; puisne judges; surveyor-general; archdeacon or bishop; colonial engineer; medical officer; and superintendents of police, convicts and slaves. As appointments worth less than roughly two hundred pounds per annum were dealt with almost wholly within the colony, it is senior officials (whether directly appointed, or rising via junior colonial positions) about whom most evidence of metropolitan connections remains. These were the officials who most successfully employed metropolitan networks; and who additionally formed the nucleus of colonial social elites.

The sources drawn on in this chapter include both public and private papers. While colonial officials were not allowed to communicate directly with the Colonial Office on public business (all official correspondence went to London through the governor), until 1835 it was perfectly acceptable, indeed encouraged, for colonial officials to write unofficially to a member of the Colonial Office on either private or public business. Thousands of such letters remain extant: at the Colonial Office in 'private letter files'; in the private collections of the secretaries and under-secretaries of state; or in the collections of colonial officials and their families.

Historiographically, colonial officials subordinate to the level of governor remain relatively unexamined as a group, although several studies of prominent individual public servants exist.[5] This chapter brings these biographies and primary sources together with the literature which examines the culture of early nineteenth-century metropolitan government. The struggles of individual colonial officials for security and advancement fit within metropolitan debates on 'Old Corruption' and patronage, as well as into the confusion surrounding the nature and responsibilities of the metropolitan and colonial civil services. This discussion draws on a range of colonies, although the Cape Colony and New South Wales are considered in most detail.

Colonial public office

Colonial offices were poorly defined in the 1820s and 1830s. The duties, importance and rewards of office varied between colonies and over time: neither between nor within colonies were there standard techniques of recruitment, conditions of service, or pension arrangements. While such ambiguities and inconsistencies troubled both colonial and metropolitan authorities, no agreement could be reached about the best remedy. Change occurred slowly: whether generally in response to larger transitions in colonial societies; or piecemeal in response to particular crises. Uncertainty about both the desired nature and composition of colonial society, and the role and responsibility of civil servants contributed to the failure to implement projected plans for an imperial civil service or to generate an idea of 'empire' to which colonial officials could be loyal.

In the very early nineteenth century colonial public servants were senior military staff, but by the 1820s the civil functions of colonial crown government demanded a senior civil service, although it remained the case that many civil officials had begun their careers in the army or, less commonly, the navy. As discussed in chapter three, the metropolitan impulse to check governors' autocratic power led to the introduction of colonial judicial, executive and administrative institutions from 1820. While crown colonies were still ruled by governors with significant executive powers in 1845, these governors' influence was considerably tempered, by an increasingly independent judiciary, an expanded administration, and representative legislative and executive councils. New South Wales, for example, added six new departments to its establishment between 1820 and 1825, and increased the number of public servants from 789 in 1821 to 1,760 in 1840, as well as introducing representative councils.[6] As civil government expanded, military influence decreased, although veterans continued to dominate the technical disciplines of surveying and engineering, and the coercive roles of policing and convict supervision. In the 1830s civilian-orientated offices – such as colonial secretary or treasurer – were more likely to be filled by a military officer in the Cape than in New South Wales: a bias which seems to have arisen from a combination of the colony's frontier problems and slower adoption of English civil institutions.

Although considerable changes in government were instituted, the demands of growing settler communities for representation – whether political or in the most senior public offices – were less carefully addressed by the Colonial Office. Important government offices were routinely and deliberately filled from Britain by existing expatriate officials, and considerable metropolitan resistance to popular representation remained into the 1840s. While it was more likely that a colonist would occupy a senior position at the Cape than in New South Wales (a result of the British policy of incorporating the conquered Dutch population), even there colonists filled very few of the highest government offices, despite forming a prosperous and respectable community. More typically, colonists were found in relatively junior offices, as landdrosts, civil commissioners, police magistrates, commissioners of crown lands, justices of the peace, assistant surveyors and clerks. Even these positions, however, were frequently filled from Britain: they provided an avenue for young Britons to acquire colonial experience which could lead to promotion. Consequently, colonial competition for these offices was fierce, with any suspected bias felt keenly.[7]

The Colonial Office did advocate the need to 'educate' colonists in anticipation of the introduction of British institutions, and, with this in mind, municipal government was established in both colonies during the 1830s. Nevertheless, the Colonial Office did not truly embrace settler involvement in either the Cape or in New South Wales. As discussed in chapter one, colonial society was designated 'immature', lacking the stability provided by a hereditary aristocracy. Some saw the creation of an upper class as a solution: Bishop Broughton, for example, dreamt of the extension of 'the principle of hereditary rank' to the colonies; and schemes for colonial honours were advanced, but floundered until the 1840s.[8] In fact, the Colonial Office's concerns about colonial societies were more profound. At the Cape, it was slavery, the perceived 'backwardness' of Dutch law, and the Dutch settlers' hostility to the colonial government. Although warned that the Dutch were becoming alienated from the British-dominated administration as early as 1826, the Colonial Office's 'pains to anglicise the colony' made most potential remedies 'extremely absurd'.[9] In New South Wales, convictism coloured metropolitan visions of society. Commissioner Bigge had identified an unacceptably high number of convicts or ex-convicts in the public service in 1821, Governor Darling reported the same situation in 1826, and discussions through the 1830s about juries and political representation were dominated by the spectre of former convicts participating fully in civil society.[10]

While the exertion of greater metropolitan control over colonial institutions and appointments, and references to 'Anglicisation', suggest that the Colonial Office was intent on unifying systems of government, at least in the crown colonies, the progress of Robert Hay's scheme for an empire-wide civil service demonstrates the problems such a task encountered.

Hay initiated discussion in 1826 by writing to several colonial governors and public servants. He suggested the introduction of a civil service that broadly resembled the Ceylon model, itself a replica of the East India Company's service on the sub-continental mainland. The plan was described in most detail to Sir Richard Plasket, the Cape's colonial secretary. An imperial civil service, Hay suggested, offered the opportunity of 'efficiency' in the civil government of conquered colonies. The only way to secure good public servants was to 'train them up collectively from an early age, not with a view to their filling particular offices, but for the service generally'. Young British writers would be attracted by reasonable salaries, a well-structured pension fund, and the opportunity of advancement. Their first years would be spent being 'fitted for higher situations'; these would become available as older men retired to collect their guaranteed pensions, avoiding the existing problem of the retention of office until death. Hay hoped to attract 'young men of average capacity to enter our Colonial Service as readily as they would . . . adopt any of the established professions'.[11] The imperial service would be professional, peripatetic and disinterested, although Hay spent more time discussing the details of pension schemes than the training which would best equip civil servants for colonial governance. Plasket and others responded warmly to Hay's suggestions, discussing the economic viability of the scheme, and how it might be implemented.[12]

But this discussion also highlighted general confusion about colonial government and society, and officials' tendency to frame responses in terms only of their colony's situation. Governor Bourke wrote that an imperial civil service would 'tend most powerfully to keep up the separation between English and Dutch [at the Cape], or rather to exclude the latter almost entirely'. He emphasised the importance of fixing the establishment at 'the lowest number of persons but with decent salaries to each', and appointing a fair mix of Dutch colonists, British settlers and British expatriates.[13] Governor Darling, only recently arrived in New South Wales, but already interested in the problem of colonial government, argued for the creation of a colonial civil service which would not only make colonial government more efficient, but also improve the quality of colonial society.[14] Darling recommended a system that would attract respectable and capable young men not through its pension scheme or high salaries, but through the provision of colonial land grants. The benefits of such a scheme were its low cost (at least for New South Wales with its abundance of land), and the potential to plant a much-needed 'respectable' society. Thus Darling's scheme was the opposite of Hay's. Rather than encouraging peripatetic disinterestedness, he would ensure that public servants were interested in the colony, in the hope that their continuing presence would increase 'the respectable class of society and . . . encourage their friends and connexions to come out and try their fortune'.[15]

Darling's ideas were unfashionable: in a sensitive climate they conjured up visions of a corrupt and land-hungry oligarchy. Via initiatives like the Ripon land regulations of 1831 which restricted free land grants, the Colonial Office emphasised that public servants should devote themselves to their offices, improving efficiency and avoiding the possibility (or appearance) of any conflict of interest. When an Australian civil servant complained that his official duties interfered 'very materially' with his 'agricultural pursuits' in 1829, the metropolitan response was terse: 'civil servants ought to be restricted from these pursuits'.[16] The aims of improving the nature of colonial society and retaining efficient civil servants were never to be officially united in imperial policy.

Hay's plan, which offered long-term efficiency if at short-term expense, was not adopted either, although better arrangements for pensions were gradually introduced. The expansion of colonial government in the 1820s was expensive; in an era of retrenchment, further expansion, especially when confused by arguments between disinterested and interested models of civil service, was too difficult.

As suggested in chapter three, the diversity of the crown colonies made imperial uniformity seem impossible. Both governors and the Colonial Office left larger questions about governance and responsibility unresolved, instead demanding greater detail and volume in reporting and more accountability from junior administrators. Debates over colonial officials' loyalty, duties and conditions did not lead to considered or significant change. The piecemeal and reactive nature of reforms can be seen in two examples: the membership of executive and legislative councils; and the role of the colonial secretary. Both reveal the high level of tension which existed within colonial administrations and which the Colonial Office refused to diffuse by specifying rules or standards.

The formalisation of councils of advice into executive and legislative councils was intended to provide advice and support to the governor, to mimic representative institutions, and to protect the colonies against gubernatorial despotism. As Bathurst observed, the necessity of consultation would give the governor time to reflect; moreover, parliament would 'more willingly trust Authority to a Governor when they know this security against its abuse'.[17] Yet the tension between the supportive and the restrictive purposes of councils led most governors to regard them with suspicion. Any hint of official dissent could send a governor rushing for assertions of metropolitan support and confidence.[18] As nominated settlers were added to councils, their structure increasingly (if crudely) resembled government and opposition, further complicating issues of official loyalty.[19] Sir Richard Plasket, the Cape's colonial secretary, had clashed with Richard Bourke in the council of advice in 1827 over loyalty; later, colonial secretary Alexander McLeay had similar problems with Bourke in New South Wales.[20] Thomas Mitchell, the obstreperous New South Wales surveyor-general, wrangled with every governor he worked under, but had particular difficulties with Gipps regarding his duty to support the governor in council meetings.[21]

Governors responded by exploiting ambiguities over precedence and council membership. It was not always clear, for example, whether membership was associated with particular individuals or with particular offices, an issue at the heart of questions of loyalty.[22] Broughton, who had repeatedly disagreed with Bourke in the New South Wales council, discovered this to his disadvantage when he was promoted from archdeacon to bishop. Bourke's out-of-date instructions specifically named the 'archdeacon' as a council member; thus, Bourke excluded Broughton the bishop until London intervened.[23]

Although by 1828 the remodelling of all colonial councils had 'been for some time in contemplation' in London, with the intention of introducing 'an uniform practise' in regard to membership and proceedings, the Colonial Office was reluctant to set down rules.[24] Some changes were made, as members who needed to appear more impartial (like judges) or whose official duties might conflict with council membership (like bishops) were gradually removed. Sir John Wylde, the Cape's chief justice, was instructed to intervene only on 'matters strictly relating to his profession' with the council of advice in 1828; while Chief Justice Forbes was removed from the New South Wales executive council completely in the same year.[25] In 1826 that colony's executive council had consisted of the governor, lieutenant-governor (the senior military officer after the governor), chief justice, archdeacon and colonial secretary; but by 1842, all had been removed except the governor and colonial secretary. All these changes were reactive. Hay's response to a colonial governor battling with problems of precedence sums up the Colonial Office response: the *important* question of Precedence' had never 'been settled upon any fixed principle in any of our colonies, and I really know not how to give you any assistance . . . on the subject'. He continued: 'If I were called upon to advise however, I should say you would act wisely in turning a deaf ear to all applications whatever on the subject, and leaving matters entirely to their courses.'[26]

Defining the role of the colonial secretary in the crown colonies was another area which exposed imperial confusion and inconsistency: was the colonial secretary a virtual premier; or merely the governor's amanuensis? By the mid-1830s the colonial secretary's office had emerged as the most central department in the crown colonies; co-ordinating government activity and oversight of government correspondence gave it an unbeatable overview. Both governors and colonial secretaries were aware of the importance of a strong relationship to their success. The 1825 recall from New South Wales of both the governor, Sir Thomas Brisbane, and the colonial secretary, Frederick Goulburn, after their professional relationship broke down completely, was a salutary lesson. Governor Arthur reported from Van Diemen's Land in 1829, for example, that he was careful to keep his colonial secretary, Burnett, fully informed, discussing all but the most intimate subjects, 'by the desire to avoid the state of things which so unhappily occurred between Sir Thomas Brisbane and Mr Goulburn'.[27]

But the relationship was not, by its nature, an easy one. While colonial secretaries displayed a more acute sensitivity to the difficulties which insubordination posed for a governor than many colonial civil servants, they were also well-enough informed to have their own views on colonial policy. Cape colonial secretary, John Bell, was aware of the 'evils of a captious and systematic opposition to a governor on the part of the Secretary'.[28] His predecessor, Sir Richard Plasket, knew he had 'no right to complain' about how the governor conducted his business, although this did not stop him from doing so.[29] Sir John Franklin's difficulties with his colonial secretary, John Montagu, led to the governor's recall in 1843.

Despite several requests, the Colonial Office was reluctant to define the role of colonial secretary. If a governor's instructions were too closely prescriptive, they could become quickly redundant.[30] Governors Bourke and Darling had both asked the Colonial Office to state where the responsibilities of public servants lay (with the clear implication, in both cases, that a public servant's duty was loyalty to the governor).[31] In the absence of instructions, the colonial secretary's role depended largely on each individual governor's style. Plasket complained that Bourke was 'extremely *uncommunicative*' never asking for the colonial secretary's advice or opinion and communicating only via 'dry memoranda'.[32] Governor Gipps, by contrast, left most of New South Wales' correspondence to his colonial secretary, Edward Deas Thomson; while at the start of the 1830s Governor Lowry Cole used his private secretary to deal with almost all the business of the Cape Colony, even though the colonial secretary was his brother-in-law, John Bell.[33]

Although Bell acknowledged 'no ambition to go beyond the proper bounds' of his 'official duty', and knew 'the danger of nice definitions on such a subject', he privately lamented to Hay that the governor had made him a 'mere cypher'. 'I regret', continued Bell:

that I have never yet had the means of ascertaining exactly what [my duties] are: whether to advance my own conscientious opinions for the good of the public service and of the Colony . . . – or to be the mere official instrument of carrying the Governor's commands into effect without comment.[34]

Lowry Cole kept the colony's public correspondence in his Cape Town residence, rather than in the office of the colonial secretary. Bell complained that it was thus impossible to 'possess at all times a clear and uninterrupted view of the public business in the course of its transaction', as he felt obliged to do.[35]

In a private response to Bell, Hay went some way towards defining the role of the colonial secretary. As 'one of the first officers of importance' in the colonial government, the colonial secretary was 'entitled to expect that the Governor should consult him in all matters connected with the affairs of the Colony'; additionally, the colonial secretary should, under the governor's instructions, be responsible for the preparation of the colony's official correspondence.[36] The colonial secretary's responsibility for securing correspondence between metropolitan and colonial administrations was stated in a number of circulars on correspondence from 1830 and was further enshrined in the *Rules and regulations* for the colonial service which first appeared in 1837.[37] The replacement of the colonial secretary by a private secretary undermined these functions, giving the governor too much unchecked power. Lowry Cole was reprimanded unofficially by both Hay and the secretary of state, Viscount Goderich; he had already been advised against the same practice while governor of Mauritius. Duties which 'properly belonged to a more responsible officer' should not be given to a private secretary, who was 'likely to prove a serious obstacle to the dispatch of public business at the time, and eventually to lead to the greatest possible embarrassments hereafter'.[38] Nevertheless, no official statement was made by the Colonial Office.

The Colonial Office's unwillingness to make categorical statements on topics of precedence, council membership and the responsibilities of civil servants (either collectively or individually) contributed to an atmosphere of unease and tension in both the Cape Colony and New South Wales. Even the Colonial Office's *Rules and regulations* concentrated more on questions about correspondence and council procedures than on defining the roles of civil servants.

The colonial civil servants

So who were the colonial civil servants? They came from all over the British Isles, although Scotland and Ireland were particularly well represented: partly because more desirable metropolitan positions often went to better-connected English candidates; and partly because there were some advantages for Roman Catholics and Protestant dissenters in the ecclesiastically less regulated (although often extremely bigoted) colonies. The 1830s' law officers in New South Wales, Roger Therry and John Hubert Plunkett, for example, were both Irish Catholics; while the Catholic Christopher Bird chose to avoid taking the oath of allegiance in 1818, becoming Cape government secretary rather than the more prestigious secretary at war in Ireland.[39] Those who sought and obtained colonial office shared some common characteristics in social background. Almost all aspired to be (and many were) 'respectable' members of the class broadly defined as gentry. They seem to have matched Bourne's characterisation of seekers of public office in Britain: that is, they belonged to the 'pseudo-gentry', a financially insecure class that was without property, but nonetheless attempted to live in a manner requiring considerable income. The civil service was regarded as a respectable means of acquiring this income, and applicants believed that a colonial office would pay well.[40]

In the era of post-war retrenchment, not only sinecure positions, but also efficient offices were threatened. Such retrenchment placed the pseudo-gentry in an awkward situation. Almost all were younger sons, and many in turn had their own large families; positions had to be found for sons, and favourable marriages arranged for daughters. William Lushington, suffering from the loss of another position and 'the very questionable state of West India Property', was reduced to begging for office at the Colonial Office in order to maintain his accustomed status. 'I have been told', he wrote, that 'the office of Paymaster General in Jamaica is vacant, and that the emoluments are about £2000 per annum [and] as I have estates in that island, such an appointment might suit me very well'. Conscious too of the need to advance his family, Lushington asked for introductions to various West Indian governors for his son.[41] Similar private correspondence indicates that much time and energy was spent in securing the family and its future, and that financial and social matters were pursued (usually) delicately, but doggedly. Anecdotal evidence suggests that most Britons who were appointed to colonial office would have preferred a metropolitan position.[42] Often, however, there was simply nothing available in Britain; or colonial life was believed more economical than metropolitan; or it was thought to provide greater opportunities for land and patronage.

Appointment to office was via patronage, in a system that Finer has called 'recruitment by private recommendation'.[43] Colonial historians disagree about the extent to which patronage was exercised by colonial governors on behalf of the metropolitan government (where most patronage belonged to the Colonial Office, Treasury or Horse Guards). Offices worth more than two hundred pounds per annum were in the gift of the metropolitan authorities, although this was not officially regulated until the late 1830s.[44] McMartin argues that in New South Wales at least the governor's recommended appointee was usually simply adopted by the Colonial Office.[45] In fact, the Colonial Office files of applications for the period 1815 to 1845 suggest that while many gubernatorial recommendations were adopted, the Colonial Office took a significant interest in the process – inspired partly by a desire to avoid the appearance of 'jobbing' (either by themselves or the governor), and partly by a desire to fulfil their own considerable patronage obligations.[46] Some governors, like Darling, had enormous difficulties getting any nominees appointed; while even Bourke, who enjoyed a strong relationship with the metropolitan government, did not find that his choices were automatically accepted; and other governors, like Napier, had to concede some appointments in order to secure others.

The best patrons for aspiring colonial officials were senior politicians in the Colonial Office, or within the ministry more broadly; and the senior permanent metropolitan officials.[47] As most applicants did not have a direct link to the Colonial Office, they used intermediary connections among the great and the good. The Colonial Office records include volumes of applications for positions of all levels; most of which were merely acknowledged and filed. Unsurprisingly, powerful individuals – large landholders, political figures, military heroes, society hostesses – and personal friends of the holders of patronage, were the best connections to have. The fewer links in the chain between applicant and patronage holder, the greater the chances of success. Bourne has examined metropolitan patronage in considerable detail, demonstrating how complex the relationships between client, broker and patron could be.[48] Such relationships were understood and manipulated by all links in the patronage chain. As a family friend wrote to a young army officer in 1812, it was always important for him to behave so that his 'Circle of Friends and Patrons' was enlarged.[49]

The influence of older relatives or in-laws in acquiring patronage supports the contention advanced by both Bourne and Harling that patronage was more likely to be a reward for services rendered than an attempt to secure future loyalty.[50] John Deas Thomson, for example, a Leith merchant and (during the Napoleonic Wars) an Admiralty official, managed after considerable trouble and an extensive programme of calling in old favours, to have his elder son appointed naval storekeeper in the Cape Colony; and his younger, clerk to the councils in New South Wales.[51] Dudley Perceval, fourth son of Spencer Perceval, was appointed clerk to the Cape's council of advice in 1825 through his friendship with Bathurst; within three years he had been appointed auditor-general at a salary of one thousand pounds per annum. Older applicants used the connections they had forged in earlier government positions to gain access to the ranks of colonial administration. Alexander McLeay, for example, worked at the Transport Board during the French wars, but was pensioned off in 1817 when he had a large family to support. McLeay used his connections within the Tory administration to secure the colonial secretaryship of New South Wales in 1825.[52] Bishop Broughton was initially appointed as archdeacon on the recommendation of his patron, the Duke of Wellington. Broughton had carefully fostered a close relationship with the Duchess of Wellington after his appointment to a living close to the Wellington residence at Strathfield Saye.[53]

A very close connection to a governor or his senior officials could also lead to colonial appointment. However, by the 1830s, the metropolitan desire to distance colonial administrations from charges of nepotism, and metropolitan pressure to find offices for the avalanche of British candidates, meant that appointments originating in the colonies were regularly disallowed in London. Hay told Governor Darling's brother-in-law that his close connections to the governor would prevent him gaining an official appointment in New South Wales.[54] The Colonial Office had been alerted several times to Darling's alleged nepotism – most vociferously by direct rivals to Darling's connections.[55] While Governor Bourke's campaign to have his son-in-law, Edward Deas Thomson, appointed colonial secretary in New South Wales, was successful, it highlighted the Colonial Office's concern about appearances in London and the colony. A few years later, Governor Napier's efforts to have his brother-in-law, Mr Craig, appointed to a Cape position, indicate that Colonial Office regulations were still fluid. In 1841 Napier wrote privately to Lord Stanley, requesting that Craig be appointed colonial secretary. Craig was 'so perfectly well calculated in every particular for the confidential and important situation', 'totally unconnected with local parties either public or private', and the only person in the Cape in whom Napier could have the confidence 'so absolutely necessary to subsist between' the colonial secretary and governor. Napier noted that he had never before appointed a 'friend or relation to any vacant office in this colony'. Despite this, Stanley declined to appoint Craig, citing his near connection to the governor, and appointing a candidate with metropolitan patrons instead. Nevertheless, when Napier again brought forward Craig's name, this time for the appointment of clerk to the councils (noting that this office could not 'be deemed subject to the immediate control or influence of the Governor, and therefore . . . not liable to the [earlier] objection'), Stanley was prepared to concede – but only after his protégé, Leveson Gower, was offered Craig's existing position of private secretary to Napier. In this case, so keen was Stanley to find Leveson Gower a position, that he also reversed the 'rule' by which he had been 'invariably guided', that is refusing to make provisional appointments to situations which were not yet vacant.[56] In earlier years, such sensibilities had carried less force. Harry Rivers, from 1816 successively wharf-master, landdrost of Albany, landdrost of Swellendam, colonial treasurer and paymaster-general of the Cape Colony, gained his initial appointments through his brother-in-law, the Cape government's secretary, apparently without remark.[57]

Applicants, or their patrons, either applied to the Colonial Office for a particular position or – more generally – for any available colonial office. Most patrons and candidates sensed correctly that the Colonial Office's selection procedures favoured early (and repeated) applications; consequently, the merest rumour regarding an impending colonial vacancy could provoke dozens of enquiries. The majority were unsuccessful, a typical response summed up by the secretary of state's minute: 'General answer – we get so many claimants – I can hold out no expectation.'[58] Occasionally, as with the introduction of English law (and a supreme court) to the Cape in 1827, or the expansion of the New South Wales colonial survey in the late 1820s, the Colonial Office would ask senior professionals to recommend suitably qualified candidates. Hay requested that the solicitor-general of Scotland provide him with a list of potential judges for the Cape, from which he chose William Menzies to be one of the puisne judges.[59] Similarly, Sir George Murray was invited to recommend qualified military surveyors for New South Wales.[60] Such cases, however, seem to have been quite rare, and selection procedures in general were unsystematic.

Senior colonial officials were rarely appointed to their most important office straight from Britain. A subordinate position in the central colonial bureaucracy – such as assistant colonial secretary, clerk to the councils, or deputy surveyor-general – was a more likely beginning, although some began seeking promotion immediately. As most officials acquired property, interests and connections where they worked, they generally preferred to gain promotion in the same colony. The expense of transferring between colonies was a frequent source of complaint. Governors, of course, did move between colonies, and their entourages formed the most peripatetic set of colonial officials. Some officials, like the relatively junior Ker Hamilton, who moved from Mauritius to the Cape with Lowry Cole, moved happily, hoping for promotion; while others, like Judge William Burton, who was transferred from the Cape to New South Wales at Bourke's request, were unhappy with the change. The move disturbed Burton's interests, and took him even further from Britain.[61]

As officials rose in the colonial hierarchy, and achieved a corresponding social standing (perhaps clearly marked by a knighthood, as in the Australian cases of Sir Thomas Mitchell and Sir Edward Deas Thomson) their role in the mediation of patronage changed. Either they became patrons by distributing junior colonial positions, or they entered the chain of patronage as brokers between their metropolitan connections and the governor. Judge Burton managed to get his brother appointed master of the rolls at the Cape; while Thomas Mitchell was optimistic about the opportunities he could provide for his extended family as surveyor-general of New South Wales.[62] Colonial officials also provided social patronage within the colonial sphere: introductions were part of the fabric of both metropolitan and colonial life; and were vital within the self-conscious world of the colonial elite. Hay, Huskisson, Gladstone, Glenelg and others who had distributed colonial patronage from London, in turn expected their protégés to foster younger clients' careers and social advancement. Hay, for example, promoted many careers, including that of the young Chetwynd Stapylton whom he sent to New South Wales as assistant surveyor in 1828: not only did Hay arrange Stapylton's position; but he also informed Thomas Mitchell, and later Bourke, of his particular interest in Stapylton, requesting their support for his protégé's professional and social advancement.[63]

Senior public servants formed a colonial social elite, especially in Australia, where the non-official elite was relatively small and poorly established by the 1830s (besides possessing socially questionable links to convict society). The conventions of British society were followed closely, at times more rigidly than in the metropolis.[64] In the Cape Colony, the better-established society of Dutch settlers diluted the official clique slightly: while few colonists got top colonial jobs, they certainly intermarried with the British expatriates who did. Marriage also cemented the bonds within official cliques. All three daughters of New South Wales' colonial secretary, Alexander McLeay, for example, married civil servants – two married police magistrates (one of whom had been the governor's aide-de-camp), and a third married the assistant colonial secretary.

Colonial officials certainly regarded themselves as belonging to a different, and better, class than colonists. Thomas Mitchell, recently appointed surveyor-general, told his brother: 'I must be very reserved and aristocratic here, being one of the *Nobility*, that is Surveyor General and Chief Commissioner in the division and valuation of the territory – Justice of the Peace, &c, &c.'[65] The expatriate officials felt (not always with justification) that they were less 'interested' in colonial affairs, and thus less open to criticisms of corruption or jobbing. They believed that they had a finer grasp of manners and etiquette, as well as better connections, than their colonial contemporaries. In Van Diemen's Land, deputy surveyor-general, George Frankland, was 'agreeably surprized by the description of society' in 1827, although it was 'limited to eight or ten families', all official. His assessment rested partially on the observation that the Tasmanian ladies were 'less behind the *fashions* than they are at the Cape or in India, and that, you know, gives a civilized air to a place'.[66] The correspondence of Alexander McLeay's daughter, Fanny, indicates that 'respectable society' in New South Wales was also very small, and almost completely divided from settler society.[67] Every new member of official society was examined in detail – on grounds of marriageability, connections, family and finances. Fanny, for example, knew how much Thomas Mitchell and Edward Deas Thomson earned.[68] Officials and their families were concerned to maintain 'appropriate' relations with other sections of colonial society. Lists of invitations to dinner, or balls, or other Government House functions, were minutely examined by the colonial elites; with great emphasis put on inappropriate inclusions or exclusions. Two particularly poignant letters from Sir John Jamison to Governor Bourke discuss the exclusion of his natural daughter from Government House.[69] These distinctions match Davidoff's analysis of the evolution of British 'Society' and her observation that social formalities were most pronounced when social distinctions were threatened or unclear – as in the colonies.[70] This distance was perceived keenly and bitterly at the Cape by the 1820 British settlers, who objected to both the social airs of the official class and a perceived bias against their appointment to important colonial positions.[71]

Exacerbated by the small size and material uncertainties of colonial society, social distinctions thus took on great significance. In the search for promotion, applicants cited social reasons almost as commonly as financial reasons, although financial security was ultimately of greater importance. Campbell Riddell applied for the position of colonial secretary of New South Wales, while treasurer in that colony, because 'if any government officer now employed in the colony becomes Colonial Secretary – he will be placed over me – and I confess . . . I should not like to be supervised'.[72] Envisaging a New South Wales' administration dominated by his extended family, Henry Dumaresq admitted to his mother that 'amongst the vanities of this silly life – power and importance, rank very high with we male fools'.[73] Questions of official precedence were particularly sensitive. When New South Wales' order of precedence was changed, moving the attorney-general ahead of the surveyor-general, the latter was outraged. 'My place at Government House, which was once beside the Archdeacon is now near the foot of the table under accountants and custom house officers, who never could under different circumstances take precedence of a field officer of His Majesty's Army', he complained to London. 'Surely [my] appointment is not so unimportant as to reduce me to a less elevated place in this corner of the Empire than my military rank would procure me elsewhere!'[74] Once the Cape's supreme court had been established, the precise ranking of the judiciary caused considerable headaches for successive governors, a difficulty also experienced in New South Wales.[75]

Recognition in the form of honours was also important.[76] John Wylde, the first chief justice of the Cape's supreme court, applied for a knighthood on the basis that the previous chief justice of the colony had received that honour. Although knighthoods were 'at a discount in England', such an honour 'would be of substantial value in the Colony', James Stephen thought, recommending the knighthood which would 'launch' the new supreme court 'with some additional éclat and advantage'. Wylde was duly knighted.[77] Others contemplated the class of distinction they received, comparing their own rank with their colleagues'. Such contemplation provoked some impassioned communications with the metropolitan authorities.[78] Requests for recognition often mentioned the perceived disadvantage of a career played out beyond England, particularly in a distant colony.[79]

While many Britons were driven to apply for colonial public service positions for economic reasons, senior officials often failed to realise their hopes of financial security. Earlier colonial officials had shared the spoils of colonial land and sinecures, but by the 1830s new land regulations and salary reductions meant that financial loss from a colonial sojourn was standard, particularly if the official returned to England on retirement. Additionally, colonial elites were expected to live and entertain in a manner suitable to their position; and such a lifestyle could eat up funds.[80] In the new atmosphere of public service probity and retrenchment, salaries seemed unlikely to rise. Michell, the Cape's surveyor-general, reported that his seven hundred pounds per annum was 'barely sufficient to make ends meet';[81] while Burnett, Van Diemen's Land's colonial secretary, could not support his family 'with that degree of respectability which is expected from the rank I hold'.[82] Broughton complained that the bishop of Australia's salary was to be reduced for any future appointee. 'Compelled to rent at an expense of £300' a year, and 'subject to a very burdensome charge for life assurances . . . and the entire expenses of travelling' between the Australian colonies, the current salary barely met his expenditure.[83] For others, deep in debt and with no prospect of an adequate pension, colonial offices were hung on to grimly, even when conditions became unbearable. Fanny McLeay lamented: 'Oh! That our Father were out of debt and that he could then retire from all intercourse with such vile creatures.'[84] Her father, who considered returning to London to lobby for a pension, regarded himself as 'a much poorer man now, after six years disadvantages . . . than when he arrived'.[85]

To combat financial insecurity, colonial officials employed every means they could to gain promotion. A Colonial Office invitation to report privately on colonial affairs was an excellent chance to pursue promotion; some officials would even prematurely announce the resignation or ill health of their colleagues or superiors. As Henry Dumaresq, Darling's private secretary, sailed for Sydney in 1829, he wrote to a metropolitan patron that it was 'by no means improbable that the present treasurer of New South Wales should have "shuffled off this mortal coil" ere we reach Sydney'. Consequently Dumaresq rebuked himself for not having acquainted the secretary of state with 'the arrangements I had made . . . in the event of his being disposed to confer the appointment on me'.[86] Previously Dumaresq (acting on behalf of his brother, William) and Thomas Mitchell had jostled to secure the appointment of surveyor-general in New South Wales as the incumbent ailed;[87] while Alexander McLeay's ambiguous pronouncements in 1835 provoked a flurry of correspondence announcing his resignation to the Colonial Office from candidates for colonial secretary including Campbell Riddell, Edward Deas Thomson and Thomas Harington.[88]

The letters of colonial officials and their families often hinted at the fear of being forgotten at home. Colonial employment was insecure and political, and the sense that good metropolitan connections could help in a crisis crept into many otherwise innocuous letters. Fanny McLeay displayed this insecurity and frustration in 1829. Her father and Governor Darling were at the centre of a colonial storm: the colonists had sent indictment documents back to London. 'I need not tell you', wrote Fanny to her brother, 'that it was a vile tissue of falsehoods from beginning to end.'

> But as the truth is not always triumphant in this vile world, I have my secret fears that its reception *at home* may not be quite what it ought to be. My reasons for this are [first] the Governor having lost his friend in the Duke of York and the Duke of Wellington has of course many protégés to provide for

who will never allow him rest until he has answered their constant cry of give, give. The next is that my Father's situation is we know much coveted by Mr Barnett . . . who is a relation of the Duke of Atholl and so connected to Sir George Murray. Mr B wrote home to the Duchess that my father had resigned and she applied for the place immediately for him, a poor stupid worn out spendthrift.[89]

As we shall see, many colonial civil servants kept in touch with their metropolitan connections; from fear of being forgotten, simple gratitude, and with an eye to future patronage.

A 'case of madeira' and a 'canister of snuff': the creation and use of networks

Like others in colonial society, officials recognised that the power over their prospects was concentrated in London. Promotion, as with initial appointment, was authorised or denied by the Colonial Office (although often recommended by the governor); appeals for pay increases, military promotion, honours and pensions were also best dealt with in London. And, in a dispute with the governor, colonial officials had nowhere to appeal but the metropolitan government. To this end metropolitan patrons were wooed relentlessly, and information and small-scale colonial patronage were mediated through networks of personal connection.

Many officials belonged to established networks – that was how they had acquired their first appointment – and they did not abandon these once they had acquired office. Bourne is incorrect to argue that colonial officials wrote a couple of letters on the voyage out, and then disappeared from metropolitan view.[90] Hay's colonial protégés, for example, were particularly assiduous in their correspondence.[91] But the appropriate form of approach depended on circumstances – sometimes nothing less than a personal appearance would do – and colonial officials had to assess each situation, extending, cultivating and manipulating information and connections as opportunities presented themselves.

Assessing colonial officials' motivations can be difficult. Attempts to skew information for the purposes of personal advancement are obvious – as with the premature reports of a colleague's retirement – but distinguishing between challenges to colonial policy that were motivated by a desire to improve government, and those intended to undermine a colleague, is more troublesome, especially as most communications involved elements of both. The same networks of communication and patronage were employed for either purpose, demonstrating colonial recognition that reports and arguments that went directly to London were most likely to be influential. Usually, officials who genuinely believed a policy misguided, would challenge it regardless of whether the policy's source was colonial or metropolitan;

while those whose primary aim was self-advancement, were more likely to focus on criticism of the governor.

Perhaps the most useful way for colonial officials to make their case – whether challenging policy or for personal advancement – was to travel to London in person. While not always the most practical way to proceed, more officials than might be suspected used this approach at least once. Colonial officials usually visited Britain while on leave of absence, although occasionally they might be sent on particular business by the governor. Once in Britain, as discussed earlier, officials undertook a number of personal and public tasks. Some, like Mitchell, the Australian surveyor-general, spent a remarkable proportion of their careers as colonial officials on leave in Britain.

William Broughton, New South Wales' archdeacon, travelled to London in 1834 to put his case on church lands to the Colonial Office. Broughton thought Governor Bourke's employment of a government agent to manage church lands, and desire to spend the profits generally, on the Irish model, wrong.[92] He argued instead that church lands should be kept as a perpetual trust, with profit spent exclusively on the Church of England. Broughton appealed for assistance to the bishop of London, Charles Blomfield, and decided his case would be best made in England. As the colonial government refused to give Broughton financial support, the archdeacon sold his belongings to fund his passage.[93] Once in Britain, Broughton contacted his friends and patrons, attending a celebration at his old school with the Duke of Wellington and William Howley, the archbishop of Canterbury, where he sought their support.[94] At an official level, Broughton encountered difficulties: while Spring Rice was colonial secretary all the interviews the archdeacon arranged at the Colonial Office were postponed.[95] Once the Tories took over in November Broughton gained access to the new secretary of state. Unfortunately for Broughton, the Tory administration actually supported Bourke's plans, but as a sop they offered Broughton the first bishopric of Australia. Although Broughton vacillated for almost another year, before leaving Britain with the church lands question unresolved, he did make some headway on education and achieved personal advancement.[96] As discussed in chapter four, Broughton's presence encouraged Governor Bourke's to send his son to the metropolis, and one of Dick Bourke's first tasks was to represent to the Colonial Office the governor's view of the church and schools issue.[97]

The New South Wales judges Francis Forbes and William Burton also usefully employed sojourns in Britain by appearing at the Colonial Office. In 1824 Forbes had helped the Colonial Office draw up a new constitution for the colony, on his way between legal appointments in Newfoundland and New South Wales. Returning to London in 1836 on leave (he announced his resignation while in Britain), Forbes was consulted extensively by Glenelg and Stephen about the forthcoming New South Wales Act, and appeared as a witness before the Transportation Select Committee, also acting as personal envoy for Bourke.[98] William Burton used two years in Britain to plead his case for promotion at the Colonial Office, if not to the chief justiceship of New South Wales, then to another colony.[99] John Bell, colonial secretary at the Cape, was another official who used his leave in Britain to give his (eagerly sought) opinions on colonial affairs to Hay at the Colonial Office; while the metropolitan self-promotion of Tasmanian colonial secretary, John Montagu, was touched on in chapter four.[100]

Obviously it was often impossible for colonial officials to travel to London to communicate with the metropolitan government, leading them to enter the ambiguous world of unofficial correspondence. Although colonial officials were forbidden from writing publicly to London on public matters (unless they went through the governor), in practice this was loosely interpreted. While Dudley Perceval was reprimanded in 1826 for writing officially to the Colonial Office, as was Judge Menzies in 1829, others who wrote privately on public matters were not.[101] Many officials had been encouraged to write unofficially to the Colonial Office by Hay, or one of the other senior staff, and although these letters had a personal flavour, they certainly dealt with public as well as private business. Wilmot Horton received considerable correspondence from some colonial officials, perhaps most notably Chief Justice Francis Forbes and John Beverley Robinson, the attorney-general of Upper Canada.[102]

Just as for governors, a personal connection within the department was the best way to initiate a correspondence. Those who were not lucky enough to have existing connections could work to create them. Sometimes this was done very explicitly. Judge John Willis's cultivation of Hay and Lord Stanley through the provision of botanical and zoological specimens, for example, was documented in chapter two. Others, like Judge William Menzies at the Cape, and Governor Sir Frederick Adam in the Ionian Islands, sent presents to the under-secretary, Hay, without any pretence of scientific interest. Interestingly, Menzies' case of madeira was rebuffed by Hay, who claimed that he routinely declined presents for fear of compromising his independence. Such a lofty approach was undermined by Hay's acceptance (in the same month) of high-quality Mediterranean snuff from Adam. The correspondence suggests that Hay perceived Adam's snuff as a genuine gift from a friend, while Menzies' present was seen merely as an unwelcome attempt at ingratiation.[103]

Form and etiquette were clearly major concerns when writing to the Colonial Office. Officials were more likely to write to Hay than to the secretary of state, even on occasions when they hoped that their concerns would reach the highest level. Sensitive intelligence was provided, or a delicate request framed, with a hint that its substance, or direct extracts, should be put by Hay before the colonial secretary. As already seen, the secretaries to colonial governments best appreciated the presumption of corresponding directly with the metropolitan government. John Bell hoped he would be excused 'the liberty' of addressing Hay on a matter which was of a 'half public, half private nature', while Alexander McLeay tried rigidly not to touch on anything relating to public business in unofficial communications with Hay.[104] Other officials were less cautious about presuming upon a personal connection. John Montagu wrote to Hay in 1834 asking him to support his application to become colonial secretary of Van Diemen's Land. The Australian colonies were not within Hay's portfolio at this time, but Montagu drew on Hay's 'kindly disposition', because the appropriate under-secretary, Lefevre, was unknown to him. Montagu thought that the decision of the secretary of state, 'like that of his predecessors', would be influenced by Hay's opinion, regardless of Hay's portfolio. He approached Hay with 'much confidence', and indeed was duly appointed.[105]

Colonial officials who regularly corresponded with the Colonial Office included Campbell Riddell, Thomas Mitchell, and Sir Richard Plasket. Riddell wrote frequently and extensively to Hay, who was his patron and a family friend, and not only kept the under-secretary informed of his progress and opinions, but also severely criticised the administration of Governor Bourke in the early 1830s.[106] Like Riddell, Thomas Mitchell was at times awarded his own section in the incoming private letter books, so copious was his correspondence with Hay. Falling out with every governor he worked under, and believing himself responsible to the crown and public before the colonial administration, meant that Mitchell had plenty to write about. His letters cover personal ambition, slights (real and imagined) from other colonists and officials, the organisation of government, his peers' and superiors' qualities, land policy, surveying and exploration. It must have been a relief for the Colonial Office in 1831 when Governor Darling (another official who wrote extensively and frequently) was recalled before his long-running dispute with Mitchell had to be resolved. The correspondence on the subject already ran into hundreds of pages.[107]

When private channels of communication to the Colonial Office failed, colonial civil servants could write to the metropolitan authorities officially, through the governor. As such correspondence was read by the governor and placed on the public record in London, it entailed significant disadvantages. However, for an official who regarded himself as truly aggrieved, or was particularly arrogant or clever, it could be a powerful tool. Governors were obliged to forward such correspondence, so, for those convinced of their case and with metropolitan allies, writing through the governor was an assertion of confidence. Governors in turn exercised their power by delaying the despatch of complaints and grievances, sometimes for years. Mitchell sent accounts of his grievances to the secretary of state 'in the regular manner' through Governor Darling, but also sent copies directly to Hay at least three times. 'As the Governor seems in no hurry to send home the originals', Mitchell thought himself 'entitled to forward copies direct to the Secretary of State'. The 'propriety of submitting a duplicate or not' to the secretary of state was left to Hay's 'kind consideration'.[108]

Andries Stockenström, lieutenant-governor of the Eastern Cape in the late 1830s, attempted to use his official correspondence with Governor D'Urban as a means of communicating with the metropolitan government. Although Stockenström was correctly regarded by D'Urban as a metropolitan-sponsored check on his administration, and a means of controlling policy on the Eastern Cape frontier, Stockenström's instructions forbade him from communicating directly with the Colonial Office. All official communication was to go via the governor, who was obliged to forward it to London. Although Stockenström had a personal connection with several of the Colonial Office staff (including James Stephen), he took up his position after private communications between officials and Colonial Office staff were banned, so he had no alternative direct avenue to the London authorities. The relationship between Stockenström and D'Urban quickly broke down, and Stockenström's despatches to the governor were correspondingly written, in practice, for London.[109] Unfortunately for Stockenström, D'Urban delayed sending his correspondence to the metropolitan government, claiming that understaffing prevented the necessary copies from being made until well after a year from the date of writing.[110] Such difficulties meant that, where possible, private and unofficial letters to Colonial Office staff were preferred over public communications.

Colonial officials and their families also extended and consolidated their networks of metropolitan contacts outside the Colonial Office. Friends and family in Britain were put into service as intermediaries between officials and the Colonial Office – directly if they had useful connections, and indirectly if not. As for governors, even where a direct link with the office existed, some sensitive matters were best approached through a patron. A number of colonial officials routinely sent their unofficial correspondence to the Colonial Office twice: one copy directly and one travelling via British-based family or friends, as a means of simultaneously guarding against lost mail, and emphasising a request through repetition. Campbell Riddell came from a moderately well-connected Scottish family: his best connection in the Colonial Office was Hay, but Glenelg was also a family acquaintance. In addition to private letters which Riddell sent directly to the Colonial Office, he asked his family (usually his brother, Sir James Riddell) to communicate their accounts of his progress to the metropolitan government. As these accounts corresponded closely with what Riddell sent directly to the government, it seems that their purpose was to emphasise, rather than to elaborate on, his information, views and requests. John Deas Thomson continued to keep the Colonial Office informed of his son's progress in New South Wales, forwarding extracts and summaries of Edward's letters. When an opportunity for Edward's promotion arose, Thomson senior seized it in a sequence of letters to his former colleague Hay.[111] Even when there was no close personal connection with the Colonial Office, family members in Britain often lobbied the government for their relatives' promotion, or for the redress of grievances. The brother of Quebec's deputy adjutant-general, for example, wrote to the Colonial Office when he discovered that his brother's position was to be combined with that of the deputy quartermaster-general, making one of the incumbents redundant. He requested that Hay 'just give me a hint that we may, if we can, get a little word in my brother's favor whispered in Ld Hill's ear'.[112]

Bishop Broughton also employed connections beyond the Colonial Office throughout his colonial career. In 1839, outraged by Governor Gipps's decision to receive the Roman Catholic bishop at a colonial levee, Broughton wrote to his friends Dr Pusey and the Reverend Edward Coleridge. He told Coleridge – who conveniently taught Peel's sons at Eton – that he had sent copies of his correspondence with Gipps to 'Sir Robert Inglis, and through him to Lord Lyndhurst [the Tory lord chancellor], and if I had been acquainted with your friend Mr Gladstone would have done the same to him'. Broughton had already hinted to Coleridge that he should interest Gladstone in the question of New South Wales' church lands earlier in 1839.[113] By engaging metropolitan support Broughton hoped he was increasing the odds in his favour, for in the colony he had 'no *effective* support' and the administration was 'fearfully against me'.[114] In 1842 Broughton expressed his conservative views on Australian society to Coleridge, hoping that he could

> put this into the head of some one of your friends, who has talent and station to qualify him for working out this conception, and who would devote himself to it, as we have seen frequent instances of men in parliament attaching themselves to some great object, and never ceasing till they had carried it.[115]

Through his connection with Peel, Coleridge ensured that this letter appeared on the desk of the colonial secretary, Lord Stanley.[116] Coleridge also obtained metropolitan legal opinions for Broughton: 'I know you have access to the best', wrote Broughton.[117]

Patrons remained an important resource to be cultivated even after a colonial appointment had been taken up. Whether in or out of office, Sir George Murray, Thomas Mitchell's patron from the Peninsula, continued to promote Mitchell's interests. Called on by Mitchell to advance his case for variously promotion, extension of leave, land grants, payments and a knighthood, Murray generally seemed happy to comply throughout the 1820s and 1830s.[118] Given that Mitchell was involved in several controversies –

over his management skills, insubordination and wanton execution of Aborigines among other things – it is likely that Murray's championship helped to keep Mitchell in office where a less well-connected individual might have been recalled.[119] Henry Somerset, commandant of the Cape's eastern frontier, was another notorious incompetent. However, as the grandson of a duke and son of the colony's former governor, Somerset managed to keep his position and even to be promoted, apparently through his good connections.[120] When requesting promotion or honours an indirect approach – ideally through a patron – was typical. Patrons employed their knowledge of metropolitan government to make the best timed and pitched approach to the Colonial Office: as when Sir George Murray told Mitchell that it was better that he did not approach the Colonial Office in the current political situation; or when Lord Melville wrote to Hay on behalf of one of his clients, instead of bothering the secretary of state.[121] On other occasions, as many avenues as possible were employed.

The Peninsular network was particularly important when it came to colonial officials' hopes of military advancement or reward for military services (sometimes in the distant past). Such requests were directed to the military staff at the Horse Guards, and encouraged a parallel (although overlapping) system of networks and patrons to those of the Colonial Office. At the Cape, where civil administrators continued to have strong military connections through the 1830s, more emphasis was placed on connections in the Horse Guards' sphere for colonial officials, as well as governors. The extra degree of remove between the Horse Guards and the Colonial Office was a disadvantage for officials attempting to achieve civilian promotion. Increasingly through the 1830s, decision-making was concentrated in the Colonial Office (although the Treasury continued to slow things down), and the Whig administrations of that decade, with fewer military connections, cut down the traditional Colonial Office–Horse Guards intercourse.

Not all colonial officials used private channels of communication effectively, even in the period up to 1835 when direct private correspondence with the Colonial Office was not only permitted, but actively encouraged. Those who did fell into three categories. First were those who had personal connections with the Colonial Office, either through family, patrons or their own long service. This class included Campbell Riddell, Edward Deas Thomson, John Bell, and Sir Richard Plasket. A good proportion of these men had been specifically asked by Hay or Wilmot Horton to keep in touch privately with the Colonial Office, an invitation that was often alluded to by way of introduction in correspondence from relatively junior colonial officials.[122] Second were those, like William Broughton and Thomas Mitchell, with sublime metropolitan connections outside the Colonial Office – the Duke of Wellington, a government minister, or one of a few members of the landed aristocracy. Such connections typically predated colonial appointments or even interest, resting rather on the Peninsular network or perhaps the Anglican church. The third category included those with sufficient confidence to establish new links with individuals within the metropolitan government – Hay, in the vast majority of cases between 1826 and 1835. Judge John Willis (the 'naturalist'), is a typical example; while John Beverley Robinson, the Upper Canadian who rose to be chief justice, managed to establish strong personal links with successive metropolitan governments throughout the 1820s and 1830s. The legal background of both these men is not surprising: the judiciary, more than any other group within colonial administrations, exercised their independence from the governor. On the whole judges were well educated (or felt themselves to be), ambitious and persistent in pursuing their aims. They had a keen sense of hierarchy and precedence, and were likely to have strong views on both the nature of colonial society, and their rightful place within (or above) it.

The impact of private correspondence

Private correspondence and personal connections did not, of course, guarantee success. Some colonial officials misjudged the favour in which they were held by the metropolitan government: someone like Hay, after all, had many protégés who frequently competed against one another. Hay, like others in the Colonial Office and colonial administrations, was also concerned that those forwarded for position or promotion were capable and responsible. Campbell Riddell, who correctly judged that Hay was interested in his career, came up against this problem in his application for the office of New South Wales' colonial secretary in 1835. The successful candidate, Edward Deas Thomson, was better connected: his father was a friend of Hay's; and, as demonstrated in chapter four, he had the weight of the Bourkes behind him. Hay's letter to Riddell on the subject suggested rather disingenuously that he 'interfered as little as possible in regard to the Patronage' of the Colonial Office, but promised 'to bear testimony in your favor should I be consulted on the subject'.[123] By this time, Hay was marginalised in the Colonial Office, but he had begun to distance himself from Riddell's application some eighteen months earlier, telling Riddell's brother that

> for so very responsible a situation as that of Colonial Secretary, in such a settlement as New South Wales, the Secretary of State must, in just service to the Public, and to his own character, institute a very rigid inquiry into the comparative merits of the candidates . . . whenever the place may become vacant.[124]

[117]

Promises from the Colonial Office to keep an individual 'in mind' were not always hollow – especially if the applicant's patron was titled – and obligations were fulfilled where possible.

The Colonial Office's unsystematic approach to appointments meant there was a significant advantage in being first to make a claim or put your side of a dispute, as the case of Judge James Dowling illustrates. Dowling was a puisne judge in New South Wales, a rival of William Burton's for the chief justiceship when Francis Forbes retired. Although Burton was Bourke's preferred candidate, a falling out between the two men, and Dowling's seniority within the New South Wales judiciary, led Bourke to appoint Dowling as acting chief justice when Forbes returned to Britain, ostensibly on leave, in 1835. When it became apparent that Forbes would not return, the Macarthur family lobby in London combined with Bourke's son, Dick, and others interested in New South Wales, to promote Burton's claims to the chief justiceship. However, Dowling's brother had already managed to obtain a promise from the Colonial Office that Dowling would be promoted.[125] Consequently a decision which the Colonial Office seem to have regretted – as they were generally supportive of Bourke, and attempted to be ostentatiously so in this period – stood.[126] Although inconsistently applied, it was the Colonial Office's general policy to place confidence in a governor's judgement; even when a colonial official provided strong evidence that the governor was mistaken. Nevertheless, there were still cases where governors felt (rightly) that they had not been awarded an appropriate degree of trust by the London government.[127]

The impact of subordinates' correspondence on governors could be devastating: occasionally resulting in recall or a dramatic change in policy. Even private correspondence that had little metropolitan influence could considerably undermine a governor's confidence and hence his ability to govern. By this measure, any report not sanctioned by the governor undermined his authority; not just reports of intra-government conflict or incompetence. Colonial newspapers were damaging enough; and their perceived impact can be traced through the efforts in the 1820s of governors in Mauritius, the Cape, New South Wales and Van Diemen's Land, to restrict the press. At least governors could deny newspaper reports, or reject them as ignorant and biased; accounts from government insiders were more difficult to dismiss. Darling, faced with combined press and government opposition, wrote that it was 'obvious' that if 'men filling the highest stations'

> whose duty it is to afford support to the Government . . . become instrumental to the abuse and degradation of that Government, through . . . opposition papers . . . it must destroy that confidence which the people generally ought to place in the Government; and in a colony composed as this is, produce, if not checked, anarchy and revolt.[128]

[118]

Both Bathurst and Hay had previously reassured Darling that his government's actions would be 'judged by their own intrinsic merit', and that Darling could 'repel with perfect confidence any charge which may be brought against [the Colonial Office] of attaching more weight than is due to information which may be derived from any other than official quarters'.[129] However, the Colonial Office actually did judge Darling and other governors on the basis of the unofficial information they gleaned from colonial officials and others.[130] It took very little to provoke Hay, for example, to comment on a governor's performance to a colonial subordinate. Responding to John Bell's request that he define the proper relationship between governor and secretary, Hay noted that as Bell had 'alluded to the mode in which the public business at the Cape is carried on by Sir Lowry Cole, I can have no hesitation in discussing that subject'.[131]

The letters exchanged four years earlier between Hay and Sir Richard Plasket, Bell's predecessor, also indicate the weight the Colonial Office accorded to unofficial correspondence, and its effect on colonial governors. Plasket, previously chief secretary to the governments of Malta and Ceylon, was appointed to the Cape in 1824. When the relatively inexperienced Bourke took over as acting governor in 1826, Plasket's disapproval of Bourke's liberal policies soon became clear, and on several occasions he opposed the governor in the Cape's advisory council. Additionally, Plasket outlined his criticisms of Bourke's government in a series of private letters to Hay. Plasket noted a definite cooling in Bourke's attitude to him, as the typically close relationship between governor and government secretary was reduced to a series of 'dry memoranda' sent down from Bourke's residence. The 'only reason' for this change that Plasket could think of was that Bourke was 'not pleased' with his correspondence with Hay. 'You will recollect', he told Hay.

> [a] private letter that you wrote to me about his having interfered with Lord Charles [Somerset's] system of Treaties Defence which you left at my discretion to shew him or not . . . I had no hesitation in shewing it to him because I was aware that he had acted from the best motives. You are also aware that on one or two points of public business in which I differed from him I wrote to you for explanation as to whether I was right or wrong in my opinion, and I thought it but fair to [Bourke] to show him both my letters to you and your replies.

'All these', concluded Plasket, the governor had 'received very coolly – and . . . it is from this period I think that his official behaviour to me has altered'.[132] Unofficial correspondence between officials and the metropolitan government thus severely tested a governors' self-confidence – regarding not only his competence to rule, but also the influence of his metropolitan connections and the extent to which they supported him.

[119]

Colonial officials' use of private and unofficial channels to communicate with Britain could also be damaging in the colony itself. John Montagu managed to leak documents about Franklin's Tasmanian administration in the colony before Franklin had received official correspondence from London.[133] Lieutenant-Governor Stockenström, frustrated by his conflict with Governor D'Urban, resorted to leaking documents to the editor of the *South African Commercial Advertiser*, John Fairbairn. After sending a copy of one despatch to Fairbairn, Stockenström admitted: 'I know it must appear *ungovernorlike* in me to make such use of these documents; but such is the unnatural state of our community that there is no other way of counteracting villainy and falsehood'.[134] Stockenström believed that the leakages went both ways: he alleged that D'Urban sent confidential metropolitan despatches, which Stockenström had not been shown, to the rival *Graham's Town Journal*.[135] Such action fostered division within the colonial administration, slowed decision-making processes and dispute resolution, and created a general lack of confidence in the governor.

Unofficial correspondence with colonial officials also had metropolitan ramifications. Hay remarked wearily that a great deal of the Colonial Office's time was spent resolving disputes between colonial personnel.[136] Not only did the climate before 1836 encourage colonial officials to put their case directly to the Colonial Office, rather than relying on colonial resolution, but it seems to have encouraged volubility: the crisp Colonial Office précis on the back of a twenty-page missive provides a sharp contrast. Although the difficulties of copying documents were sometimes exaggerated in order to make a political point, copying did consume a large proportion of colonial and metropolitan resources. When coupled with the time it took for the Colonial Office to collect governors' comments on officials' complaints, the delays were significant.[137] Hay suggested in November 1835 that the reason for ending unofficial correspondence was that it had been 'found productive of so much inconvenience'.[138] While, as argued in chapter three, it was the breakdown in relations between Hay and Stephen that precipitated the ban, the resultant prospect of streamlining colonial correspondence must have been gratifying.

The metropolitan effects of unofficial correspondence with colonial officials were clearly not all bad. Many of those encouraged to keep in touch informally were personally known to members of the Colonial Office, and therefore while their testimony was not always accepted at face value, at least its worth could be quite confidently assessed. Through unofficial accounts the Colonial Office was offered a variety of perspectives on the colonial situation: sometimes these merely served to give the metropolitan government greater understanding; at other times they served as a warning of a coming crisis. The Colonial Office ran the risk, however, because of metropolitan uncertainty and ignorance, of becoming too dependent on the accounts of those individuals who did manage to communicate with them, even though they were biased, or deliberately misleading.

Unofficial correspondence between colonial civil servants and members of the metropolitan Colonial Office was one of the most important strands in the web that constituted colonial governance. Although it was never referred to in any official despatch or statement, unofficial correspondence from governors, civil servants and private citizens formed the basis of the Colonial Office's understanding of colonies, and their sense of what might be feasible in any situation. For colonial civil servants, like other colonists, private correspondence fulfilled a variety of functions: informative, psychological, and professional. Also like other colonists, civil servants used any available connections, whether already established or specifically developed, to secure their future. But private correspondence also played a deleterious part in colonial governance. If even one of his subordinates was a protégé of the metropolitan administration, a governor could not but help worrying about the impact of competing reports at the Colonial Office. Private correspondence also triggered and extended a plethora of disputes and disagreements between civil servants, in most cases probably slowing down their resolution.

By the 1830s it was difficult to separate the good consequences of private correspondence from the bad, although both were recognised by the metropolitan government. In a climate of uncertainty – about the role of government, the duties and loyalties of colonial civil servants, and the purpose of imperialism – the metropolitan Colonial Office failed to develop any more sophisticated response than the enforcement of a crude blanket ban on all private correspondence from the colonies, and even this was provoked more by internal departmental problems than imperial considerations.

Of course, private correspondence did not end immediately, and even its arch-critic, James Stephen, continued to receive unofficial letters on public business from governors and colonial officials into the 1840s.[139] Most department heads received more private correspondence than ever: Lord Stanley's private correspondence as secretary of state in the early 1840s far outweighs (year by year) that of his 1833–34 term.[140] The effect of the ban, however, was to give even more value to pre-existing patronage relationships and ties of friendship, military service and political alliance, while reducing the opportunities for outsiders to open up links with the Colonial Office. In addition, the illicit status of private correspondence from colonial officials meant that the information contained in private letters no longer received wide attention within the department.

The Colonial Office's concern with colonial officials' disruptive power was marked in October 1839 by the decision to reconfigure their tenure. Colonial officials no longer held their offices 'during good behaviour', but could be replaced 'as often as any sufficient motives of public policy', including a change of governor, made it expedient.[141] This rendered officials a much less threatening presence for governors, and as a by-product, served to bolster notions of the responsibility of elected representative councils where they existed. This transition, combined with the general transferral of power and patronage from London to the colonies with the advent of representative and responsible government, meant officials in the settler colonies would focus their efforts in the colony from the 1840s on.

Notes

1 CO 201/219, fos 46–72, Darling to Murray, separate, 28 March 1831.
2 TLM, A293, p. 615, Mitchell to Grey, 21 September 1848; Cumpston, *Mitchell*, p. 199.
3 Appendix three contains brief details of the colonial officials discussed here.
4 Ward, *Colonial self-government*, pp. 27, 58.
5 McMartin, *Public servants*, constitutes a significant exception to the lack of consideration of the group as a whole for New South Wales; Fryer's *Government* is a less useful study of the Cape. Studies of individual colonial officials are more numerous for Australian public servants than South African.
6 McMartin, *Public servants*, pp. 48–9, 293–4.
7 E.g. *Philipps letters*, pp. 72, 90, 99–100, Philipps to King, 20 October 1820, 25 April 1821; Philipps to Harries, 15 July 1821.
8 ML, Broughton Papers, FM4/225, pp. 153–6, Broughton to Coleridge, 17 February 1842. Knox, 'Democracy, aristocracy and empire', 248–50, 253–4, 263–4.
9 CO 324/80, pp. 234–5, Hay to Lowry Cole, 23 September 1828; CO 323/144 [unpaginated], Bourke to Hay, private, 27 August 1826. Sturgis, 'Anglicisation'.
10 Neal, *Rule of law*.
11 CO 324/76, pp. 214–17, Hay to Plasket, 31 March 1826; CO 324/85, fo. 50, Hay to Darling, private, 14 June 1826; CO 324/78, pp. 56–60, Hay to Hankey, 1 March 1827.
12 CO 323/144 [unpaginated], Plasket to Hay, private, 8 August 1826.
13 *Ibid.*, Bourke to Hay, private, 27 August 1826.
14 McMartin, *Public servants*, pp. 143–64, 178–9.
15 CO 323/149, fos 172–8, Darling to Hay, 6 February 1827.
16 CO 323/162, fos 310–12, E. Thomson to J. Thomson, 1 January 1829, encl. in J. Thomson to Hay, 7 March 1830.
17 BL, Bathurst Papers, vol. 65, pp. 110–24, Bathurst to Somerset, 29 October 1824, cited in King, *Bourke*, p. 72.
18 E.g., ML, Arthur Papers, A2167, Darling to Arthur, 15 January 1826; King, *Bourke*, p. 215.
19 CO 201/260, fos 44–6, Bourke to Glenelg, 3 January 1837.
20 CO 323/148, fos 237–53, Plasket to Bourke, 20 December 1827, encl. in Plasket to Hay, private, 22 December 1827; CO 323/151, fo. 98, Plasket to Hay, 7 January 1828. BP, A1738, pp. 333–5, Bourke to McLeay, 9 May 1835.
21 *Gipps–La Trobe correspondence*, pp. 282–3, Gipps to La Trobe, 17 August 1844; CO 201/347, fos 400–2, Gipps to Stanley, 18 August 1844.
22 Shaw, *Patriarch*, n. 20, p. 287; CO 201/225, Stephen minute on Bourke to Goderich, 2 January 1832. Franklin, *Private correspondence*, i, pp. 82–4, 87–8, Sir John to Lady Franklin, 17 May 1839, 22 May 1839.
23 CO 201/253, fos 252–60, 350, 467–8, Bourke to Glenelg, 11 June 1836, 18 June 1836, 25 July 1836.
24 CO 324/80, pp. 77–8, Hay to Lowry Cole, private and confidential, 19 June 1828.
25 *Ibid.*, p. 74.
26 CO 324/78, p. 133, Hay to Ponsonby, private, 3 April 1827.

27 CO 323/157, fos 169–70, Arthur to Hay, private and confidential, 26 January 1829.
28 CO 323/165, fo. 227, Bell to Hay, 24 June 1831.
29 CO 323/148, fos 237–8, Plasket to Hay, 22 December 1827.
30 CO 324/83, p. 240, Hay to Bell, private, 27 October 1831.
31 CO 201/260, fos 44–6, Bourke to Glenelg, 3 January 1837.
32 CO 323/148, fo. 237, Plasket to Hay, 22 December 1827.
33 Foster, *Colonial improver*, pp. 50–63.
34 CO 323/165, fos 226–7, Bell to Hay, private, 24 June 1831.
35 *Ibid.*
36 CO 324/83, pp. 230–41, Hay to Bell, private, 27 October 1831.
37 Colonial Office, *Rules and regulations*, p. 87. CO circulars: CO 854/2, fos 84, 85, 20 April 1830, 30 January 1831; CO 854/1, fo. 8, 17 November 1831; CO 854/2, fo. 82, 24 November 1837.
38 CO 324/83, pp. 230–41, Hay to Bell, private, 27 October 1831.
39 *DSAB*, i, pp. 76–7.
40 By 1857 seven genteel occupations could be identified: church, medicine, law, army, navy, mercantile marine, and public civil service. Bourne, *Patronage*, pp. 88–90.
41 CO 323/173, fos 131, 133, Lushington to Hay, 3 March 1834, 9 March 1834.
42 E.g., see ML, Broughton Papers, FM4/225, pp. 3–4, 7–11, Broughton to his mother, 27 October 1828, 4 November 1828; ML, Broughton Letters, FM3/789, Broughton to the Duchess of Wellington, 25 May 1829.
43 Finer, 'Patronage', 329.
44 CO 854/2, fos 180, 181, circulars, August 1838; CO 854/3, fos 114–15, circular, 15 June 1842; Colonial Office, *Rules and regulations*, 2nd edn, pp. 16–20.
45 McMartin, *Public servants*, p. 49.
46 See CO 323/121–175 for 1825–35. Many other applications remain in the private collections of senior Colonial Office staff.
47 E.g. *Philipps letters*, pp. 254–6, Philipps to King, 15 January 1826.
48 Bourne, *Patronage*, pp. 5–7, 63, 79.
49 TLM, A290, p. 90, Roebuck to Mitchell, 8 April 1812.
50 Harling, 'Old Corruption', p. 129; Bourne, *Patronage*, pp. 79–80.
51 CO 324/84, fo. 88, Hay to D'Urban, 18 December 1833; CO 324/85, fo. 16, Hay to J. Thomson, 2 November 1825; CO 323/155, fo. 258, E. Thomson to Hay, 13 May 1828; Foster, *Colonial improver*, ch. 1.
52 King, 'Man in a trap'.
53 ML, Broughton Letters, FM3/789, Broughton to the Duchess of Wellington, 14 March 1826, 2 June 1826, 1 October 1826, 25 May 1826. ML, Broughton Papers, FM4/225, pp. 3–4, 7–11, Broughton to his mother, 27 October 1828, 4 November 1828; WO 80/2, Wellington to Murray, 29 October 1828.
54 CO 324/86, fo. 33, Hay to Dumaresq, 19 April 1828.
55 E.g., CO 201/215, fos 262–3, Graham to Murray, 15 April 1830; CO 201/198, fos 71, 110, Mitchell to Hay, private, 30 September 1828, 15 December 1828.
56 LRO, 920 DER (14) 138/7, Napier to Stanley, 19 November 1841, 16 September 1842, 25 March 1843, 27 May 1843, 16 September 1843.
57 *DSAB*, ii, pp. 586–7.
58 CO 323/224, fos 401–2, Hamilton to Glenelg, 17 July 1838.
59 See CO 324/78, pp. 237–9, Hay to Horton, private, 25 June 1827.
60 CO 324/85, fo. 96, Hay to Murray, 31 January 1827.
61 CO 201/235, fos 46–7, E. Burton to Hay, 12 June 1833; *ibid.*, fos 63–5, William Burton to Hay, 6 September 1833.
62 CO 323/125, fos 93, 95, C. Burton to Bathurst, 4 April 1827, C. Burton to Hay, 16 April 1827; TLM, A291, pp. 355, 378–80, 385–6, Thomas to John Mitchell, 25 January 1828, 1 November 1828, Houston to Thomas Mitchell, 24 November 1828.
63 CO 324/86, fo. 71, Hay to Mitchell, 10 November 1828; CO 324/87, fo. 18, Hay to Bourke, private, 15 May 1831. On introductions, see also McKenzie, *Scandal*, pp. 46, 55–6.
64 E.g., Lady Bourke's failure to conform to social conventions. ML, A4301, p. 465, Fanny to William McLeay, 6 May 1832.

65 TLM, A291, p. 376, Thomas to John Mitchell, 30 October 1828.
66 CO 323/149, fos 489–90, Frankland to Hay, 15 August 1827.
67 ML, A4300, pp. 163, 169, Fanny to William McLeay, 21 April 1826, 9/10 May 1826; ML, A4301, p. 318, Fanny to William McLeay, 7 January 1829.
68 ML, A4301, pp. 259, 318, Fanny to William McLeay, 12 November 1827, 7 January 1829.
69 BP, A1738, pp. 511–13, 515–19, Jamison to Bourke, 19 July 1836, 20 July 1836.
70 Davidoff, *Best circles*, pp. 16–17. For the colonial case see McKenzie, *Scandal*.
71 *Philipps letters*, pp. 106–7, Philipps to King, 25 December 1821.
72 CO 323/175, fo. 168, Riddell to Hay, 13 June 1835.
73 ML, A2571, fo. 143, 25 November 1825.
74 CO 201/207, fos 293–4, Mitchell to Hay, private, 18 October 1829. See also CO 201/244, fos 78–80, Memorial encl. in Broughton to Spring Rice, 1 September 1834, regarding Broughton's move from third to fourth in colonial precedence.
75 CO 714/36, fo. 128, Bourke to CO, 8 December 1827; CO 714/37, fo. 254, Napier to CO, 7 July 1843. CO 201/247, fos 270–9, Bourke to Glenelg, 3 October 1835; CO 201/248, fo. 178, Bourke to Glenelg, 1 December 1835.
76 Knox, 'Democracy, aristocracy and empire'.
77 CO 323/148, fo. 261, Stephen to Hay, 28 May 1827.
78 CO 323/174, fos 225–7, 228–9, Darling to Hill, 6 February 1835, encl. in Darling to Hay, 6 February 1835; Darling to Hay, 16 February 1835.
79 TLM, A292, pp. 521–2, Mitchell to Somerset, 19 February 1839.
80 E.g., CO 323/149, fos 469, 488–90, Burnett to Hay, 27 January 1827, Frankland to Hay, 15 August 1827.
81 TLM, A292, p. 118, Michell to Mitchell, 19 March 1831.
82 CO 323/149, fo. 469, Burnett to Hay, private and confidential, 27 January 1827.
83 ML, Broughton Papers, FM4/225, p. 17, Broughton to Coleridge, 8 September 1837.
84 ML, A4302, p. 466, Fanny to William McLeay, 6 May 1832.
85 ML, A4301, p. 449, Fanny to William McLeay, 11 November 1831.
86 ML, A2571, fo. 185, Dumaresq to Winn, 9 April 1829.
87 TLM, A291, p. 337, Mitchell to Hay, 9 June 1827; CO 324/85, fo. 119, Hay to Mitchell, 13 June 1827; CO 323/155, fos 113, 127–8, Dumaresq to Hay, private, 21 March 1828, 10 November 1828; CO 324/86, fo. 24, Hay to Dumaresq, 21 March 1828.
88 CO 323/175, fos 168, 174–5, C. Riddell to Hay, 13 June 1835, J. Riddell to Hay, 6 November 1835; CO 201/247, fos 3–5, Bourke to Aberdeen, 1 August 1835; CO 201/253, fos 356–9, Harington to Glenelg, 8 June 1836, encl. in Bourke to Glenelg, 1 July 1836.
89 ML, A4301, p. 331, Fanny to William McLeay, 6 June 1829.
90 Bourne, *Patronage*, p. 99.
91 CO 323/144–175.
92 Shaw, *Patriarch*, pp. 77–81. Ridden, 'Making good citizens', chs 2–3.
93 CO 201/235, fos 433–8, Broughton to Blomfield, 30 September 1832, encl. in Blomfield to Stanley, 3 May 1833; CO 202/29, fo. 165, Stanley to Blomfield, 17 June 1833; Stanley to Broughton, 8 November 1833, cited in Shaw, *Patriarch*, p. 81.
94 *The Times*, 25 September 1834; CO 323/172, fo. 137, Broughton to Hay, 6 September 1834; Shaw, *Patriarch*, pp. 83–4.
95 CO 201/244, fos 74, 84, Broughton to Spring Rice, 29 August 1834, 3 September 1834; *ibid.*, fos 86, 107, Broughton to Grey, 10 September 1834, 13 September 1834. ML, Arthur Papers, A2172, Broughton to Arthur, 13 October 1834.
96 Shaw, *Patriarch*, pp. 87–97.
97 BP, A1736, p. 212, Bourke to Spring Rice, 12 March 1834.
98 BP, A1738, pp. 543–6, 561–7, 593–601, 603–6, Forbes to Bourke, 6 September 1836, 28 October 1836, 25 February 1837, 1 May 1837.
99 See CO 201/257, fos 42–5, Burton to Grey, 29 March 1836; CO 201/285, fo. 164, Gipps to Glenelg, 9 March 1839; CO 201/309, fos 371–2, Stephen minute, 12 October 1841, on Gipps to Russell, 28 May 1841.

100 CO 324/84, fo. 79, Hay to Bell, 25 July 1833; CO 323/172, fo. 125, Bell to Hay, 26 June 1834.
101 CO 324/76, pp. 269–71, 275, Hay to Perceval, 27 May 1826; CO 324/81, pp. 155–6, Hay to Menzies, 30 April 1829.
102 ML, A1819 Forbes–Wilmot Horton correspondence; Brode, *Robinson*, pp. 80–1, 89.
103 CO 324/81, p. 155, Hay to Menzies, 30 April 1829; CO 323/151, fo. 87, Menzies to Hay, 16 December 1828; CO 323/159 [unpaginated], Menzies to Hay, 26 January 1829. CO 324/81, p. 139, Hay to Adam, private, 9 April 1829.
104 CO 323/165, fo. 226, Bell to Hay, 24 June 1831; CO 323/162, fo. 197, McLeay to Hay, private, 19 August 1830.
105 CO 323/173, fos 183–4, Montagu to Hay, 20 September 1834. See also CO 323/162, fos 188, 200, Montagu to Hay, 13 March 1830, 5 October 1830; CO 323/166, fo. 374, Montagu to Hay, 20 April 1831.
106 See, e.g., CO 323/173, fos 342–8, Riddell to Hay, 3 August 1834; CO 323/175, fos 166–8, Riddell to Hay, 24 March 1835, 13 June 1835.
107 Darling's 26-page despatch recommending Mitchell's dismissal was accompanied by 238 folio leaves of supporting documents. CO 201/219, fos 46–311, Darling to Murray, separate, 28 March 1831.
108 CO 323/162, fo. 250, Mitchell to Hay, private, 19 December 1830; CO 323/166, fo. 444, 7 February 1831; CO 201/224, fos 190, 223, 14 February 1831, 20 March 1831.
109 CO 48/194–195, particularly, CO 48/195, fos 17–20, Stockenström to D'Urban, 11 October 1837.
110 CO 48/187, fo. 214, D'Urban to Glenelg, 20 January 1838; CA, A50/4, Stockenström to Fairbairn, 29 December 1837.
111 CO 323/167, fo. 49, J. Riddell to Hay, 23 July 1831; CO 323/171, fo. 327, J. Riddell to Hay, 3 April 1831; CO 323/175, fos 174–5, J. Riddell to Hay, 6 November 1835. CO 323/162, fos 306, 310–12, 316, 318, Thomson to Hay, private, 18 February 1830, 7 March 1830, 1 April 1830, 15 June 1830; CO 323/167, fos 357, 371, Thomson to Hay, 31 May 1831, 12 August 1831.
112 CO 323/175, fo. 46, Moore to Hay, 17 March 1835.
113 ML, Broughton Papers, FM4/225, pp. 55–6, 66, 84–5, Broughton to Coleridge, 15 February 1839, 13 September 1839, 3 April 1840.
114 *Ibid.*, pp. 73, 78, Broughton to Coleridge, 14 October 1839.
115 *Ibid.*, pp. 153–4, Broughton to Coleridge, 17 February 1842.
116 Shaw, *Patriarch*, p. 146.
117 ML, Broughton Papers, FM4/225, p. 93, Broughton to Coleridge, 15 February 1841.
118 TLM, A291–293.
119 E.g., LRO, 920 DER (14) 137/9–9A, Murray to Stanley, 13 April 1843, 24 July 1843, 13 April 1842.
120 Dracopoli, *Stockenström*, pp. 41–3; Harington, *Smith*, pp. 21–2, 231, 236; Scott, *British solider*, pp. 130, 143–4, 155. CA, A1415/77/8, pp. 155–9, Hare to Napier, 23 January 1843.
121 TLM, A293, pp. 101, 105, 144–5, 257, Murray to Mitchell, 24 June 1840, 30 June 1840, 11 August 1840, 11 May 1842. CO 323/173, fo. 210, Melville to Hay, 3 December 1834.
122 E.g. CO 324/76, p. 275, Hay to Perceval, 27 May 1826; CO 323/149, fos 472, 488, Burnett to Hay, secret and confidential, 18 March 1827, Frankland to Hay, 15 August 1827.
123 CO 324/87, fo. 122, Hay to Riddell, 14 November 1835.
124 CO 324/94, pp. 39–40, Hay to J. Riddell, 25 April 1833.
125 BP, A1739, pp. 214–15, Dick to Richard Bourke, 27 May 1837; CO 201/257, fos 408–10, J. Dowling to Brougham, 7 March 1836, encl. in V. Dowling to Glenelg, 26 August 1836.
126 See, e.g., LRO, 920 DER (14), 125/1, Goulburn to Stanley, 10 September 1841; *ibid.*, 174/1, p. 17, Stanley to Goulburn, 10 September 1841; *ibid.*, 128/14, Ripon to Stanley, 22 December 1843, Stanley to Ripon, 23 December 1843.
127 E.g., CO 111/98, fo. 123, Stephen to Twiss, 25 August 1830; CO 48/171, fos 225–30, 233–4, D'Urban to Glenelg, 15 March 1837.

128 CO 201/182, fo. 188, Darling to Bathurst, 18 April 1827; CO 201/213, fos 430–1, Darling to Murray, private, 1 December 1830.
129 CO 324/85, fo. 55, Hay to Darling, 17 July 1826.
130 CO 201/218, fos 75–6, minute on Darling to Murray, 21 January 1831.
131 CO 324/83, p. 234, Hay to Bell, private, 27 October 1831.
132 CO 323/148, fos 237–9, Plasket to Hay, private, 22 December 1827.
133 Fitzpatrick, *Franklin*, pp. 267–72, 341, 346–7.
134 CA, A50/4, Stockenström to Fairbairn, 11 August 1837; see also *ibid.*, Stockenström to Fairbairn, 21 October 1836; early May 1837; 15 September 1837; 22 September 1837; 26 October 1837; 29 December 1837.
135 *Ibid.*, Stockenström to Fairbairn, 7 September 1837.
136 CO 324/79, pp. 324–5, Hay to Taylor, private, 19 April 1828.
137 E.g., CO 324/84, fo. 139, Hay to St John, 30 June 1835.
138 *Ibid.*, fo. 145, R. Hay to E. Hay, private, 2 November 1835.
139 E.g., *Arthur papers*, i, p. 206; ii, p. 282; iii, p. 37, Arthur to Stephen, 25 June 1838, 15 October 1839, 16 April 1840.
140 Comparison based on LRO, 920 DER (14) 167/2; 170; 174/1; 174/2; 175/1; 175/2; 176/1, Stanley's Letter Books.
141 CO 854/2, fos 300–2, 344, circulars, 16 October 1839, 3 March 1840.

CHAPTER SIX

Colonial lobbyists: tactics and networks

... take no part in Colonial Politics on any consideration. Party politics there will not for fifty years have any real influence upon its affairs. It is *here* [in London] that the decisions will be made. (Edward Macarthur, 1834)[1]

Edward Macarthur, like all the colonial lobbyists and officials considered in this book, regarded metropolitan influence as critical for colonial concerns. Even those who did not manage to obtain influence often participated in debates about how it might be acquired. The most successful lobbyists developed networks of personal contacts in the metropolitan government, which were utilised over a number of campaigns and maintained by permanent representatives in the metropole. This chapter considers lobbyists campaigning on the Cape Colony or New South Wales, demonstrating that lobbyists who dealt with quite different issues nevertheless shared an understanding of colonial power and how it might be manipulated.

Colonial pressure groups faced many of the same challenges as those with purely British concerns, and employed many of the same tactics, adapted to the imperial situation. Eastwood's observation, for example, that lobbyists outside parliament achieved more success in 'self-contained areas of policy' than in 'highly charged areas', holds true in the colonial arena;[2] metropolitan ignorance of colonial affairs meant lobbyists were well advised to limit their message and ambitions. Although there has been considerable investigation of pressure and interest groups operating in nineteenth-century domestic British politics, and some work on eighteenth-century transatlantic interest groups, little systematic investigation of colonial interest groups in the nineteenth century has taken place, nor comparative work between colonies.[3]

Like their domestic counterparts, colonial pressure groups faced the dilemma of whether to concentrate their lobbying on the traditional loci of power – parliament, government, the crown – or whether to risk an appeal to the increasingly powerful sphere of public opinion. Hollis argues that in the 1830s domestic pressure groups regarded the direct and personal manipulation of members of parliament and government as the most effective means of influence; followed by indirect lobbying through commercial or religious 'interest' groups. It was only after such methods had failed that appeals to the public were considered: first in the form of general education campaigns; and then through the formation of a 'national voice', via associations with regional branches and a wide social base.[4] Colonial pressure groups also followed this progression, believing that 'personal communication' was more effective than circuitous appeals through 'the press and public opinion'.[5] But, grappling with vast distances and considerable British ignorance and indifference, colonial lobbyists were reluctant to attempt to create a national voice. Although skilfully employed, their methods were conservative in comparison to the radical project to legitimise popular opinion's place in the political system.[6] Colonial lobbyists, with minimal electoral power and less recourse to public opinion if their first lobbying attempts failed, typically took more care than their domestic counterparts to support the status quo and appear socially respectable.[7]

Thus before the 1840s, lobbyists on crown colonies concentrated on influencing and infiltrating government, through both official and unofficial channels. Primarily, lobbyists dealt in information, hoping that its transmission, publication or threatened release would encourage the metropolitan government to reverse governors' unpopular and unjust decisions, provide compensation, or introduce imperial legislation which protected particular colonial interests. This metropolitan focus resonates with Olson's work on eighteenth-century American interest groups. While different political structures and levels of autonomy separate the pre-Revolutionary American colonies from the nineteenth-century crown colonies, there are many similarities. Both looked to London to overcome local colonial discrimination; to access metropolitan resources for use against colonial opponents; and to resolve internal conflict.[8] Both also explored maintaining metropolitan representatives. The nineteenth-century lobbyists, like their official counterparts, had to balance the advantages of a well-connected metropolitan agent against the experience and understanding of a colonial expatriate.[9] Colonial pressure groups developed informal networks as assiduously as did the colonial officials already considered, with significant effect. In some cases they employed the same networks as government agents. Colonial lobbyists outside government were less immediately affected by the changes in Colonial Office administration than governors and colonial officials, simply because they never enjoyed such easy access to the heart of government.

Although Hollis's and Olson's studies of lobbyists have much to offer the colonial historian, not all the same assumptions hold. Hollis's division of domestic pressure groups into 'interest' and 'cause' driven, and Olson's classification of interest groups by the nature of the bonds between members, tend to obscure rather than clarify in the colonial case.[10] Motivation and internal connection do not emerge as defining features of colonial lobby groups; longevity and strength of metropolitan connections were more important. Hollis's collection, *Pressure from without*, does highlight an important feature for any study: an almost equal division between essays on individuals, specific organisations, and broader movements. So it is with this examination of colonial pressure groups before the advent of representative government. In New South Wales, the focus is on the Australian Patriotic Association, which campaigned for representation and greater political rights for emancipists; and on the Macarthur family, the leading free emigrant family and self-appointed protector of the colonial elite. At the Cape, Grahamstown merchants provide a less clearly defined pressure group in the 1830s; while opponents to the colonial government's frontier policy are virtually encapsulated by the names John Philip and Thomas Fowell Buxton.

How should the success of extra-governmental colonial lobbyists be gauged? Traditionally, historians have considered 'colonial outcomes' to be the important and clear indicators of success. For this project, however, with its focus on the transmission of information and power through networks of connections, and the centrality of London, conceptions of success are perhaps more subtle, and certainly more short term. From this point of view, a network is judged by its transmission of information; the creation of a metropolitan framework in which pressure groups could influence metropolitan policies; and the engagement of parliamentary, governmental and other representatives; as much as by eventual colonial success. The success of lobbyists must also be viewed in the context of the metropolitan government: to what extent were lobbyists manipulated and managed by the imperial authorities, and in particular the Colonial Office? As the networks of colonial lobbyists overlapped, opposed one another, and sometimes collaborated, the chapter looks first at the activities of those lobbying on New South Wales, and then at those associated with the Cape Colony.

Political representation in New South Wales

The burning questions for New South Wales' lobbyists in the 1820s and 1830s were political representation and transportation. Representative government was not introduced to the colony until 1843, but it was under discussion through the 1830s: encouraged by a rapidly growing population; an expanding economy; and the imminent expiry of the New South Wales Act (which formed the constitution) in 1836. The debate about the effects of transportation on both convicts and settlers connected economics, social policy and politics. The metropolitan government was reluctant to consider granting political representation while the system of convict assignment persisted. Yet many colonists depended on cheap convict labour in the era before mass emigration.

Non-convict New South Wales society could be crudely divided (and it was by its inhabitants) into free emigrants, or 'Exclusives', and emancipated convicts, their families and supporters (collectively 'Emancipists'). Free emigrants, attracted by the generous land grants of an earlier period, and the possibility of advancement offered by a new society, strongly defended their political and economic power. They occupied the great majority of nominated non-official positions on the legislative council, and controlled most of the colony's wealth. A few particularly wealthy families, most notably the Macarthurs, presented themselves as a landed elite, as a de facto aristocracy. The Emancipists, who comprised the majority of the population, had a different experience. Shut out from political power and opportunities for economic and social advancement, they increasingly advocated the need for a directly elected representative assembly, and a reduction in the concentration of power in the hands of the few. While the form of colonial government was still very much under discussion in both New South Wales and Britain, the divisions between Emancipists and Exclusives – crudely Whig and Tory – were starkly apparent and vigorously defended.

Until the late 1830s, both groups hoped to secure the governor's support for their cause and to increase their own power at the expense of the governor's. Yet, as Ward has argued, after the first elections in 1843, Emancipists and Exclusives coalesced as wealth became more important than background.[11] 'Australian' colonists then perceived the British government and the governor (the representative of imperial power) as greater opponents than each other. There is a rich literature on the transition to representative and then responsible government in New South Wales, which this chapter does little more than touch upon: here, the focus is the lobbying of Exclusives and Emancipists before 1843 as seen through their competing – and sometimes overlapping – networks.[12]

De facto aristocracy? The Macarthurs in London

The Macarthur family, probably the wealthiest and most powerful of the Exclusives, had well-established and useful connections in London.[13] First used to advance the family's commercial interests, in the 1830s, as the Macarthurs' interests converged with the interest of the New South Wales Exclusives more broadly, these links were used for political lobbying. This section traces the Macarthurs' reflections on the nature and legitimacy of political lobbying over the next fifteen years.

The *Dictionary of national biography* described John Macarthur as 'the father' of New South Wales. Macarthur arrived in Sydney in 1790, a lieutenant in the 102nd foot. A major beneficiary of the land and convict labour available in the colony, by 1801 he had accumulated more than one thousand acres and one thousand sheep, as well as being a leading participant in the unofficial rum trade and paymaster of the colonial corps.[14] Sent to London by Governor King after a duel with a superior officer in 1801, Macarthur resigned his commission and used the trip to raise interest in the nascent colonial wool industry. On the voyage to Britain he befriended the son of Sir Walter Farquhar, physician to the Prince of Wales. This connection gave Macarthur and later his sons (Edward, John, James and William) their entrée to influential metropolitan circles.[15] Macarthur returned to New South Wales with a Colonial Office order granting him a further two thousand acres of land. He continued to consolidate his position as a leading settler into the 1820s, despite leading the 1808 rum rebellion which ended Bligh's governorship.

The Macarthurs' powerful position in the colony made them a sort of quasi-aristocracy, a situation they were keen to preserve. By the later 1830s letters of introduction for hopeful new colonists were provided to the Macarthurs as well as to the governor and crown officers. William Gladstone provided a letter of introduction to James Macarthur for a Mr Blair; while Viscount Howick hoped that the Macarthurs would find Lady Sefton's nephew 'and his family an accession to Australian society'.[16] When the legislative council was introduced, John Macarthur was among the non-official members.[17] The Macarthurs viewed this seat as virtually hereditary: when the ailing Macarthur senior stepped down in 1831, his son, Edward, asked that his replacement be a Macarthur, 'considering the property possessed by my family in that country, together with their long and intimate connexion with it'.[18]

Such confidence often reaped its own rewards, but the Macarthurs' political and economic power concerned the government, straining the relationship between the family and the governor. This growing tension was one reason that the Macarthurs looked to London as not only more powerful, but also more ignorant – and thus amenable – than the colonial government. The question of the Macarthurs' council seats provoked much correspondence between colonial and metropolitan governments, with Governor Bourke particularly uncomfortable with the number of near Macarthur relations on the council. This discomfort was displayed ambiguously: the colonial and metropolitan governments blocked a family replacement for Macarthur senior, but Bourke's reluctance to appoint Philip Parker King (a Macarthur in-law) to the council in 1837 was closely related to his desire to bring the under-represented Emancipists into the political process.[19] When Governor Gipps appointed King to the council in 1839, he justified the appointment carefully to Downing Street, acknowledging metropolitan concern about Macarthur influence. Gipps emphasised that he was 'driven almost by necessity' (three others had refused the seat), that King could be considered 'the Representative of the large body of naval and military settlers' in the colony, and that despite his family ties, King was 'liberal in his politics, as well as prudent and moderate in his general bearing'.[20] Gipps soon after also appointed James Macarthur to the council.

John Macarthur's second son, also John, acted as the family's commercial agent in London from 1818 while he first studied for the bar and then began his career. Hazel King's work demonstrates that John junior understood clearly the importance of metropolitan contacts to his family's interests. As his father before him, John joined the Athenaeum Club and also the Society of Arts, in 1823 becoming chairman of the society's committee for colonies and trade.[21] In 1825 he attempted to gain a seat in parliament to enable him to secure colonial land grants for his younger brothers, and military promotion for his elder brother, Edward. Despite encouragement from Wilmot Horton, John was unable to raise the necessary money to cover a parliamentary election campaign.[22] He engineered an introduction to Commissioner Bigge when he returned to London from New South Wales, by befriending Bigge's secretary, Thomas Scott. John also befriended Edward Barnard, the New South Wales government agent, and, before they left for New South Wales, Ralph Darling and Alexander McLeay.[23] He sent presents to the colonial secretary, Bathurst, and successfully lobbied in London for a grant of five thousand acres for his father, which Governor Macquarie had refused. John's best Colonial Office connection was Wilmot Horton. Through him, John became 'a persona grata at the Colonial Office', invited to speak 'frankly on Australian affairs', including the legislation which established the New South Wales legislative council. John was involved with the appointments of Thomas Scott as archdeacon and Saxe Bannister as attorney-general to the colony. King documented how Macarthur used his contacts, particularly Wilmot Horton, to establish the Australian Agricultural Company (AAC) in London. The preliminary meeting of the AAC attracted eight directors of the Bank of England, including the chairman, and three directors of the East India Company.[24] This overview demonstrates that John's primary aim was to promote Macarthur family interests, which he did extremely successfully. The metropolitan political and government figures he mixed with, however, did not identify him with any wider colonial group beyond the Macarthur interest.

John died prematurely in 1831, but the Macarthurs' London network was firmly established. John's brother, Major Edward Macarthur, had lived in Britain since 1798 and, despite several trips back to Australia, would remain based there and in Ireland until 1851.[25] Edward had fought in the Mediterranean, the Iberian Peninsula, and Quebec, and served with the army of occupation in France. He too had useful contacts, such as Sir Herbert Taylor, who, while military secretary at the Horse Guards, secured

Edward his majority.[26] Before John died, Edward concentrated on securing promotion for himself, first in the army and then in civil society. 'I do not neglect any channel that may lead to preferment' he assured his father in 1830. Edward's friendship with Lord Cholmondeley led to his appointment as secretary in the lord great chamberlain's office in the House of Lords, from where he conducted Macarthur business.[27] Less acutely aware of the importance of networking to the family interest than his brother, and far more wary of politics, it took Edward some time to develop into his role of family agent and representative.

Cultivating the elite political and social circles in which he moved, however, did not pose a problem, and Edward smoothly extended his attention to prospective colonial officials. He met governor-elect Bourke at the Queen's Drawing Room in 1831, and introduced himself, being 'kindly and courteously addressed in return'.[28] Several years later, Edward and his brother James met with Governor Gipps before he left for New South Wales; while in 1836 Edward reported a visit from Maurice O'Connell, an old friend of his father's, before he left to command the forces in New South Wales.[29] Current and past colonial officials in London on leave were also valuable allies. In London during the 1830s Edward – and James in 1837 and 1838 – met several New South Wales officials including judges Francis Forbes and William Burton; surveyor-general, Thomas Mitchell; treasurer, Campbell Riddell; and Bishop Broughton.[30] James had 'unrestrained conversation' with Forbes in London in 1837 regarding the establishment of a local New South Wales legislature, ways to promote emigration, and their shared distrust of the colonial reformers.[31] In 1840, when he was lobbying on emigration, Edward found Judge Burton's presence 'fortunate'; Burton had increased parliamentary support for the cause. Past governors were no less useful. Edward corresponded with Arthur after the latter's departure from Van Diemen's Land; while Darling drafted a letter on emigration which a Macarthur-led deputation presented to the Colonial Office in April 1840.[32] In July 1842 Edward dined at the United Services Club two nights running with Bourke, who promised to enlist the help of Spring Rice on emigration.[33]

Through Mr Estcourt, the MP for Oxford ('a very influential man'), Edward learnt what passed at the in camera hearings of the 1831 Select Committee on Secondary Punishments. The continuation of transportation was of great importance to the Macarthurs who were among the largest employers of convict labour in New South Wales, and Edward had earlier given evidence before the select committee himself. Edward persuaded Estcourt of the Macarthur view: large proprietors, who could best enforce convict discipline and provide economies of scale, must be encouraged.[34] Edward recognised the 'philanthropic' Buxton interest as a threat to transportation, and consequently to the Macarthurs' interests. This group

had 'completely' encompassed Goderich in the early 1830s and threatened
to overtake Howick. It was this threat that made Edward more overtly
bolster his position at the Colonial Office, primarily by presenting himself
as a privileged and impartial source of information. He was able, for example,
to reassure the Colonial Office that worrying reports of convict rebellions
in 1831 were 'destitute of any foundation commensurate with that alarm'.
'My own advices from the Colony are to the 23rd December', he wrote,
emphasising his superior sources of intelligence.[35] Edward also acted as a
conduit for colonial protests, in 1832 presenting the Colonial Office with a
letter from fifty-two major colonial landholders protesting against Governor
Darling's demand for quit-rent payments. He accompanied the letter with a
private note to Robert Hay and a present of fine cloth made from Macarthur
wool for Goderich, an 'illustration of the mutual relationship and interest
of Great Britain and the Australian colonies'.[36]

For all his apparent lobbying – creating and maintaining networks of
useful contacts, providing and correcting information about New South
Wales, appearing before select committees, advising the Colonial Office –
Edward did not regard himself as involved in *politics* until about 1839.
Earlier, he was wary of explicitly adopting a political stance. To Edward,
acquiring and exerting influence was distinct from and vastly preferable to
political involvement. The employment of influence was neutral and
'statesmanlike', while 'politics' denoted a less respectable activity. Edward
regarded himself as possessing influence, which he employed impartially
and beneficially for New South Wales. 'I never', he wrote, 'in any way interfere
in the affairs of the colony excepting by [conveying] to those who may
desire it information . . . without any reference to party whatsoever'.[37]
Edward's private and public correspondence indicate that he believed he
provided neutral information and corrected inaccurate accounts rather than
engaging with actual opponents.[38] The 'truth' would 'ultimately prevail' in
metropolitan government, without the need for 'political broils'.[39]

Edward regarded London, not Sydney, as the centre of power in New
South Wales' affairs. More particularly, decisions which affected the
Macarthur interest were made in Whitehall. Of a new governor, Edward
wrote in 1831: '[E]xcepting to administer his Government with wisdom
what have we to desire from him besides? There is nothing that he can do
for us! Therefore let us build no hopes upon his appointment.'[40]

Edward's distinction between 'influence' and 'politics' and his assessment
that critical decisions were taken in London made him nervous about brash
interference in colonial politics by his more hot-headed relatives. He exhorted
his father and brothers to be 'moderate' and 'exceedingly cautious' in colonial
politics; struggled to explain 'proper interference in the affairs of the colony';
and urged 'an observance of the duties of life and the weight of good example'
over 'clamour and intrigue'.[41] Once, in frustration, Edward recommended

that William and James should 'take no part in Colonial Politics on any consideration'. This anxiety was particularly fuelled by the behaviour of his cousin, Hannibal Macarthur, a member of the legislative council. While Hannibal was right to express his views in council, he should not do so 'in the spirit of a partisan'.[42] Edward's distress was connected with style as well as content. In 1831 he had urged his father not to seek Bourke's favour 'too anxiously and eagerly', nor to be 'over anxious about impressing him with your own opinions of Colonial Policy'.[43] The almost patronising tone in these letters to John senior, combined with his instructions for Hannibal, reflect Edward's understanding of power and influence. If power lay in London, the Macarthur family had nothing to gain from political wrangles in Sydney. Moreover, reports of brash colonial interference could detract from Edward's standing in London and his ability to employ influence on behalf of his family.

During 1837 and 1838 Edward was joined in London by his brother James, who arrived with a petition to parliament from the Exclusives. James had family tasks to perform – he raised a £10,000 loan, negotiated the purchase of some land, and made a very fortuitous marriage to Miss Amelia Stone[44] – but he also pursued a more explicitly political course of action than Edward. He quickly cultivated strong contacts at the Colonial Office and in parliament, and was clearly identified by contemporaries, including James Stephen, as an 'agent' for the Exclusive party of New South Wales.[45] James used Macarthur networks to interfere in matters of colonial personnel, such as the unsuccessful attempt to block the appointment of James Dowling and promote William Burton as chief justice.[46]

The petition James presented addressed the form of government appropriate for the colony. James established a London committee to manage the petition which included Edward and several directors of the AAC.[47] The committee left negotiations to James, but provided funds and lent his campaign political weight. Despite the simultaneous presentation of a petition from the opposing Emancipists with more than twenty times as many signatures, James made quite an impact in London. Edward had arranged a meeting for him at the Colonial Office, reporting that James could 'have access to the Head of the Department when necessary. Everything looks as promising at the outset as it could possibly do'.[48] Financial assistance from the petition committee allowed James to publish *New South Wales: its present state and future prospects*. In it, James proposed measures which would secure land, political power and labour to the Exclusive interest.[49] To justify keeping power from the emancipists, James portrayed New South Wales' society as ridden by crime and immorality (a picture he reinforced in his evidence before Molesworth's Select Committee on Transportation).[50] Given the colony's depravity, James was prepared to accept a gradual diminution of transportation, bringing the colony 'the moral and religious

[135]

character of a British community'.[51] A consequent labour shortage would be avoided by promoting assisted migration under the scheme James outlined in *New South Wales*. The book compiled a mass of statistics and other evidence to support the Exclusives' claims, and, in the absence of other sources, was taken at face value for rather longer than it deserved.

James was pragmatic, willing to compromise with his colonial political opponents to achieve the best possible result for the Macarthur interest. Thus he worked with Charles Buller – the poorly informed and badly managed representative of the Emancipists' Australian Patriotic Association (APA) – framing a Bill for the establishment of representative government in New South Wales. He told the Colonial Office that although he supported representative institutions in principle, New South Wales was not ready for them; at most the colony should have a 'blended' legislature of nominated and elected members.[52] Nevertheless, he assured the government that he would 'cheerfully acquiesce' in whatever form of government was instituted, and would work to promote it in the colony.[53] If there had to be an elected representative assembly, the Macarthurs favoured a system of double election with a narrow franchise rather than the alternative of direct elections with a broad franchise favoured by the Emancipists. Exploiting Buller's ignorance of the APA's wishes, James convinced him to lobby for a doubly elected legislature as well. James realised that if he could not prevent representative government altogether, he could at least influence its form.

James's successful visit to London coincided with, and probably caused, a development in Edward's approach to colonial affairs. While Edward continued to believe that the Macarthurs would do best if they were cool, rational and fair in their dealings with government, he became more willing to interfere in political affairs. 'I am doing all I can to urge the Govt to increase the number of emigrant labourers', he reported in 1839. Edward had 'individually made one very earnest representation to the Colonial Office, and another to Lord Howick'; organised a group to meet with Glenelg; and asked his brothers to provide more and better evidence. 'You may depend upon it, I will keep the throng in movement, both by means of the press, and by private representation.'[54] Edward was also in regular contact with Sir George Grey (who enquired fondly after James), and 'plied both him and Lord Howick well with Papers' about the deficiency of labour in the colony.[55] Throughout 1840 Edward lobbied both Lord John Russell and the Colonial Land and Emigration commissioners on emigration and land-pricing policies; when he felt he was making no progress, he contacted Sir Robert Peel.[56] When Stanley became colonial secretary, Edward wrote to him criticising Russell for having pronounced New South Wales 'a society contaminated in its infancy, and fed with new streams of pollution in its progress'.[57] Stanley, in contrast, responded favourably to the Macarthur view, and Edward soon thought that 'All that the colonists can in reason expect with regard to territory, Lord Stanley is disposed to concede'.[58] Edward remained well-informed about the government's policies on New South Wales and in contact with Stanley, Peel, Gladstone and Hope during 1842.[59] It was always a struggle to ensure New South Wales' issues were heard, amidst the 'variety of questions' – both imperial and domestic – which beset the government. In the late 1830s Edward drew consolation from the possibility that the Canadian crisis might ultimately produce a blueprint for 'all colonial questions of a similar nature'.[60] However, once the new New South Wales Act was passed, Edward found it even more difficult to keep the colony at the forefront of metropolitan concern, although he continued to lobby Stanley, and then Grey, on emigration and colonial issues.[61]

Edward did maintain some of his former caution. In 1840, while instructing his brothers to 'continue to remonstrate' on emigration and '[r]esist every attempt to throw a British burthen upon you', Edward warned that their appeal should employ 'temperate, but firm language'. 'Endeavour to make a *just* division of those parts of the expenditure . . . created for British purposes, and those . . . Colonial', he continued.[62] After a particularly unrestrained petition from the colony about the potential partition of Port Phillip from New South Wales, Edward rued the colonists' action. The matter was one 'for the Mother Country and not for the colonists . . . a subject not of colonial but imperial policy'. 'The petition should have done no more than calmly show the impropriety of dividing the territory if impolitic it be.'[63] In private comments about the Macarthurs, their political opponent Bourke described them variously as 'sincere', 'just' and 'gentlemanly', indicating that Edward's desired image of the Macarthur family was successfully projected.[64]

From the later 1830s, Edward increasingly appreciated the influence of the City and the British press. He advocated the establishment of a London association of 'men of capital' interested in investing in Australia 'in the same mode that has been affected with great success in the United States'. His communications of the 1840s refer to the importance of the City's influence on government action, with emigration, in particular, presented in London as an economic issue which would affect the strength of investments in the colony. In both 1839 and 1840 deputations went to the Colonial Office to 'remonstrate on the suspension of Emigration', presenting letters which had been passed around interested City parties.[65]

In 1839 Edward, with William Burton, felt the 'necessity of interesting the public press of [England] in favor of the Colony'. Edward had encouraged his metropolitan connections to subscribe to the *Colonial Gazette* as it supported the Macarthurs' view of colonial affairs.[66] In 1842 he asked his brothers for colonial 'statistical returns' which could then be placed strategically in the English newspapers, although he cautioned that 'the public press' was 'a two edged sword which cuts both ways'.[67] In 1841

Edward published *Colonial policy of 1840 and 1841*, a criticism of Russell's New South Wales policy intended to demonstrate the 'mistaken course of the Home Government in adopting the recommendations of Colonization Commissioners in London, without previously advising with the Local Government'.[68] Edward sent copies to the Colonial Office officials, Vernon Smith and Stephen among others.[69] In many ways, the book epitomised Edward's movement from a gentleman officer dabbling in colonial affairs through his social networks to a skilled political operator who appreciated the need to manipulate governments both in the metropolis and in the colony.

Edward's politicisation also made him aware of the importance of a reliable, well-informed and articulate parliamentary advocate. Witnessing an 1839 parliamentary debate on New South Wales he thought the APA representative, Buller, 'a very inefficient advocate and wholly unequal to Lord Howick'.[70] A better way of informing and influencing parliament would be to have 'one of [the colonists'] own body' elected. Unless funds were subscribed for 'that and other purposes, such as influencing the press, obtaining legal advice and so forth, they will be oppressed and reduced to mere vassalage'. His earlier ambivalence was cast aside as Edward offered his own services as parliamentary advocate.

> The long time I have been about the public offices here, my general acquaintance with men of all parties and the never having committed myself to any political influence would certainly . . . give me weight and consideration in the House of Commons. You would not then be plundered in any way.[71]

This offer was never taken up, although the New South Wales legislative council would appoint the barrister and MP, Francis Scott, as its parliamentary agent in September 1844.[72]

Although they operated quite independently of any colonial control, the Macarthurs' London networks were very important. The efforts of John, Edward and James Macarthur secured the family land, colonial political power and significant commercial advantage. As lobbyists, the Macarthurs successfully transferred their attention from causes which benefited their family directly to the broader political concerns of their class: transportation, the form of government and emigration. Simultaneously they advanced the family fortune through appointed office and land grants. They were important sources of information for the Colonial Office, and the wider government, during successive administrations. Edward's assessment of the inevitability of the concentration of political power in London may have been flawed, but, when the time came in the mid-1840s, the Macarthurs quickly transferred their primary efforts back to the colony where they all pursued successful careers: Edward with a knighthood and periods as acting governor of Victoria and military commander of Australia; William and James elected five times to the New South Wales legislative council between them.[73]

The convict stain: the Australian Patriotic Association

Despite their influence, the Exclusives represented only a small section of New South Wales' population; whereas their political opponents could raise between ten and twenty times as many signatures for a petition.[74] The Emancipists included not only emancipated convicts and their families, but many others who supported the introduction of greater political representation and trial by jury.[75] Their leaders were educated professionals with considerable resources: only one of the most prominent in the 1830s, William Bland, was an emancipated convict, and he had been transported for killing a fellow naval officer in a duel. Others – William Wentworth, Sir John Jamison, John and Gregory Blaxland, John Stephen, Thomas Potter Macqueen and John Mackaness – were variously substantial landholders, lawyers, doctors and politicians with English educations and colonial aspirations. While they appreciated the importance of metropolitan connections their fiery litigiousness and political radicalism meant several had burnt useful bridges in both Sydney and London. Jamison, despite being a major landholder, was on a Colonial Office blacklist because of the unproven allegations he made of convict immorality. (His seven illegitimate children also attracted unwelcome colonial attention.) Both John and Gregory Blaxland, friends of Sir Joseph Banks, fell out with successive governors from William Bligh onwards; while John Mackaness, appointed sheriff of New South Wales in 1824, alienated Governor Darling by chairing meetings which demanded elected settler representation and trial by jury.

Despite public meetings, petitions and pamphlets that advocated political and legal rights, little headway was made until the 1830s. The arrival of Bourke, who supported many of the Emancipists' arguments, encouraged a renewed effort. Gregory Blaxland had delivered a petition to Britain in 1827 (alongside samples of his prize-winning Australian wine), but more were drawn up in 1830 and 1833.[76] In part, this increased activity was inspired by the growing metropolitan distaste for transportation to New South Wales. Metropolitan commentators like Archbishop Whately compared convict assignment to slavery and argued for the introduction of Benthamite penitentiaries. Australian society was condemned as evil, the whole population contaminated by convictism.[77] But an end to assignment, or transportation, would have serious consequences for the colony's economic prospects. Most of the leading emancipists, indeed most free settlers, relied on cheap assigned convict labour to run their farms and manage their homes. Almost eighty per cent of the twenty-seven thousand convicts in New South Wales in 1836 were on assignment; any change would seriously affect the colonists' livelihoods.[78]

The 1833 petition was presented to parliament by a metropolitan sympathiser, Henry Lytton Bulwer, in July 1835. By then a public correspondence between Bulwer, Jamison and Wentworth (the editor of the *Australian* news-paper) had inspired the May 1835 formation of the Australian Patriotic Association (APA).[79] The APA would gather information and raise funds to make the case for political representation to the metropolitan and colonial governments. Although the Emancipists had, relatively, mass Australian appeal, the APA had only 416 subscribers in 1835 and struggled finan-cially.[80]

On 20 March 1835, the *Australian*'s editorial noted the necessity of appointing an agent in London to advance colonists' interests.[81] A letter from Bulwer, published on 24 March, suggested that he should be appointed as parliamentary agent. In Britain, 'apathy and indifference' to New South Wales reflected a more general ignorance of colonial affairs, exacerbated by the lack of reliable information: 'no one hears – no one cares – no one thinks'. 'You will become a matter of English interest', Bulwer told the colonists, 'when you blend yourself with England's daily affairs'. Once 'public men' in London were interested in the colony's affairs, they would rouse the government and public, overcoming the damaging criminal stereotype of the Emancipists created by Whately and others hostile to the extension of political rights. Bulwer would also tackle the problem of providing reliable and regular information: the colonists should form a permanent committee in New South Wales to keep the London agent informed. 'Thus armed', the agent, 'with the current confidence of an important Colony' would possess 'a weight both with the minister and the press, that would grow with every new instance of oppression that he proved – and redress that he obtained'. Bulwer required no salary, merely the provision of a London office, 'an intelligent secretary, and the postage of all letters'. He was confident of success; 'but there must be activity – there must be exertion'.[82]

Bulwer's confidence in 'prompt and energetic means' did not lead him to enormous exertion. He did speak in the infrequent Commons' debates on the Australian colonies: in March 1835 debating trial by jury in Van Diemen's Land; in July presenting the Emancipists' petition, and initiating a short debate on the possibility of representative institutions for New South Wales. The following July, Bulwer reminded Sir George Grey that the government had promised to consider the colonies' constitutions during the 1836 session, and identified land and the use of funds raised from the sale of land as issues which needed to be addressed. Grey asked for and received a year's deferral of the subject. When Grey again asked for a year's extension in June 1837, Bulwer pointed to several further petitions, and emphasised that while the 'more liberal' colonists desired an 'elective assembly', even the Exclusives 'objected to the existing Legislative Council, as furnishing . . . nothing like a fair or well constituted body for the purposes of impartial legislation'.[83] While reflecting the feelings of the APA, these were Bulwer's only parliamentary contributions on its behalf.

Bulwer joined the Transportation Select Committee during its first session in 1837, but only attended four of eighteen days' hearings in that session. Despite being primed with information by the APA he asked questions only of the Reverend Lang.[84] He had also joined the Select Committee on Waste Lands, and been a member of the committee which inquired into Darling's governorship, but made little impact and could not be regarded as a central member of either.[85] In 1837 he left England abruptly to pursue a diplomatic career in Europe.

Bulwer's resignation highlighted the role of Edward Eagar who called himself the 'ordinary' (that is, non-parliamentary) agent of the APA between 1837 and 1842.[86] From 1837 Eagar sent a series of letters to the APA which were published in first the Sydney *Monitor* and then the *Australian*. He urged the colonists to establish 'a duly *authorized* working agency'. This would remedy the ignorance of the metropolitan government, and meet the challenge of the 'colonial *Tories*', who, in the form of James Macarthur had an agent 'with abundant funds at his command, and a powerful London committee to assist him'.[87] While Eagar was not officially appointed by the APA, his letters to William Bland provide useful evidence on the perceived role of a metropolitan agent, including the details of payment and regular tasks.

Eagar was an emancipated convict who had lived in London since 1821 when he arrived carrying letters of introduction to Earl Bathurst provided by Governor Macquarie. His intention then was to defend the emancipists against Commissioner Bigge's report.[88] Eagar claimed to have attended the Transportation Select Committee 'from day to day', encouraging Bulwer to become a member as there was 'literally no one to raise a finger [on the APA's] behalf' and supplying Bulwer with information to combat attacks on the colony. Eagar presented himself as the main conduit for information flowing in both directions between Sydney and London. He also claimed to have 'collected and arranged all the scattered papers and documents' when the APA was 'between' parliamentary advocates in 1837.[89] Although Charles Buller wrote that Bulwer 'entrusted' the position to him personally, Eagar claimed that he had 'introduced' Buller to the agency, 'instructed him in all matters respecting the Colony, and enabled him to treat with the Government of the day respecting [the APA's] interests'.[90] Eagar's relationship with Buller may not have been as close as the former claimed, or Eagar may simply have been a poor servant of the APA. An effective 'ordinary agent' who had completed the tasks Eagar claimed to have fulfilled would have kept Buller well-informed of the APA's position, yet Buller appeared ignorant and 'a very inefficient advocate' in an 1839 debate on New South Wales; and he fell easy prey to James Macarthur's arguments which directly contradicted the APA position on representative government.[91] From Buller's own correspondence it is apparent that he was not formally employed as agent until 1839, although he first acted as such in early 1838.[92] An able parliamentary performer, Buller had access to the Colonial Office and potentially useful connections to the 'colonial reformers'. He was not, however, particularly reliable. Between April 1838 and early 1839, before his APA position had been confirmed, he accompanied Lord Durham to Canada. What the Sydney committee termed 'the unfortunate interval' in parliamentary representation between 1837 and 1839 ensued.[93] Before he left for Canada, Buller met with James Macarthur, who convinced him that the Exclusives' plan for a legislative council composed of a mixture of nominated and indirectly elected members, would meet the demands of the APA. Buller sent a paper outlining such a scheme to Lord Glenelg in early 1838.[94] Meetings with Glenelg, and later with Sir George Grey, led Buller to believe that the plan, submitted to cabinet in the form of a draft Bill, would meet with government approval. However, in April, the cabinet expressed implacable opposition to representative government for a penal colony. About to sail for Canada, Buller convinced the Colonial Office that no permanent constitutional changes 'alien' to the feelings of the APA should be made before the future of transportation was decided. Sure that no legislation could be enacted inside a period of two to three years, Buller did not think the extension of the existing New South Wales Act until 1841, or his departure for Canada, would have particularly adverse effects on the colony and had not therefore transferred the agency to another MP. The APA could correspond with Buller's father in his absence.[95]

The APA committee were, needless to say, horrified that their ignorant parliamentary advocate had been hoodwinked by James Macarthur into proposing a system which was inimical to their aims of broad representative government, low land prices and assigned convict labour. Buller's scheme would have the effect of creating a 'colonial plutocracy, without one of the redeeming features of the aristocracy of England'. The APA found themselves 'compelled to confess' complete disagreement with every aspect of Buller's plan. 'You will at once perceive', continued the APA:

> how utterly at variance your notions of a local Government for this colony are with ours. This circumstance we attribute to no absence of due regard for public liberty – the constitutional rights of British subjects – but solely, to your unavoidable want of correct information respecting the social state of this Colony, and its political capabilities.[96]

Nonetheless the APA maintained Buller as its advocate. Presumably, this decision was based on Buller's good connections and willingness to act on the colonists' behalf, as he continued to hold independent views which conflicted with the APA throughout the period to 1842.[97] Buller was, after all, one of the colonial reformers, a group which the APA thought intelligent, wealthy and influential, and increasingly 'wrong'.[98]

The APA's first two letters to Buller were published in Sydney in 1839, and transmitted to both the colonial authorities and 'a considerable number of different parties in England' as an 'indispensable resource' in an attempt to correct the misrepresentations of New South Wales current in Britain.[99] The letters emphasise Sydney frustration with metropolitan ignorance and the ease with which the Macarthur family, in particular James, propagated their 'violent libels' of the colony and its society.[100] Macarthur was condemned for publishing his 1837 book only in England, and further limiting its circulation 'exclusively, as far as possible, to his own friends and party'. Clearly Macarthur hoped the book would take effect 'long before' it was possible his account 'could be *read* in this Colony, much less *refuted*'.[101] The APA attempted to expose the Exclusives' motivations, rebut their 'alleged grounds of attack', and provide an alternative proposal for representative government, encompassing continued, and indeed increased, transportation. Their vision was almost utopian. If their plans were followed, England would gain a colonial empire rather than a colony, 'a *fulcrum* . . . from which she might diffuse her language, her institutions, her religion, and every desirable blessing, on at least one half of the globe. The loss of the West Indies, the loss of Java, or of any other Colony, would no longer be felt'.[102] But, as Ritchie has demonstrated, the argument about assignment had been lost in London in 1836. Even without Molesworth's Transportation Select Committee, senior members of the government, in particular Russell and Howick, had decided that systematic colonisation could generate enough colonial labour for the assignment system – so roundly condemned in London despite its many colonial supporters – to be ended immediately.[103]

The APA continued to argue for greater political representation. In September 1840 James Macarthur led a group which intimidated Governor Gipps into withdrawing a Bill on municipal institutions which was supported by the APA. Furious, the APA fired off letters to Buller in London, while Jamison and Blaxland warned Gipps of the perils of bending to Exclusive demands, insisting that their letter be forwarded to the secretary of state. It was written for both audiences: fortifying Gipps by reminding him that Bourke, 'assailed' by the Exclusives in a similar way, had nonetheless 'eventually carried every measure, which they . . . denounced'; yet drawing Colonial Office attention to the past misdemeanours of prominent Exclusives – 'Governor Bligh was violently deposed by these people'. The letter also recalled other aggressive assertions of Exclusive power which would offend metropolitan sensibilities, including the 'right of *systematic slaughter* of the *aborigines*' in a reference to the highly controversial Myall Creek massacre of 1838.[104]

As Buller's letters were received in return, the APA became convinced that, because of implacable metropolitan opposition to representative government in a convict society, they would have to compromise on assignment to achieve their greater aim of 'free institutions'. In fact, the metropolitan government had already suspended transportation to New South Wales, and in other respects the Bill introduced in 1841 met many of the APA's demands: reduced disabilities for emancipists; a wide franchise; direct elections to the legislative council; and the introduction of civil juries. Partly this success may be attributed to James Macarthur's assertion in February 1841 that he was prepared to work for a common cause and no longer supported distinction between emancipists and free settlers; partly to Westminster's recognition that granting representative government was easier than refusing it; and partly to the growing wealth and conservatism of the APA's leaders. Like the Macarthurs, leading emancipists would benefit from systematic colonisation. Nevertheless, progress was also dependent on the communications between Buller and the APA; and these convinced the latter that compromise was necessary.

The APA were a colonial interest group who very consciously acquired a parliamentary agent to overcome their lack of good contacts in the metropolis. Their parliamentary advocates did draw metropolitan attention to the APA's views in parliament and the Colonial Office, improving the flow of information both to and from the colony. Again, perhaps because of their weak government connections, the APA and its agents demonstrated an awareness of public opinion: publishing correspondence; circulating petitions; and tapping into contemporary colonial sensibilities. Nonetheless, the difficulty of overcoming simultaneously both the immense temporal and spatial distance between colony and metropolis, and their metropolitan advocates' fundamental ignorance about colonial affairs, proved serious obstacles.

The Eastern Cape Colony – settler and indigenous competition

In 1820 four thousand British migrants were planted in the Eastern Cape Colony to increase frontier security and establish a farming community that replicated English society.[105] Failing as agriculturalists due to poor techniques, disease and unsuitable soil, many of these settlers soon left the Eastern Cape, while others turned to the government in search of more land, access to public office, and improved infrastructure.[106] The Commission of Eastern Inquiry spent two months in the Eastern Cape's main town, Grahamstown, in 1824, eventually recommending a separate eastern political, administrative and judicial establishment. The metropolitan government rejected this plan, introducing an alternative commissioner-general system in 1828, which was abandoned in 1833. British settlers in the Eastern Cape remained frustrated by the lack of representation, access to patronage, investment in Grahamstown, and migration to the district.[107] But it was their relationship with the Cape's indigenous peoples that made settlers an object of metropolitan disapprobation.

Like their Australian counterparts, Cape settlers wanted access to land and labour. Barred from keeping slaves, and unable to attract European migrants,[108] the 1820 settlers turned to the Khoi people (first incorporated into the Cape economy by the Dutch) as cheap and pliable labour. Settlers' attempts to coerce and discipline the Khoi attracted substantial humanitarian criticism, brought to metropolitan attention in 1828 and 1834 by John Philip, the director of the London Missionary Society (LMS) in the Cape. Philip drew on anti-slavery sentiment and rhetoric to encourage successfully some legal protection for the Khoi. Such metropolitan intervention was seen by most settlers as a betrayal, but encouraged Philip and his supporters to look to the imperial, rather than the colonial, government to secure the rights of other indigenous groups within society.[109]

The humanitarian and evangelical impulses of the LMS and its sympathisers extended also to the Xhosa people, whose desirable grazing land overlapped the Eastern Cape's frontier. In December 1834 the sixth in a series of wars broke out between Xhosa and settlers. Tensions had increased with a resurgence in the colony's 'commando system', whereby settler posses made forays into Xhosa land, officially and unofficially, to recapture allegedly stolen cattle. Critics of the commando system condemned it as 'an instrument of intimidation, of terror, and of arbitrary cattle seizure' with punitive action taken against an entire community for the acts of a few individuals.[110] The Xhosa had also been repeatedly expelled from their land between the Kei and the Fish rivers – the so-called 'ceded' or 'neutral' territory – with troops destroying Xhosa crops and homes on each occasion.[111] In 1835 colonial and imperial troops would seize the 'neutral' territory and a larger area beyond between the Kei and the Keiskamma rivers, renaming it Queen Adelaide Province. In victory, Governor D'Urban demanded tens of thousands of cattle in reparations from the Xhosa, and, on 17 September 1835, declared them subjects of the British Empire. The motivations, course and outcome of the war were contested in Britain and the Cape, where the majority of settlers supported D'Urban, while the opposing minority were led by Philip.[112]

Eastern Cape settlers and philanthropists alike employed networks and counter-networks during and after the 1834–35 war. Their actions illuminate contemporary understandings of imperial power and information, as well as demonstrating how colonial lobbyists shaped their appeals to complement metropolitan concerns like anti-slavery.

'Furnish me with facts, give me facts'

John Philip and Thomas Fowell Buxton together form the focus of the philanthropic influence in the Cape Colony during the 1830s. Although based in Cape Town, Philip travelled extensively within the colony and beyond its frontiers, also making two extended trips to Britain in 1826–29 and 1836–37. Buxton, the parliamentary leader of the anti-slavery movement, never visited the Cape Colony, although he maintained networks of contacts there and throughout the empire. Both men were motivated by a combination of religious and, broadly speaking, 'humanitarian' concerns. Unlike many later imperialists and evangelicals, both regarded all men as essentially equal – at least in potential – and they were horrified by the degradation and violence faced by indigenous peoples in the empire. In addition, they were religious proselytisers, convinced that Britain's most important reparation for imperial destruction should be the bestowal of Christianity and civilisation upon indigenous communities.

Buxton first collaborated with Philip during the 1820s' campaign to secure the same legal rights for the Khoi as for Cape settlers. In the early 1830s, concerned about the persecution faced by the Xhosa, Philip renewed his contact with Buxton. As a veteran parliamentary campaigner with wide-ranging experience, Buxton saw the Cape Colony within its broader imperial context. Philip, on the other hand, focused on the Cape, bringing to the collaboration a more detailed knowledge and extensive Cape contacts. Aside from their different focuses and networks, Philip and Buxton's tactics, perceptions of the use of information, and of metropolitan society were informed by their different lobbying experiences.

Information came to Philip in Cape Town about the commando system, border clashes and settler iniquities from missionary, settler and indigenous sources, many of whom operated networks of their own. Philip's inflated reputation for being influential in Britain encouraged many of his colonial correspondents to believe that Philip would use the information they provided more effectively than anyone else in the Cape.[113] Apart from his missionary contacts, Philip's relationship with the Eastern Cape's commissioner-general, Andries Stockenström, proved particularly fruitful; while Philip's son-in-law, John Fairbairn, provided him with an extended network of sources, and also, as editor of the *South African Commercial Advertiser*, with a colonial platform.[114] From these connections, and meetings with the Xhosa leaders Maqoma, Tyhali and Sandile in 1832, Philip became convinced that the system of retributive commandos demanded colonial and metropolitan attention.

Like other critics of the commando system, Philip advocated a policy which recognised the rights and responsibilities of both the Xhosa and the settlers and abandoned the British habit of dealing with a constructed Xhosa 'paramount chief'.[115] Clear and intelligible written treaties between the colony and the various border tribes were needed. As another sympathiser would write:

> a just and comprehensive system . . . must maintain a *steady, uniform* character . . . Fixedness of character . . . will be indispensably necessary to remove suspicions from the minds of the [Xhosa], and inspire them with confidence in the principles and intentions of the Colonial Government.[116]

Philip sent the information he collected to Buxton in England. Since their collaboration on the Khoi, links between the Buxton family and Philip had strengthened, based on warm correspondence about political, domestic and missionary subjects. The Buxtons handled some of Philip's personal and financial affairs, and raised money for his missionary activities; they also treated him to the 'Buxton view' on politics and family confidences. He was urged in return to send information on missionary progress, especially with respect to education.[117]

After the passage of the 1833 Emancipation Act, Buxton turned his attention to the Cape. Despite several meetings, he found Stanley, the colonial secretary, unhelpful and feared that he would do little 'without open war and public opinion'. Consequently, Buxton became 'very anxious to make himself Master of the subject' before the next session of parliament; Philip was asked to supply 'all the *facts* and authentic documents you can without any delay'.[118] By December 1833 Buxton was contemplating a select committee: the collection and publication of accurate information would 'drag the truth to light', shaming the government into action.[119]

In mid-1834 Buxton called daily on the new colonial secretary, Spring Rice, his 'old friend . . . on Mauritius and slavery matters'.[120] Spring Rice agreed to support a parliamentary motion drawing attention to Britain's responsibility to indigenous peoples in the colonies, although he did not think an inquiry was warranted. On 1 July, Buxton proposed his motion, and Spring Rice gave modified support. Undeterred, Buxton collected more information from Philip, begging him to 'furnish me with facts, give me facts to confute Rice's statements . . . and I will . . . aim an effectual blow at them'.[121] A year after his first motion, in July 1835, Buxton successfully moved that a select committee be appointed to inquire into the condition of indigenous peoples throughout the British colonies.[122]

Buxton's call for an imperial select committee, rather than the projected inquiry into southern Africa, requires some explanation.[123] He was probably influenced by the information he received both through his networks and the press of attacks on indigenous welfare elsewhere. Plans to colonise New Zealand were widely reported, for example, and Buxton had received news from Governor Arthur and the Quaker James Backhouse about the decline of the Tasmanian Aborigines.[124] The elation of the Emancipation

Act – and the subsequent emotional vacuum – together with Buxton's religious conviction that Britain had both the opportunity and the duty to convert millions to Christianity also contributed.

The anti-slavery campaign influenced Buxton and Philip in terms of tactics and attitudes. In the heady days of 1833 and 1834, both emphasised the power of British public opinion, and the importance of imperial legislation. As Philip wrote to Buxton just after emancipation, the Xhosa's position was 'a question on which it must be an easy matter to raise England at the moment, the great struggle for the liberty of the slaves is a recent occurrence, the arguments which have been employed on this subject are yet fresh in the memories of the people'.[125] However, compromising to get the Emancipation Act through parliament provoked a rancorous split in the anti-slavery movement, and demonstrated to Buxton that legislation was ultimately more reliable than fickle and demanding public opinion. While Philip would continue to advocate the importance of publications, lecturing tours and appeals to the people into 1837, Buxton turned more determinedly to persuading individuals within the government and parliament of his case.

This difference in emphasis altered the relationship between Buxton and Philip. While before 1835 they had been reasonably equal partners, each with his own sphere of influence and expertise, after this point Buxton primarily used Philip as a source of information. The Buxton family trawled through Philip's letters, whether straightforward, passionate, flowery or restrained, taking information and quotations as they thought best, sometimes using whole letters and at other times substantially repackaging the information. While Philip had access to the Colonial Office in the 1820s, his 1834–35 conflict with the Cape administration made him too controversial to be received personally by the imperial government. His reliance on Buxton was therefore increased.[126]

Despite his faith in imperial action, Philip devoted some time to colonial lobbying in 1834 and early 1835. The new governor, Sir Benjamin D'Urban, seemed open to Philip's concerns about the Xhosa. D'Urban referred favourably to an 1833 Colonial Office interview on the subject; he met with Philip more than once; and gave him access to government documents. Philip reciprocated with 'memorials' on frontier policy.[127] In August 1834 Philip travelled to the eastern frontier to initiate treaty negotiations with the Xhosa chiefs, who he assured of the governor's 'justice and humanity'.[128]

At the outbreak of war, however, Philip and his supporters were accused by the Grahamstown settlers of inciting a Xhosa invasion. The philanthropists countered, arguing that the greedy and ruthless settlers had 'no notion of settling the affairs of the Caffres but by powder and lead'.[129] Ahead of the military, the settlers became the focus for critics of colonial policy. As D'Urban travelled to Grahamstown, the philanthropists feared that the settlers' false accounts would blind him to the real circumstances of the frontier.[130] To combat this pernicious influence, Philip thought D'Urban would need not only great strength of character, but intelligent and well-informed support from the metropolitan government.[131] Thus Philip increased his correspondence, so that Buxton could exert greater pressure on the Colonial Office. D'Urban's untimely proclamation of 10 May 1835, which declared the war won and his Xhosa opponents 'irreclaimable savages', provoked a further reassessment by Philip. From this point on (although he continued to hope that the governor would come to his senses) Philip by-passed the colonial elite altogether, concentrating on lobbying London.[132]

Until December 1834 Philip's correspondence could be characterised as informative, rather than passionate. By providing the government and public with a 'true account', Philip believed – much as Edward Macarthur did – that a positive response would automatically be generated. Accordingly he wrote numerous and extensive letters to his contacts in London, privileging Buxton over the LMS because of his government contacts, and because of LMS unease about Philip's involvement in 'politics'.[133] Although Philip thought public opinion important, he agreed that change could be hastened by the application of personal pressure and information to the government. As he became more frustrated, Philip sent Buxton not only more information but also suggestions on how it should be used, pressing Buxton to call for commissioners of inquiry to be sent to the Cape.[134]

Philip's loss of faith in D'Urban after the May 1835 annexation encouraged him to put even greater effort into providing information for London. First-hand missionary, Khoi and Xhosa accounts were appended to Philip's letters. Buxton, Philip wrote, was 'at perfect liberty to put my documents . . . into the hands of Ministers and to let them know that I am fully prepared to prove all that I have stated'. Like other colonial lobbyists, official and unofficial, Philip emphasised his superior sources of information and privileged position in the Cape: 'the Government must feel that as I was the medium of the communication between the Governor and the Caffre Chiefs . . . and . . . was on the Frontier two months immediately before . . . the war I must be well acquainted with the whole subject and that my statements . . . are not to be trifled with'.[135]

In late May, Philip heard of the Xhosa chief Hintsa's death while in Harry Smith's custody. Hintsa, wounded and defenceless, had allegedly begged for mercy before a colonial volunteer shot him in the head at close range. After death, Hintsa's body was mutilated: his ears cut off and displayed in Grahamstown by settlers. These reports outraged Philip and his informants, generating a new wave of correspondence written explicitly for its ultimate Colonial Office audience, although sent through Buxton and William Ellis at the LMS. There is, for example, a marked difference in tone between the description of Hintsa's death in Philip's letter to Buxton of 29 May 1835 and a letter written the next day. The 29 May account of the death was calm and concise; the 30 May letter was full of passion. These letters were rich in analogy as well as attacks on the home and colonial governments for allowing the national honour to be brought into such disrepute.[136] 'How long is this state of things to continue? It will continue till England faces by its decision the guilty stain upon the ruthless perpetrators of this foul deed. Till England pronounces the death of Hintsa to be *Murder*!'[137] Most powerful was Philip's careful selection of direct excerpts from the colonial intelligence he received. The testimony of Klaas on Hintsa's death, as first related to a missionary, provided a typical example.

> Hintsa stood up and cried out to the corps of guides – Tahu Amapakati; which is to say, Take me as your prisoner; which the corps of guides *heard and understood*. After this, one of the name of Southey blew the upper part of his head off. William Southey then cut off his ears. The Corps of Guides all exalted at the exploit.[138]

Philip's increased flow of letters coincided with Buxton's efforts to give the newly appointed Aborigines Select Committee a pan-imperial remit. As news of the conflict between Xhosa and colonists arrived in London, Buxton shifted the committee's focus back to the Cape. Of forty-six witnesses, twenty-seven gave evidence exclusively on the Cape, and a further three on the Cape as well as other colonies. Buxton also lobbied personally at the Colonial Office: a task which was made easier for him in April 1835 when the return of a Whig government brought Glenelg and Grey into the Office. Buxton's daughter wrote, as Glenelg became secretary of state: '[My father] went yesterday to commence his persecution of the new Colonial Secy . . . whom he found fully conformable about the savages'. Buxton's relationship with Glenelg was as strong as that he had enjoyed with Spring Rice the previous year.[139]

Buxton and his family also appreciated the uses of colonial information and, particularly, the importance of its presentation. During 1835 the information they possessed proved especially powerful as D'Urban's official despatches fell almost completely silent about the war. This unlikely situation created a vacuum of official information which Ross has aptly described as 'one of the most extraordinary episodes of British colonial history'.[140] The combined labour of Buxton, his unmarried sister Sarah Maria, cousin Anna Gurney, daughter Priscilla, and her husband Andrew Johnston (an MP and member of the Aborigines Select Committee), enabled the Buxtons to collect, collate and repackage large quantities of colonial information.[141] Much of it came from Philip and other contacts, but Buxton, drawing on his anti-slavery experience, also lobbied the Colonial Office in private and through parliament for documents on the Cape and 'aborigines' in general. When Aberdeen complained about the volume of papers requested,

Buxton told him 'that if slavery had been abolished by any one thing it was by sly motions for papers', and that 'he always made the net as wide as he could, in hope of sweeping in some good things by accident'. 'I wish you had the copying of them yourself', was James Stephen's rueful response in 1837 when Buxton moved for yet another batch of documents.[142]

Much of the collation was done by Anna Gurney and Sarah Maria Buxton in Norfolk. Gurney's 1835 compendium on the Cape was 'the most valuable and the only thing in use'; which 'might save a nation of 100,000 beings and several flourishing missions'.[143] Daughter Priscilla described how she sat in the family's London house 'copying and culling' from Anna's collation, while her husband collected copies of debates from the Commons, in preparation for one of Buxton's speeches.[144] Thus the information provided by Philip might be revised more than once before it was presented to parliament or privately to the Colonial Office.

Buxton used his metropolitan networks and connections to get information to the right places. As noted earlier, Philip's conflict with D'Urban meant he was unable to make direct contact with the Colonial Office, who were determined to appear unbiased. But, in the absence of official despatches from the governor, the information Buxton received from Philip and passed to the Colonial Office became incorporated into policy. Philip's information also travelled via Ellis at the LMS, who Buxton was also careful to keep up to date.[145] Buxton used Ellis to deliver documents to the Colonial Office when he was out of town, and the two men discussed delicate issues such as the propriety of using a confidential testimonial which described Hintsa's mutilation. The Colonial Office's response to Ellis's independent communications, however, was far more muted than when he accompanied Buxton.[146]

As reports of Hintsa's death arrived in Britain, Buxton increased his personal letters and visits to the department where he emphasised the seriousness of such a death in British custody. Buxton told Glenelg directly that 'the life or death of many, many thousands of human beings' depended on the secretary of state's actions.[147] Armed with Gurney's collation and Philip's letters, Buxton and Ellis visited Glenelg in late September. Buxton then gave Glenelg 'a lecture to my heart's content on the treatment of Savages – the death of Hintza – the atrocities of white men, and above all on the responsibilities of a Secretary of State'.[148] Buxton credited his passion and Gurney's skilful and arresting collation of edited documents with sparking Colonial Office interest in their cause. These efforts 'changed to blood' the response of Glenelg, Grey and Stephen. By late November 1835, after two months of Buxton's most intensive lobbying, the officials appeared convinced.[149] A month later, on 26 December 1835, Glenelg sent a despatch to D'Urban which criticised his actions and language, and asked him to justify the retention of the annexed territory. Shortly afterwards,

Stockenström was despatched as the Eastern Cape lieutenant-governor, with instructions to restore stable and friendly relations with the Xhosa based on written treaties. Queen Adelaide Province was abandoned in 1837.

Buxton's Select Committee on Aborigines (British Settlements) began hearing evidence in mid-1835 becoming in many respects a de facto inquiry into the Cape Colony. Buxton kept a close control over proceedings, preparing amenable witnesses like Stockenström and Philip with lists of questions, keeping the missionary officials on side, and making sure he chaired every session.[150] From September 1835 he negotiated with the LMS and the imperial government to bring Philip to London, battling against the LMS's desire to remain apolitical, and the Colonial Office's reluctance to appear biased.[151] Confident of eventual success and in anticipation of Philip's evidence, Buxton decided in September first to 'avoid South Africa', and then 'abruptly' to adjourn the committee until Philip arrived. Although Stockenström's evidence was compelling, he had left the colony before the war. With D'Urban's supporters – some with first-hand experience – present at the hearings, Buxton needed a well-prepared Philip to counter them. He sent Philip confidential copies of the existing evidence. 'Come well prepared', he instructed, 'your facts clear and well substantiated – *in lucid order* – the questions which I am to ask you in the Committee . . . well digested. Your plan for the safe, economical just Government of the Colony, so far as the Natives . . . are concerned fully weighed & prepared'.[152] Philip brought with him Dyani Tshatshu (a Xhosa chief) and Andries Stoffels (a Khoi convert to Christianity), as well as the missionary James Read and his son. Philip appeared before the committee on five days between 15 June and 1 August 1836, and on a further four days in May 1837. Tshatshu, Stoffels and both the Reads also gave evidence and met with government officials, although their hopes of meeting William IV were not realised.[153] Philip and Read senior returned to traditional methods of extra-governmental lobbying during their period in Britain, embarking on intensive lecture and preaching tours to raise public support, during which the presence of Stoffels and Tshatshu drew crowds and donations.[154] The three major missionary societies also collaborated to publish the select committee testimony of William Ellis, and his counterparts at the Wesleyan and Church missionary societies, in pamphlet form in 1837.[155]

The select committee report was drafted in January 1837 at Buxton's Norfolk home. Along with most of the Buxton family, Philip was present, although the primary author was Anna Gurney.[156] Although the Buxtons were pleased with the result, the report's subsequent progress was not smooth. In March a fire at the printers destroyed part of the original manuscript; and committee members, William Gladstone and John Bagshaw, forced Buxton to reconvene the committee to hear defensive evidence on behalf of the Eastern Cape settlers.[157] Most seriously, in June the Colonial Office produced documents 'a yard in height' which 'modified the views of Lord Glenelg' on the Cape.[158] With William IV on the verge of death, and parliament thus on the cusp of dissolution, distributing the new papers to committee members ran the risk of a far longer delay. The committee might not even be reappointed in the following session. Pragmatically, Buxton agreed to the significant changes demanded by the Colonial Office in lieu of incorporating the new evidence. Even a diminished report would 'save half a dozen nations from extermination', he argued, agreeing to 'cut out and hack away at all in S Africa which related to the late war' to avoid 'the murder of the whole'. Despite this setback, Buxton remained optimistic, he had, after all, split the anti-slavery movement in the early 1830s with a compromise.[159] The revised Cape section revolved around official documents, reducing controversy.[160] In the last scramble to bring out the report the Buxtons stopped keeping Philip informed, again indicating the altered relationship between the lobbyists. Philip had served his primary purpose by providing information, but was no longer regarded as a good tactician by the Buxtons. The report was printed before William IV's death, although critics since have derided its importance because of this last-minute emasculation.

Philip and Buxton's lobbying was effective. Through his colonial networks Philip collected copious and startling intelligence, the Buxton family collated and repackaged this information to best influence the metropolitan government, and Thomas Buxton used his knowledge and connections to present the evidence personally to the right people. Although their cause was aided by D'Urban's failure to keep the Colonial Office officially or unofficially informed, the whole effort underlines, as Elbourne has observed, the small-scale nature of politics in this period, and the impact which personal networks could have.[161] Moreover, the Colonial Office used the information Buxton provided. Glenelg's despatches to D'Urban of 26 December 1835 and 1 May 1837 not only concentrated on the issues which Philip, Buxton and Gurney highlighted, but used their language in direct, if unacknowledged, quotes.[162] In concrete terms, Queen Adelaide Province was relinquished (although reoccupied in the 1840s), D'Urban chastised and Stockenström appointed. It is true, as Ross has argued, that Philip failed to get Buxton to advocate his hopes with respect to the location of the borders of the Cape Colony.[163] But this underlines Buxton's importance to the proceedings, Philip's lack of personal access to the Colonial Office, and the lack of immediate impact of the select committee's recommendations on the Cape. Buxton certainly regarded himself as successful. After losing his parliamentary seat in 1837, he drew up a list of the questions which had interested him during his public career. Numbers eleven and twelve were 'Aborigines' and 'Adelaide restored': both received ticks to indicate satisfactory completion.[164]

The select committee's report was undermined by the changes forced in mid-1837. Nevertheless, the minutes of evidence, which were printed in 1836 and 1837, had already been used effectively by Buxton – alongside Philip's letters – to persuade the government of his case. In broader terms, the report and the publicity which Philip in particular pursued, made 'Aborigines' a metropolitan issue.[165] As Porter has argued, the report 'identified clearly the areas and issues which were to preoccupy British administrators throughout the century', and should not be dismissed as 'merely rhetorical or cosmetic'.[166]

The short-term success of the lobbyists, as well as their long-term failure, indicates how important it was for colonial lobbyists to gain influence both in London and in the colonial sphere. The critical nature of the link between Philip and Buxton to this success is indicated by contrast with New South Wales. There, the leading missionary voice on settler depredations against the Aboriginal people, the LMS's Lancelot Threlkeld, catalogued violence against Aborigines, reported his concerns and proposed remedies to his superiors in London, and publicised them in the colony. Yet Threlkeld's efforts received little attention in Britain. His poor relationship with the LMS and leading colonial religious figures, Samuel Marsden and J. D. Lang, meant that a much more benign assessment of inevitable 'decay', rather than Threlkeld's 'war of extirpation', was presented to the Aborigines Select Committee.[167] As Lester has observed, Threlkeld was seriously hampered by his failure to '[insert] himself within the powerful humanitarian networks to which Buxton was key'.[168] While general metropolitan disapprobation of the Cape settlers undermined settlers' claims for compensation, Buxton's link to the Colonial Office was critical to the government decision to renounce Queen Adelaide Province.

'The libels against us': the Grahamstown settlers

Most settlers – especially in the Eastern Cape – supported the retributive war against the Xhosa, viewing the philanthropists' campaign with horror and anger. Although both Dutch and British communities supported the war, the discussion here focuses on the group of primarily British settlers whose views were shaped and expressed by the weekly *Graham's Town Journal*.

Grahamstown was a growing commercial centre in the 1830s: its merchants trading with the Xhosa as well as within the colony.[169] Many of the traders were 1820 settlers, others had based their success on that influx of British immigrants.[170] As commercial ventures consolidated, some turned to the acquisition of land and political representation. In religion, the Wesleyan Methodists were influential, if not numerically dominant: their leading minister was the Reverend William Shaw, and the Wesleyans retained a strong grip on the Grahamstown trader class throughout the nineteenth century.[171] When the war began, many of these settlers signed up to serve in the Grahamstown volunteers.

From December 1834 until mid-1835, the Grahamstown settlers concentrated on lobbying within the colony. Less than two weeks after the first fighting, 360 settlers pledged to boycott the Cape Town published *South African Commercial Advertiser* because it blamed the settlers for the war. The eastern-based *Graham's Town Journal* provided their alternative rallying point. Established in 1831, and largely sustained by agricultural and commercial notices, its political bias was stridently anti-Philip and anti-Fairbairn. From January 1834 its editor was Robert Godlonton, a failed agriculturalist and minor civil servant, who would become one of the most powerful people in the colony.[172] Through 1835, the *Journal* took a strong pro-settler line: it advocated compensation for claimed war losses; the opening up of conquered territory for settlement; an increased frontier military presence; and an eastern seat of power in the colony. The *Journal*'s reconstruction of the Xhosa as savage and inferior provided the settlers with moral justification for their claims.[173] The *Journal* was highly critical of the imperial and colonial governments, which were condemned as possessing 'an unaccountable credulity . . . in believing the statements of visionaries and theorists, in preference to the complaints, the remonstrances, the recommendations and the warnings which have been so often reiterated by men residing on the spot'.[174]

The settlers employed traditional tactics of pledges, public meetings and petitions to lobby the colonial and imperial authorities. In February a committee of Grahamstown merchants and traders petitioned the governor for loans against possible future compensation for property lost in the war.[175] In June, Godlonton published in Grahamstown the first section of the *Irruption of the Kafir hordes*. This volume purported to reveal the truth of the conflict between Xhosa and settlers, and, like the *Journal* articles it was based on, detailed the failures of the imperial government, the duplicity of colonial 'philanthropists', the innocence of the Grahamstown settlers, and their right to compensation. Godlonton was convinced that the settlers' case needed to be made, the 'truth' established. The second and third parts of the *Irruption* were published in early 1836.[176]

Lobbying the colonial administration was made easier by the governor's presence in the Eastern Cape from early January 1835. D'Urban was surrounded by Grahamstown men who worked hard to establish personal relations with him. Although he would become frustrated by the local government officials, D'Urban formed close links with the settlers which endured beyond his governorship. Many were encouraged to write to him confidentially, and their viewpoints and information influenced the governor.[177] In 1835 D'Urban held out the promise of land grants in the captured territory to prominent Eastern Cape families, in appreciation of their services and support.[178] Theophilus Shepstone took the lead among Wesleyan missionaries in providing counsel and interpreting services for the governor, although the widespread colonial Wesleyan support for the governor and leading missionaries' calls for retribution against the Xhosa caused deep embarrassment for the parent missionary society in England.[179]

By mid-1835 negative metropolitan reactions to the war had arrived in the colony with the British newspapers. Philip and other 'philanthropists' appeared to have convinced the British government and public that the colonists were to blame for the crisis. The Grahamstown settlers thus faced a hostile metropolitan reception before they had even begun to defend themselves. Their campaign was further hampered by D'Urban's poor relationship with the imperial government and a lack of powerful metropolitan supporters. The London-based Cape of Good Hope Trade Society advised the colonists that as metropolitan opinion was so firmly against them, appeals for financial support should only be directed to the British government – the metropolitan public was lost.[180]

The settlers' reception at the Aborigines Select Committee was hostile. Thomas Philipps, a settler who had left the colony before the war, and the Wesleyan missionary, William Shaw, strongly defended the eastern settlers, but were overshadowed by Andries Stockenström, the former commissioner-general. Although Stockenström had also left the Cape before the war, his evidence that the settlers and colonial government were to blame coincided with Buxton's own views; Stockenström also made twelve appearances before the committee, compared to Philipps' two and Shaw's three. As the committee's evidence appeared in the *Graham's Town Journal* from mid-December 1835, it confirmed to the settlers the immediate need to reverse British views of the Cape. In 1836 the 'British Immigrants of 1820' published an attack on the philanthropists in London. The book – probably written by D'Urban's ardent supporter, John Chase – made its aims explicit:

> we have hitherto been wasting our strength. The Enemy wrote for *England*, – We contented ourselves with exposing him in the *Colony*, – We have seen our error, and this Pamphlet, the first fruits of the discovery, is intended for the same field as the libels against us – *OUR MOTHER COUNTRY*.[181]

The settlers' frustration is redolent of the APA's criticisms of James Macarthur for publishing only in England and not in New South Wales.

In June and July 1835, a rash of settler petitions to the governor, the House of Commons, and William IV were drawn up, coming not only from Grahamstown but also from the other Eastern Cape towns – Uitenhage, Bathurst, Graaf Reinet and Port Elizabeth – and Cape Town.[182] These petitions took a common form. R. M. Beverley, whose 1837 book opposed the war, made the illuminating, if partial, assessment that the petitions shared a 'similar style of solemn nonsense' and 'fumigated' D'Urban, 'sometimes mixing piety with adulation, and generally enlarging upon two topics, "the merciful forbearance" of his Excellency, and "that great act of philanthropy and humanity" ' which freed the Mfengu people from Xhosa bondage.[183] The petitions did indeed make a rather crude appeal to British anti-slavery sentiment by comparing D'Urban's questionable 'emancipation' of the Mfengu with the emancipation of slaves.[184] They also emphasised the widespread support for D'Urban's annexation of territory, the wanton devastation caused by the Xhosa, and the destructive opposition to his policies from the philanthropist minority. Many petitions attracted a considerable proportion of the population as signatories. In Grahamstown, for example, with a total population of about three thousand, more than seven hundred adult males signed some petitions.

Most petitions were sent to Britain through the governor, although some were presented to parliament via the Cape of Good Hope Trade Society. The presentation of a petition from Albany (the district in which Grahamstown lay) by the Trade Society was probably managed by Thomas Philipps after his appearance before the Aborigines Select Committee. Philipps had already delivered a statement from the landholders and traders of Albany to the Colonial Office, which dated from before the war.[185] The Trade Society, established in London in 1825 in the presence of several important Cape Town commercial figures such as John Ebden, William Venning and Abraham Borradaile, had a history of moderately successful intervention on mercantile interests at the Board of Trade, the Treasury, and the Colonial Office; particularly in relation to wine and grain tariffs.[186] The society was experienced, under the chairmanship of Borradaile, in the usual metropolitan lobbying techniques of interest groups: deputations met with ministers; private letters were exchanged with Robert Hay; petitions from the colony were presented; members of parliament were contacted and canvassed; information was provided; and liaison occurred with the Cape Colony government agent, Courtenay.[187] But the Trade Society's closest and strongest connections were with the Cape Town Commercial Exchange, not the Grahamstown merchants, and much of the society's impetus came from the western Cape.[188] Certainly, it was the Commercial Exchange that received the Trade Society's advice during 1835 about the hostility of the British public to the Cape settlers. Nevertheless, the Trade Society took the Grahamstown settlers closer to government than any other means available.

Between July and December 1835 the Trade Society sent five letters to the Colonial Office about the war: these concentrated on the innocence of the settlers, their economic importance to the colony, and their right to compensation.[189] A deputation from the society, headed by Borradaile, met with Glenelg on 5 October and (probably) in late December. Alongside the colonial petitions, the society presented a series of its own resolutions to the Colonial Office on 15 October. Borradaile hinted to the Colonial Office at the importance of his private sources of colonial information, but presented his official representations on the basis of intelligence gleaned from the Commercial Exchange.[190] The Colonial Office's response to the society was rather cool. A Captain Aitchison had reported that the Trade Society had asked him to attend a meeting 'with a view to my furnishing information touching the late Caffre irruption'; Aitchison declined as his intelligence was the 'property of His Majesty's Government'.[191] This cannot have made the government expect much new information from Borradaile, despite his private sources. James Stephen wrote on the Trade Society's first claim that it was an 'unsatisfactory representation', and it took two unanswered letters before the Colonial Office agreed to the 5 October meeting.[192] The Trade Society followed up the meeting with four resolutions: that the colonists were entitled to compensation; that the society supported D'Urban and his eastern frontier policy; that the annexation of Queen Adelaide Province and the emancipation of the Mfengu people were vital to the viability of the Eastern Cape; and that the resolutions should be published in five metropolitan newspapers including *The Times*. While earlier letters were couched in commercial and economic terms, heavily emphasising the financial importance of the Eastern Cape, its settlers and trade, the October resolutions clearly employed a language of humanitarianism, hoping for the 'extension of Trade, Civilization and Religion which it is the most anxious wish of the Colonists to promote among their coloured neighbours', and asking the government to adopt the 'spirit of peace and conciliation'.[193]

The Trade Society, despite receiving a grudging hearing at the Colonial Office, did not have much impact. Nor, given the general anti-settler climate in Britain, is it likely that they could have altered public opinion greatly even if they had tried more forcefully. They had no established networks beyond the City of London, and no experience of raising public awareness. The philanthropists had won this war of opinion before the settlers started. The society continued to lobby the Colonial Office on Cape affairs with little effect through the later 1830s – in particular sending three letters during 1838 regarding the commercial opportunities at Natal.[194]

While little direct evidence remains, the successful 1837 demand by two members of the Aborigines Select Committee that additional evidence be heard defending the Eastern Cape settlers, suggests that Philipps, John Chase, and other colonial settlers and former officials in London were able to utilise some connections in the metropolis. In this case, William Gladstone and John Bagshaw ensured that George Greig, the Cape Town printer and associate of Godlonton, gave evidence before the select committee on two occasions. As Greig asked to be excused after giving only a little evidence, his contribution was not actually very important.[195] Gladstone continued to lobby for the settlers after the select committee: he wrote to Chase in December 1837 detailing two interviews with the Duke of Wellington at which they had discussed D'Urban's situation and the Albany petitions. However, no action was taken in anticipation of D'Urban's return to London.[196]

Although colonists focused on the metropolitan government from mid-1835, campaigning also continued in Grahamstown. Petitions were raised, works which vindicated the settlers were published, and opposition to the new lieutenant-governor, Stockenström, was palpable and damaging. Throughout 1838 and 1839 Godlonton seized on (and exaggerated) the Dutch exodus from the colony as evidence that relinquishing Queen Adelaide Province had been wrong-headed. A group of sixteen leading colonial citizens, including Ebden, met in Cape Town during February 1837 and commissioned an official documentary record which would once and for all set history 'straight'. Although Donald Moodie's Record had little effect on the settlers' claims for compensation, it would prove to be the basis for later nineteenth-century and early twentieth-century accounts of the period.

In some limited respects the settlers achieved their aims: D'Urban advocated the establishment of a political power base in the east, and this was, to a certain extent, instituted, although to the Grahamstown settlers' dismay, the first lieutenant-governor was Stockenström, and he chose to make his base at Uitenhage, not Grahamstown. Within ten years the territory returned to the Xhosa was once again incorporated into the colony, never to be relinquished, while gradually the frontier area was militarised, leading to an expansion of trading interests in Grahamstown. But in 1835 and 1836 the Grahamstown settlers were hampered by the unpalatable nature of their aims. Demands for compensation and soldiers, and for the oppression of indigenous peoples did not go down well in a metropolitan climate both fiscally repressive and evangelical. To have won such a case, the settlers would have needed an almost impossibly good network of metropolitan contacts.

Conclusion

Extra-governmental colonial lobbyists in both New South Wales and the Cape Colony viewed the acquisition and utilisation of influence in London as crucial in the era before representative government. Although colonists developed their metropolitan networks in a range of ways – from the long-term maintenance of a family representative in London by the Macarthurs, to the indirect use of the Cape Trade Society by the Grahamstown settlers – all the lobbyists shared basic conceptions of how lobbying might and should be employed. Colonial lobbyists expected more from personal contacts within government than from appeals to the public in the 1830s. The increasing recognition of the need to win metropolitan public opinion, as demonstrated by the anguish of both the APA and the Grahamstown settlers at their misrepresentation, shaped the arguments used by colonial lobbyists – as, for example, appeals to anti-slavery sentiment from philanthropists, Cape settlers and anti-transportation campaigners demonstrates. But this recognition rarely translated into expensive wide-ranging campaigning. Even when partisan publications appeared in Britain, their circulation was typically small and targeted at members of the government and other opinion-makers. Edward Macarthur's *Colonial policy*, for example, was as much (if not more) a means to marshal vital information for a few, as to win over the masses.

The development of lobbyists' networks was typically slow. Relationships developed through shared experience, the interdependence of lobbyists and government on the information they provided, and increasing confidence. The frequent changes in Colonial Office personnel from the late 1820s forced lobbyists to be flexible and pragmatic if they were to maintain influence. Political longevity was a significant factor in the success of the networks of Thomas Buxton and the Macarthurs. Yet while networks were gradually established, colonial crises could provoke a rapid evolution in strategy, as seen in John Philip's marshalling of information during the 1834–35 war.

More than anything else, however, the colonists' networks demonstrated the smallness of the world of colonial governance in this period. Knowing a very few metropolitan government figures gave lobbyists considerable potential for influence. In a climate of metropolitan ignorance, it was significant to be merely a favoured supplier of information, even if the Colonial Office was not persuaded of a particular point of view. This difference marked out Philip's success from the Grahamstown merchants or the APA. Philip, a figure too controversial to be welcomed at the Colonial Office by 1836, was nonetheless able to use the determined and conscientious Buxton to pass on his message; while Edward Eagar, former convict, was forced to make use of the less reliable Bulwer and Buller. The Grahamstown merchants lost the battle to win metropolitan respectability early on, and thus lost vital ground at the Colonial Office; while even though the Macarthurs' opinions were treated with healthy suspicion by government, their information was privileged because of their successful integration into London society.

The development of lobbyists' understanding of the power of information has been a prominent feature of this study. Initially all groups were convinced that merely a clear, rational statement – 'the truth' – could convince metropolitan or colonial authorities of a point of view. Information was the basis for any decision, and in London colonial intelligence was in short supply. This was the clear message of Henry Bulwer's letter to the Emancipists, and indeed, as noted above, the opportunity to provide information where little alternative provision existed was important. The studies of Edward Macarthur and the philanthropists, however, show most explicitly the development of an understanding that information alone was not sufficient: for the desired effect it had to be packaged correctly (in terms of both style and content) and presented carefully. This recognition helped transform colonists from interest groups into sophisticated lobbyists.

But, as the next chapter will demonstrate, the world of colonial governance did not stand still. As government embraced statistical over narrative information from the late 1830s, a transformation in the very structure and style of government was precipitated. Having developed their techniques of lobbying and personal contacts over the 1820s and 1830s, colonial lobbyists were again forced to reassess and adapt to the ever-expanding metropolitan and colonial bureaucracies. For some, this transition would take decades.

Notes

1 MP, A2914, fo. 145, Edward to James Macarthur, 26 December 1834.
2 Eastwood, 'Social legislation', 204.
3 Hollis, *Pressure from without*; Eastwood, 'Social legislation'; Olson, *Making the empire work*; Kammen, *Rope of sand*.
4 Hollis, *Pressure from without*, p. 3.
5 GRE/B130/2B, fo. 1, Wakefield to Howick, 5 September 1831.
6 Hollis, *Pressure from without*, p. 3.
7 Eastwood, 'Social legislation', 204.
8 Olson, *Making the empire work*, p. 72.
9 *Ibid.*, p. 155; Kammen, *Rope of sand*.
10 Hollis, *Pressure from without*, p. viii; Olson, *Making the empire work*, pp. 2–4.
11 Ward, *Colonial self-government*, pp. 166–71.
12 On the development of self-government see: Neal, *Rule of law*; Hirst, *Colonial democracy*; Ward, *Colonial self-government*; Hirst, *Republican manifesto*; Atkinson, *Muddle-headed republic*.
13 King, *Colonial expatriates*; Ellis, *Macarthur*; Ward, *Macarthur*.
14 Macintyre, *Concise history*, p. 39.
15 King, 'John Macarthur', 178; King, *Colonial expatriates*, pp. 11–12.
16 MP, A2922, pp. 173, 176–7, Gladstone to Macarthur, 26 November 1839, Howick to James Macarthur, 3 February 1840.
17 Macintyre, *Concise history*, p. 47.
18 CO 201/236, fo. 8, Macarthur to Goderich, 8 February 1833.
19 CO 201/260, fos 375–6, 379–82, Bourke to Glenelg, 16 May 1837, 17 May 1837; CO 201/261, fos 13–15, Bourke to Glenelg, 3 June 1837; NSW Archives, 4/1303, Glenelg to Gipps, 24 October 1837.
20 CO 201/285, fos 149–51, Gipps to Glenelg, 5 March 1839.
21 King, 'John Macarthur', 181.
22 John Macarthur to his father, 18 July 1826, quoted in King, *Colonial expatriates*, pp. 34–5.
23 King, *Colonial expatriates*, pp. 22–6, 31, 34.
24 King, 'John Macarthur', 180–5; Ward, *Colonial self-government*, pp. 137, 145.
25 King, *Colonial expatriates*.

26 MP, A2913, fo. 215, Edward to William Macarthur, 13 November 1826.
27 *Ibid.*, fo. 251, Edward to John Macarthur, 23 September 1830. King, *Colonial expatriates*, p. 38.
28 MP, A2913, fo. 293, Macarthur to his parents, 28 May 1831.
29 MP, A2914, fo. 290, Edward to William Macarthur, 16 February 1836.
30 MP, A2914, fos 358, 362, Macarthur to his brothers, 10 August 1839, 27 September 1839.
31 CO 201/266, fos 468–9, Forbes to Stephen, 31 March 1837; MP, A2922, pp. 72–4, Forbes to Macarthur, 26 February 1837.
32 MP, A2915, fo. 6, Macarthur to his brothers, 10 April 1841; MP, A2914, fo. 399, Macarthur to his brothers, 10 April 1840.
33 MP, A2915, fo. 64, Macarthur to his brothers, 17 July 1842.
34 MP, A2913, fo. 351, Edward to James Macarthur, 24 September 1831; *PP 1831*, vii (276), Minutes of Evidence before Select Committee on Secondary Punishments, pp. 113–17.
35 CO 201/224, fo. 72, Macarthur to Howick, 26 May 1831.
36 CO 201/230, fo. 95, Macarthur to Hay, 24 February 1832.
37 MP, A2914, fo. 145, Edward to James Macarthur, 26 December 1834.
38 MP, A2913, fo. 309, Macarthur to his father, 27 June 1831; *PP 1831*, vii (276), Edward Macarthur, 'Letter on the Present System of Transportation to New South Wales', Appendix 6, p. 142.
39 MP, A2913, fo. 306, Macarthur to his father, 6 June 1831.
40 MP, A2913, fo. 293, Macarthur to his parents, 28 May 1831.
41 MP, A2914, fos 16, 145, Edward to James Macarthur, 6 May 1832, 26 December 1834.
42 *Ibid.*, fo. 145, Edward to James Macarthur, 26 December 1834.
43 MP, A2913, fos 293, 309, Macarthur to his parents, 28 May 1831, 27 June 1831.
44 King, *Colonial expatriates*, pp. 47–8, 51.
45 CO 201/285, fos 291–3, Gipps to Glenelg, 3 April 1839, and Stephen minute, 8 October 1839.
46 CO 201/268, fo. 157, Stewart to Glenelg, 29 May 1837.
47 *PP 1840*, xxxiii (211), Macarthur to Russell, 25 March 1840.
48 MP, A2914, fo. 283, Edward to Elizabeth Macarthur, 8 December 1836. See King, *Colonial expatriates*, pp. 48–9.
49 Macarthur, *New South Wales*, pp. 276–7.
50 *PP 1837*, xix (518), Qs 3024, 3333, 3339, 3356, 3363, 3371, James Macarthur.
51 Macarthur, *New South Wales*, p. 284; *PP 1837*, xix (518), Qs 4179, 4188–94, Macarthur.
52 CO 201/282, fos 301–2, Macarthur to Glenelg, 10 April 1838.
53 *Ibid.*, fo. 307, Macarthur to Grey, 10 April 1838.
54 MP, A2914, fo. 324, Macarthur to his brothers, 21 January 1839.
55 *Ibid.*, fo. 326, Macarthur to his brothers, 13 March 1839.
56 CO 201/315, fos 73–7, Macarthur to the Colonial Land and Emigration commissioners, 18 March 1840; Macarthur *et al.* to Russell, 11 April 1840; Peel to Macarthur, 28 July 1840; all encl. in Macarthur to Stanley, 3 September 1841.
57 *Ibid.*, fo. 55, Macarthur to Stanley, 3 September 1841.
58 MP, A2915, fo. 24, Macarthur to his brothers, 18 September 1841.
59 *Ibid.*, fos 54–6, 110, Macarthur to his brothers, 2 March 1842, 29 May 1842, 15 May 1843.
60 MP, A2914, fo. 326, Macarthur to his brothers, 13 March 1839.
61 MP, A2915, fos 110, 239, Macarthur to his brothers, 15 May 1843, 28 July 1846.
62 MP, A2914, fo. 399, Macarthur to his brothers, 10 April 1840, emphasis added.
63 MP, A2915, fo. 6, Macarthur to his brothers, 10 April 1841.
64 BP, A1733, p. 171, Richard to Dick Bourke, 15 May 1836.
65 MP, A2914, fo. 399, Macarthur to his brothers, 10 April 1840.
66 *Ibid.*, fo. 362, Macarthur to his brothers, 27 September 1839.
67 MP, A2915, fo. 50, Macarthur to his brothers, 4 January 1842.
68 Macarthur, *Colonial policy*, p. 17.
69 CO 201/315, fo. 53, Macarthur to Stephen, 5 June 1841; MP, A2915, fo. 12, Edward to James Macarthur, 8 June 1841; King, *Colonial expatriates*, p. 55.

70 MP, A2914, fo. 358, Macarthur to his brothers, 10 August 1839.
71 *Ibid.*, fos 399, 362, Macarthur to his brothers, 10 April 1840, 27 September 1839.
72 Burroughs, *Britain and Australia*, p. 316.
73 King, *Colonial expatriates*, chs 9–11.
74 CO 201/253, fo. 420, Bourke to Glenelg, 25 July 1836.
75 On the connection between political representation and legal rights, see Neal, *Rule of law*.
76 *Hansard*, NS, 1828, xviii, 1559; 1830, xxiii, 856; 3rd ser., 1832, xiii, 1089; 1835, xxix, 227.
77 Whately, *Secondary punishments* and *Remarks on transportation*.
78 Shaw, *Convicts*, p. 257.
79 ML, 363.06/1A1, APA Subscribers List, 1835. Melbourne, *Early constitutional development*, pp. 202–10.
80 ML, 363.06/1A1, APA Subscribers List, 1835.
81 *Australian*, 20 March 1835, p. 2.
82 Bulwer to Jamison, September 1834, *Australian*, 24 March 1835, p. 2.
83 *Hansard*, 3rd ser., 1835, xxvi, 533; 1835, xxix, 227–9; 1836, xxxiv, 1265; 1837, xxxviii, 1708–9.
84 *PP 1837*, xix (518), p. 251, Report of the Select Committee on Transportation.
85 *PP 1836*, xi (512), p. 449, Report of the Select Committee on the Disposal of Waste Lands; *PP 1835*, vi (580), p. 369, Report of the Select Committee on the Conduct of General Darling.
86 ML, Ae7/1, Eagar to Bland, 1 August 1842. McLachlan, 'Eagar'.
87 Eagar, 13 April 1838, in *Monitor*, 27 August 1838. Also letters of July 1837, 1 February 1838, 17 July 1839 in *Monitor*, 5 January 1838, 27 June 1838, and *Australian*, 19 December 1839.
88 Ritchie, *Wentworths*, pp. 192–3, 198–200, 202–3; McLachlan, 'Eagar', 431–47.
89 ML, Ae7/1, Eagar to Bland, 1 August 1842.
90 ML, A357, p. 167, Buller to APA, 21 April 1838; ML, Ae7/1, Eagar to Bland, 1 August 1842.
91 MP, A2914, fo. 358, Macarthur to his brothers, 10 August 1839.
92 ML, A357, p. 167, Buller to APA, 21 April 1838.
93 Jamison and Bland to Buller, 22 November 1840, in Bland, *Letters*, pp. 140–1.
94 CO 201/282, fos 301–2, Macarthur to Glenelg, 10 April 1838; ML, A357, p. 171–6, Buller to APA, 21 April 1838.
95 ML, A357, pp. 167–89, Buller to APA, 21 April 1838.
96 Bland, *Letters*, pp. 12, 16, APA to Buller, 20 March 1839.
97 *Ibid.*, pp. 147–50, Jamison and Bland to Buller, 22 November 1840.
98 *Ibid.*, p. 165, APA to Buller, 15 February 1841.
99 *Ibid.*, p. 89, Jamison and Bland to Buller, 29 February 1840.
100 *Ibid.*, pp. 2, 152, APA to Buller, 20 March 1839, 22 November 1840.
101 *Ibid.*, pp. 2–3, APA to Buller, 20 March 1839.
102 *Ibid.*, pp. 27–70, especially pp. 36, 69–70, APA to Buller, 29 February 1839.
103 Ritchie, 'Molesworth Committee'.
104 Bland, *Letters*, pp. 105–6, Jamison and Blaxland to Gipps, 7 September 1840.
105 Nash, *Bailie's party*; Le Cordeur, *Eastern Cape separatism*.
106 Nash, *Bailie's party*, pp. 77–9; Ross, *Status and respectability*, pp. 60–6.
107 Le Cordeur, *Eastern Cape separatism*, chs. 1–2; Thomson, *Grahamstown*.
108 Nash, *Bailie's party*, pp. 68–72.
109 *Kitchingman papers*, pp. 123–4, Philip to Kitchingman, 20 December 1834.
110 Mostert, *Frontiers*, p. 631.
111 Peires, *House of Phalo*, pp. 89–94; Ross, *Philip*, pp. 123–32.
112 Lester, *Imperial networks*.
113 CO 48/165, fos 83, 88, 186, Herschel to Philip, 24 November 1834, Read to Philip, 9 December 1834, Campbell to Philip, 22 May 1835; *Documents relating to the Kaffir war*, p. 152, Smith to Sargeant, 7 May 1835.
114 E.g., CO 48/165, fos 234–61, [Philip] to [Buxton], 4 June 1835.

115 Peires, *House of Phalo*, pp. 60–1.
116 CO 48/165, fos 33–5, 'Paper prepared by John Beecham'.
117 TFB, vol. 3, p. 19, Buxton to Wright, 10 April 1832; TFB, vol. 12, pp. 125–34, Priscilla Buxton to Philip, 20–21 September 1833; TFB, vol. 13, p. 216, T. Buxton to Philip, 16 September 1834.
118 TFB, vol. 12, p. 144, P. Buxton to Philip, 5 December 1833.
119 TFB, vol. 12, pp. 145a, 147a–b, 148–51, T. Buxton to Pringle, 5 December 1833, 21 December 1833, 14 January 1834.
120 TFB, vol. 13, p. 95, Priscilla to Sarah Buxton, 22 July 1834; TFB, vol. 13, pp. 211–12, T. Buxton to Philip, 16 September 1834.
121 *Hansard*, 3rd ser., 1834, xxiv, 1061–3; TFB, vol. 13, pp. 211–16, Buxton to Philip, 16 September 1834.
122 *Hansard*, 3rd ser., 1835, xxix, 549–53.
123 Laidlaw, 'Metropolitan, colonial and imperial histories', pp. 84–5.
124 TFB, vol. 13, pp. 356–60, 366–71, Arthur to Buxton, 18 September 1834, Backhouse to Buxton, 22 October 1834.
125 SOAS, LMS archives, CWM, South Africa, 14/2/A, Philip to T. Buxton, copy, 13 August 1834.
126 CO 48/169, fos 353–4, Stephen minute on Ellis to Glenelg, 18 May 1836; Ross, *Philip*, p. 144.
127 DP, A519/20, pp. 55, 57–9, D'Urban to Philip, 31 May 1834, 14 July 1834, private. CO 48/165, fo. 81, Philip to unknown, 21 October 1834; *ibid.*, fo. 204, Philip to Buxton, 29 May 1835; DP, A519/1, pp. 66–7, Philip to D'Urban, 18 January 1835.
128 CO 48/165, fo. 114, Philip to Buxton, 22 January 1835; SOAS, LMS archives, CWM, South Africa, 14/1/C, Philip to Wilson, 12 June 1834.
129 CO 48/165, fos 114–20, Philip to Buxton, 22 January 1835.
130 *Ibid.*, fo. 186, Campbell to Philip, 22 May 1835; *Kitchingman papers*, p. 154, Read junior to Kitchingman, July 1835.
131 CO 48/165, fo. 122, Philip to Buxton, 22 January 1835.
132 *Ibid.*, fos 321–6, Philip to Alexander, undated.
133 SOAS, LMS archives, CWM, South Africa, 14/1/C, Philip to Wilson, 12 June 1834; *ibid.*, 14/2/A, Philip to LMS, 13 August 1834.
134 CO 48/165, fos 116–23, Philip to Buxton, 22 January 1835.
135 *Ibid.*, fos 206–7, Philip to Buxton, 29 May 1835.
136 *Ibid.*, fos 200–7, 209–14, Philip to Buxton, 29 May 1835, 30 May 1835. See also: *ibid.*, fos 167, 234–62, 285–92, 295–315, 1 May 1835, 4–13 June 1835, 29 June–2 July 1835, 11 July 1835.
137 *Ibid.*, fo. 212, Philip to Buxton, 30 May 1835.
138 Testimony of Glass [or Klaas], Xhosa interpreter to Colonel Smith, 15 June 1835, repeated in *ibid.*, fo. 268, Campbell to Philip, 19 June 1835.
139 TFB, vol. 2, p. 289, Johnston to S. Buxton, 28 April 1835.
140 Ross, *Philip*, p. 137.
141 Laidlaw, 'Aunt Anna's report'.
142 TFB, vol. 13, pp. 378–80, P. Johnston to Gurney, 10 March 1835; TFB, vol. 15, p. 185c, Stephen to Buxton, 28 January 1837.
143 TFB, vol. 13, p. 377, Johnston to Gurney, 10 March 1835; TFB, vol. 14, pp. 105–6, T. Buxton to [S. Buxton], 28 September 1835.
144 TFB, vol. 13, p. 375, Johnston to Buxton, 9 March 1835.
145 SOAS, LMS archives, CWM, Home Office, 6/9/B, Buxton to Ellis, 15 December 1835.
146 TFB, vol. 14, pp. 108, 359–60, Buxton to Ellis, 10 October 1835, 27 January 1836; *ibid.*, p. 109, Buxton to Glenelg, 10 October 1835; CO 48/169, fos 349–51, Ellis to Glenelg, 12 February 1836.
147 TFB, vol. 14, pp. 109–10, Buxton to Glenelg, 10 October 1835.
148 *Ibid.*, pp. 105–6, T. Buxton to [S. Buxton], 28 September 1835.
149 TFB, vol. 2, pp. 81–3, T. Buxton to Gurney, 24 November 1835.
150 TFB, vol. 14, p. 83, T. Buxton to H. Buxton, 19 August 1835; TFB, vol. 13, pp. 186–9, 'List of questions for Stockenström', [1834].

151 TFB, vol. 14, pp. 93a–b, 98–9, 100–2, Read to Buxton, 16 September 1835, Buxton to Grey, 6 September 1835, Grey to Buxton, 20 September 1835, private; NLSA, MSB 142, p. 286, D'Urban to Smith, 8 January 1836.

152 TFB, vol. 14, pp. 94–7, Buxton to Philip, 17 September 1835.

153 CO 48/169, fos 422–3, Ellis to Stephen, private, 28 September 1836. On Tshatshu's and Stoffels' activities in Britain, see Elbourne, *Blood ground*, pp. 288–92.

154 SOAS, LMS archives, CWM, Home Office, 6/11/A, Read to Arundell (LMS), 13 August 1836. *Kitchingman papers*, pp. 167–70, 172, 174–5, Read senior to Kitchingman, 4 September 1836, 8 December 1836, 26 January 1837. TFB, vol. 15, pp. 123e–h, Philip to H. Buxton, 13 December 1836.

155 Coates, Beecham and Ellis, *Christianity*. TFB, vol. 14, pp. 155–6, Buxton to Beecham, 9 November 1835.

156 Laidlaw, 'Aunt Anna's report'.

157 TFB, vol. 15, pp. 207a–c, 208, Johnston to Gurney, 3 March 1837, Buxton to the Cottage, 3 March 1837.

158 *Ibid.*, pp. 311a–d, 319b–c, Johnston to Gurney, 8 June 1837, 9 June 1837, Buxton to the Cottage, 17 June 1837.

159 *Ibid.*, pp. 319b–f, Buxton to the Cottage, 17 June 1837.

160 *PP 1837*, vii (425), pp. 81–2, Report of the Select Committee on Aborigines.

161 Elbourne, *Blood ground*, pp. 286–7.

162 E.g., see CO 48/165, fo. 145, Philip to [?], 17 February 1835; CO 48/192, fos 33, 73–85, 269–80, Glenelg to D'Urban, draft, 26 December 1835; CO 537/145, Glenelg to D'Urban, 26 December 1835, draft.

163 CO 48/165, fo. 270, Philip to Ellis, 19 June 1835. Ross, *Philip*, pp. 140–4.

164 TFB, vol. 16, p. 91e, December 1837.

165 Cooley, 'Cape of Good Hope'; Kay, *Kaffer's case*; Beverley, *Wrongs of the Caffre nation*; Spedding, 'New theory of colonization' and 'Expedition to the Niger'.

166 Porter, 'Trusteeship', p. 208.

167 See, e.g., NSW Archives, 5/1123, Memoranda selected from 24 years of missionary engagements in the South Sea Islands and Australia by Lancelot Edward Threlkeld, Missionary to the Aborigines, New South Wales, 1838.

168 Lester, 'Humanitarians and white settlers'.

169 Le Cordeur, *Eastern Cape separatism*, pp. 41–3.

170 Keegan, *Colonial South Africa*, p. 68.

171 *Ibid.*, pp. 65–7.

172 Le Cordeur, *Godlonton*.

173 Lester, *Imperial networks*, pp. 62–7.

174 *Graham's Town Journal*, 9 January 1835. See also *ibid.*, 16 January 1835, 24 September 1835, 8 October 1835, 22 October 1835.

175 Le Cordeur, *Eastern Cape separatism*, p. 72.

176 *Ibid.*, p. 73.

177 E.g., DP, A519/22, pp. 6–8, D'Urban to Boyce, 7 November 1835; DP, A519/3, pp. 209–14, Collett to D'Urban, 15 December 1835; DP, A519/4, pp. 98–101, Robson to D'Urban, 3 March 1836.

178 DP, A519/8, pp. 163–201, applications for land grants.

179 CO 48/169, fos 442–8, 450, Bunting (WMMS) to Stephen, 9 January 1836, Bunting to Glenelg, 30 March 1836; CO 48/163, fos 277–84, 287, 287.1, Beecham to Glenelg, 3 November 1835, Bunting to Glenelg, 17 December 1835, Bunting to Stephen, 17 December 1835.

180 Minutes of Commercial Exchange, 23 February 1836, cited in Immelman, *Men of Good Hope*, p. 68.

181 British Immigrants of 1820, *Some reasons*, p. v. McGinn attributes the pamphlet to Chase. 'Chase', p. 43.

182 CO 48/162. Also Godlonton, *Irruption of the Kafir hordes*.

183 Beverley, *Wrongs of the Caffre nation*, p. 275.

184 On the Xhosa – Mfengu relationship: Webster, 'Unmasking the Fingo'.

185 CO 48/163, fos 270–3, Borradaile to Glenelg, Copy of the Resolutions of the Cape of

Good Hope Trade Society, 15 October 1835; CO 48/164, fo. 194, Philipps to Hay, 25 July 1835.

186 Immelman, *Men of Good Hope*, ch. 5.
187 CO 324/83, p. 248, Hay to Borradaile, 28 October 1831.
188 Keegan, *Colonial South Africa*, p. 68.
189 CO 48/163, fos 262–4, 266, 268, 270–2, 274, Borradaile to Glenelg, 13 July 1835, 29 August 1835, 23 September 1835, 15 October 1835, 21 December 1835.
190 *Ibid.*, fo. 262, Borradaile to Glenelg, 13 July 1835.
191 CO 48/164, fo. 2, Aitchison to Hay, 26 March 1835.
192 CO 48/163, fo. 262, Stephen minute on Borradaile to Glenelg, 13 July 1835.
193 *Ibid.*, fos 270–2, Borradaile to Glenelg, 15 October 1835.
194 CO 48/197, fos 343–55, 357, 361, Trade Society to Glenelg, 18 May 1838, 31 May 1838, 15 December 1838.
195 TFB, vol. 15, pp. 212, 220, A. Johnston to the Cottage, 6 March 1837, P. Johnston to the Cottage, 14 March 1837.
196 DP, A519/8, pp. 10–12, Chase to D'Urban, 9 March 1838, incl. Gladstone to Chase, 9 December 1837.

PART III

Agendas for imperial reform

CHAPTER SEVEN

An information revolution

To me a colony is as turtle-soup to an alderman – daily fare and hardly palatable. (James Stephen, February 1842)[1]

James Stephen's weariness was understandable. Every day Stephen and his staff at the Colonial Office faced an enormous challenge: how could a small metropolitan organisation effectively control a diverse, distant and increasingly dissatisfied empire? Colonial Office action seemed to Stephen to be contingent and limited almost by definition. As he wrote in 1836: 'It would be a very arduous task indeed to vindicate the best of our colonial schemes of Governm[en]t on the principles of political philosophy. All that can be said for them is, that they are as good as Parliament will sanction, and as the Colonists will accept.'[2] This chapter examines the change in the Colonial Office's approach to the task of colonial governance at the end of the 1830s. It demonstrates that the challenges of controlling an ever-expanding empire, when combined with personal politics, domestic pressure, and metropolitan intellectual movements, forced the Colonial Office to reassess the means by which imperial influence was exerted. As the government's attitude to personal contacts altered, a new era of information collection and centralisation was ushered in, changing the nature of colonial governance, and briefly signalling the possibility of uniform imperial action.

The private networks on which the Colonial Office drew until 1835 fulfilled a number of functions. They provided a means of creating, or strengthening, relationships between colony and metropole, thus giving governors greater confidence and allowing the Colonial Office to exert influence more subtly than via an official despatch. They were also important for the mediation of patronage. Finally, personal networks transmitted a different type of information to that conveyed officially – helping to create a more nuanced and rounded, or 'affective', sense of a colony's political climate. The banning of private communications between colonial officials and anyone other than the secretary of state in October 1835 combined with permanent under-secretary Robert Hay's departure in February 1836 seriously damaged these networks and emphasised the deficiencies in the department's institutional memory. Hay's successor, Stephen, could not merely resurrect personal networks of colonial contacts: apart from the time required, the Whigs had decried Hay's private correspondence as inefficient and verging on corrupt. Recreating that system was unthinkable; different means were needed.

Stephen attempted to exert influence over colonial governors and administrators in a more formal way than Hay: reasserting the terms of acceptable behaviour via edict rather than through unofficial influence. In 1837 Stephen prepared the first edition of the Colonial Office's *Rules and regulations*, which was distributed to each colonial government. Lord Glenelg, noted the preface, had frequently observed 'various regulations connected with His Majesty's Colonial Service, which appear to be inaccurately understood, and, on that account, imperfectly observed, in many of His Majesty's Colonies'. The *Rules and regulations* were intended to correct these misconceptions, encouraging 'the immediate introduction of a better method, and greater certainty in the despatch of the duties of the Governors and other Public Officers' in the colonies.[3] Its fourteen chapters covered all manner of colonial business, from the regulation of councils and rates of passage for officials, to the furniture in government houses, financial and statistical returns, and control of the militia. One chapter contained the rules governing official correspondence, right down to paper size and ink quality. In fact, the *Rules and regulations* consisted almost entirely of existing circular despatches, but their organisation and reissue were indicative of the metropolitan government's desire both to standardise their relationship with the colonies (whether crown or legislative) and to exert central control. The volume was constantly reworked, supplemented and reordered into the twentieth century, with the second edition, containing additional guidance on the disposal of waste lands and colonial appointments, distributed in 1843.

Collecting colonial information, 1819–36

Demands for colonial information emerged during metropolitan debates about corruption in the immediate post-war period. As Harling has demonstrated, the Tory administration attempted to diminish expenditure and sinecures to protect its public image.[4] In 1817 parliamentary demands revealed (from the sketchy information provided by the Colonial Office for thirty colonies) one hundred thousand pounds worth of annual unregulated colonial sinecures.[5] From 1823 until 1835 returns listing absentee colonial office-holders were demanded by parliament, until an 1835 inquiry reported that of 71 colonial sinecures or offices executed by deputies in 1812, 24 had been abolished and 30 remodelled, while 1 was vacant and only 4 were held by non-residents. The remaining 12 sinecures were so insignificant that they were not even recorded, indicating the campaign of reduction's determined nature.[6]

The 1817 request for a list of civil and military colonial offices demonstrated the paucity of the Colonial Office's records. From 1819 colonial administrations were instructed to return almanacs to London listing methods and dates of appointment, salaries and incumbents. In March 1822 this requirement was formalised: annual returns (which became known as 'Blue Books'), completed under categories provided by the Colonial Office, and entered on forms sent from London, were to be made beginning retrospectively with 1821.[7] A sequence of circulars expanded the categories covered by these returns. The information collected not only provided the Colonial Office with the means to respond to parliamentary inquiries, but also allowed some central checks to be placed on colonial jobbery and corruption. Colonial administrations forced to report regularly on such matters were aware that the metropolitan government (and, by extension, parliament) was observing them, and of the importance now placed on the appearance of probity even beyond Britain's shores.

Information was also collected as a means of surveillance in contemporary India, Ireland and provincial Britain. In Ireland, as in Britain and indeed Europe more widely, the prisons had provided a particular opportunity for both the collection of information and increasing centralisation in the early nineteenth century. This was extended to the population at large with the introduction of a centralised police force in 1836.[8] Eastwood has demonstrated the extent to which the British government increased demands for information from the provinces during the same period, according the changes great weight. As he has argued: 'The capacity of central government to command, filter and deploy information constituted the kernel of a revolution in government.'[9] Bayly's work on India indicates a related transition from government collection of affective information, based particularly on existing indigenous networks, to impersonal, statistical data over the first half of the nineteenth century.[10]

Events in the colonies also spurred the metropolitan collection of colonial information. The government of Lachlan Macquarie in New South Wales provides an example. Following complaints received by the Colonial Office about the treatment of convicts, Bathurst agitated for a commission of inquiry from 1817. The Home Office and Treasury compromised in 1818, agreeing that Bathurst should send former Trinidadian chief justice, J. T. Bigge, to the colony as a one-man commission. Bigge carried with him a series of formal and informal instructions from Bathurst, which directed him to investigate not only the convict establishment, but also the state of the colony more widely. Bigge was to 'furnish every information' on subjects including the function of the courts and police; provision for education and religious instruction; the effect of colonial regulations on agricultural and commercial interests; the effect of licensing a distillery; the likelihood of New South Wales being able to pay more of its own administrative costs; and the relationship between emancipists and free emigrants. Woods has convincingly argued that once Bathurst had used the complaints about Macquarie and the convict establishment (which had been raised in parliament) to justify Bigge's inquiry to the metropolitan government, he informally expanded its remit so that it became a 'genuine attempt to gather as much information as possible about the colony'.[11]

Beyond specifying areas for investigation, Bathurst instructed Bigge on what to do with his findings. Most importantly, Bigge was to return his evidence and his conclusions directly to London; releasing neither in the colony.[12] It was important for Bathurst to have first access to the evidence Bigge collected, particularly as at least a year would elapse between Bigge finishing his inquiry and Bathurst's response reaching the colony. Control of information thus became critical. The Bigge Commission set a precedent for Bathurst: another commission was sent to the West Indies; while Bigge was also involved with the Commission of Eastern Inquiry which investigated the Cape, Mauritius and Ceylon. These inquiries produced thousands of pages of evidence which the Colonial Office used to frame and justify the implementation of policies on constitutional form, advisory councils, legal systems and ecclesiastical questions.

The increasing interest in colonial information was not limited to commissions of inquiry. The Blue Books quickly expanded in scope. While at first 'nothing more was done than to get a regular detailed establishment from each colony, and an account of all the different sources of revenue', by 1837 they consisted of twenty-two returns 'on financial and statistical subjects' covering 'almost every possible subject relating to the public establishment and actual condition of the colonies'.[13] In 1822 the heads for return had covered net revenue and expenditure; a schedule of taxes, duties, and fees; and the military and civil establishments. The next year three new headings were added: population; exports and imports; and currency. Reports on geographical and topological subjects, including the details of exploration were requested in January 1827.[14]

Thus, within five years, the acquisition of previously uncollected colonial information was perceived to be of 'essential' importance to the metropolitan government. In 1827 governors were told that the current ignorance of the metropolitan administration made it impossible to 'complete with any degree of accuracy the maps deposited in this office of the distant colonies which belong to this country'.[15] The frequency with which returns were made also increased. While the Blue Books would remain annual, the Colonial Office additionally asked for half-yearly tables to be completed from 1826.

Contemporaries estimated that the quantity of information returned with the annual Blue Books increased by fifty per cent between 1827 and 1837.[16] More frequent returns enabled the metropolitan administration 'to obtain with more regularity, and at an earlier period, some part of the information' which was 'essentially necessary' for the Colonial Office.[17]

Despite the Colonial Office's assertions, much of the information collected in the Blue Books was never actually used. The returns themselves were not regarded as public documents until the later 1830s, instead forming 'a private Report of the state of the Colony in all its branches made by the Governor for [the Secretary of State's] information'.[18] The 1827 Blue Books had been printed for the use of the House of Commons' Committee on Finance, but this experiment was not repeated, nor were the 1827 returns presented to parliament. During particular colonial crises, the Blue Books sometimes yielded useful information; but there was no digest of contents, nor was the information collected passed on officially to other government bodies. Many of the returns were simple tables which were completed with a mixture of descriptive and numerical information. Although most numerical returns required only the addition or subtraction of whole numbers, problems arose in defining what categories included, and ensuring accuracy. Very little was done in the way of comparative statistics, either in the colonies – where copies of the Blue Books were retained only after 1836[19] – or in London. The Colonial Office had neither the technical capacity nor the personnel to implement comparative analysis whether between colonies, with Britain, or even over time.

From 1826 the governor was asked to accompany the annual Blue Book with a descriptive report on the colony's progress, and copies of speeches he had made to executive or legislative councils. By the early 1830s, these were regarded by the metropolitan authorities as the most useful colonial returns. The Colonial Office emphasised the narrative format of the report: it was to be 'an explanatory statement, in the nature of a short exposé of the proceedings which have taken place in your Government since the transmission of your last Statistical Tables'. A list of heads under which such statements should be organised was included. Despite these instructions, the metropolitan authorities also expected that the report would include the discussion of matters that would not normally warrant an individual despatch, in this way enabling 'a general view' of the colonial empire to be constructed.[20] In 1831 Goderich reminded governors that their remarks formed 'a useful commentary on the Blue Book', which otherwise was 'of much less practical utility than it might be'.[21] Hay explained that while the colonial secretary was 'properly responsible' for the preparation and transmission of the Blue Books, the annual report remained the responsibility of the governor, 'the only person who could adequately fulfill [sic] this important task, as he alone could be entirely conversant with all the measures of his Gov[ernmen]t which might be in contemplation as well as those actually in operation'.[22] Such discussions and exhortations suggest that the governors' reports were the only element of the Blue Books routinely used by the Colonial Office, and particularly the political staff.

Given the weight accorded to narrative summaries, why did the Colonial Office so dramatically increase its demands for other, quantitative, information? The answer seems to lie in control and appearances.[23] In addition to the expansion of the Blue Books, the number of incoming letters and despatches to the Colonial Office rose by sixty-seven per cent between 1816 and 1824, while during the following sixteen years incoming correspondence increased by a further thirty per cent.[24] By demanding ever more information the Colonial Office was demonstrating to colonial administrations its surveillance of their affairs and determination to exert central control. In the late 1830s, when information collection for its own sake was more widely celebrated, Wilmot Horton pointed to Bathurst's introduction of the Blue Books ('which name is now even adopted in Parliamentary documents') as evidence that the former colonial secretary was 'an efficient public servant'.[25]

The Colonial Office's interest in exerting control was demonstrated by the effort put into enforcing the timely completion and remittance of returns. Understandably, many colonial administrations groaned under the weight of ever-increasing demands for data, while some colonies with representative legislative assemblies were deeply suspicious of the metropolitan government's new and detailed interest in their affairs.[26] By 1831 the Colonial Office admitted that efforts to produce timely returns had proved 'ineffectual'.[27] During the next six years, circulars were more likely to demand overdue Blue Books or impose penalties for lateness or non-completion, than to expand the returns' scope.[28] This correspondence also clarified the responsibilities of various colonial officials in collecting, processing and submitting information to London. Aside from the governor's report, the Blue Book was ultimately the responsibility of the colonial secretary.[29] Unless the colonial secretary could produce certification from the governor that the Blue Book had been properly completed, or demonstrate that all possible steps had been taken to collect the necessary returns from subordinate officials, his first quarter's salary would be withheld. If a subordinate officer was shown to be responsible, the penalty would apply to him instead.[30] Hay noted that taking such a step was 'not unknown' and had 'proved effectual' when tried.[31] As Philip Souper, former colonial secretary of Trinidad, told an 1837 inquiry, he always sent home the Blue Book 'previous to the expiration of March; the orders have been made so stringent, that if it did not leave, the secretary would not receive his salary'.[32] These penalties were restated in the Colonial Office's 1837 *Rules and regulations*.

Despite all this effort, however, the Colonial Office, with its small staff, had no capacity to do anything with this information after it was collected.

The mania for classification

Before the Colonial Office's response to the challenges of the mid-1830s can be addressed, a brief consideration of a broader metropolitan trend is necessary. Metropolitan society in the early nineteenth century witnessed a renewed enthusiasm for facts, and a new interest in quantitative statistics. The revival of 'facts' – what contemporaries called a return to Bacon, and what late twentieth-century theorists described as the 'discourse of "the real"' – operated across the spectrum of British intellectual endeavour and reached a high point in the 1830s.[33] It was manifested in scientific methods, straight and satirical popular debate, utilitarian thought and government practice. Interest in the classification and recording of information was displayed practically in the reformulation of the census; the consolidation of state archives; and the establishment of statistical societies across Britain; but was also apparent in the establishment of the Ordnance Survey in Britain and Ireland; the Great Trigonometrical Survey of India; and the classification of 150,000 new species of life in the period between 1750 and 1833.[34] In the colonies, as in Britain, administrators and settlers reflected this interest through the establishment of institutions such as libraries, museums and botanical gardens, which flourished empire-wide from the 1830s.[35]

A particularly important component of the interest in 'facts' was the emerging science of statistics. The word 'statistics' became current in Britain only in the late eighteenth century, first appearing in the *Encyclopaedia Britannica* in 1797 as a 'word lately introduced to express a view or survey of any kingdom, county, or parish'. By 1839 Herman Merivale termed statistics: 'the favourite study of the present age . . . the latest birth of the inductive or Baconian system of philosophy'. Problems were now to be tackled via the explicit 'collection of facts' and the subsequent drawing of inferences.[36] For the purposes of this discussion two 1830s' trends in statistics were important. First, the growing acceptance that statistics involved the collection and comparison of quantitative, not descriptive, information. Across intellectual, political and scientific society, there was a great contemporary interest in precise quantitative data: numbers implied control over a subject, and the possibility, so important to utilitarian philosophy, of calculation.[37] Second, those involved with statistics in the 1830s struggled to demonstrate that it was both a 'science' and 'objective', rather than merely a method for proving preconceived (which implied party political) ideas. Interestingly, at this time social and political investigators were more closely associated with statistics than natural scientists, who drew on 'the language of political arithmetic', rather than the reverse.[38] Despite the interest in statistical endeavour, little statistical analysis was employed beyond the creation of actuarial tables, and most technical debates were about the collection and arrangement of numerical data.[39] British statisticians were heavily influenced both by the difficulty of collecting any, let alone reliable, data, and by the German advocacy of 'tabellenstatistik' – long columns of only slightly processed data – as the best way of presenting information.[40]

Despite these qualifications, a marked increase in the collection, arrangement and use of statistics was apparent in Britain from the early 1830s. The first British statistical societies were established in 1833 and 1834 in Manchester and London, and in June 1833 the British Association for the Advancement of Science agreed reluctantly to the formation of a statistical division, although on the condition that it remained strictly apolitical.[41] The societies published journals, most notably the *Journal of the Statistical Society of London*, which emphasised its metropolitan status by carrying reports of provincial societies' proceedings. Topics which came under statistical investigation – in books as well as articles – included the military, medicine, paupers and publishing, as well as the old staples of trade and life expectancy. R. M. Martin published the mammoth *Statistics of the colonies of the British Empire* in 1839, based on Colonial Office and other government records, and the statistical journals carried a smattering of articles on colonial subjects.[42]

While colonial topics received only limited attention in the metropolitan journals, colonists did recognise the need to present their arguments according to contemporary conventions. James Macarthur's 1837 book, *New South Wales*, included more than three hundred pages of statistics, returns and reports to support his arguments on transportation and emancipists; while Edward Macarthur urged his brothers to send him Australian 'statistical returns' to be placed in the metropolitan press.[43] Colonial governments were just as influenced by the thirst for knowledge and interest in statistics. The New South Wales legislative council's establishment of a parliamentary library, for example, was linked to the changing information order. Governor Gipps told the secretary of state of the colonists' decision to devote three hundred pounds annually to purchasing books.[44] Mirroring contemporary discussions in Britain, attention was directed to:

> books of reference of established repute as may furnish members with the means of ascertaining facts and principles connected with the most ordinary subjects of legislation, also with the most authentic records and documents of an historical character, and with information regarding Parliamentary History, Precedents and Proceedings; national, colonial and commercial law; political economy, statistics and . . . general information.[45]

Both in 1840 and again in 1843, Gipps conveyed the colonists' hopes that the Colonial Office would contribute a set of free parliamentary papers to the library: and, indeed, those deemed relevant to colonial circumstances were transmitted on James Stephen's orders in 1844, a scheme that was then extended to other colonies.[46] As Dawn Nell has demonstrated, in the Cape Colony the possession of statistical knowledge and data was entwined with arguments about agricultural progress in the mid-nineteenth century. There, the colonial government stood condemned as inadequate because of its failure, relative to other colonies, to collect statistical information.[47]

Aside from a rise in statistical enquiries, the level of public debate about the nature and value of statistics – including satirical comment – demonstrates the impact of this movement.[48] Britain lagged behind Germany and France in statistical knowledge, a position that commentators thought damaged claims of national progress. An 1835 *Edinburgh Review* article by J. R. McCulloch lamented the lack of British statistical works: 'If an individual living in Kent wishes to learn anything of Northumberland, he has nothing for it but to go there.' Similarly, 'those who wish to learn any thing of the arts, the military and naval force, constitution, etc. of the empire, must consult at least some twenty or thirty different works'.[49] Other commentary focused on statistical method, emphasising not only the importance of comparison and analysis but also basic requirements like using accurate data and the ability to understand numerical information.[50] Both McCulloch and Merivale agreed that the general public's distrust of 'tabular results' was wise. Often statistical information was inaccurate, yet numbers 'had a scientific air about them' which could be extremely misleading as 'most people' shrank from 'the irksome task of examining whether tabular statements be correct or not'.[51] Browne has demonstrated how this 'scientific air' was relished by contemporary British naturalists, whose 'tables and figures, ratios and proportions' added 'weight and an aura of "science" to their publications'.[52] In fact, historians have suggested that a familiarity with statistics did enable policy-makers to 'depersonalise' their world-view.[53] As will be seen, this was of particular importance to colonial governance.

The government was at the forefront of the British statistical movement, with politicians and civil servants prominent in the new statistical societies. In an era of reform, the need for evidence one way or the other on a number of economic and political issues alerted the government to its poor statistical resources, just as, in turn, the collection of statistical data encouraged the identification of new 'problems'.[54] While the Manchester Statistical Society arose largely from the concern to remedy social ills, the Statistical Society of London focused on the centralisation of information and was dominated by men with a government interest. The group Cullen described as the 'Whig-Liberal intelligentsia' was particularly enamoured of statistics, and did most to promote its acceptance as a science among scientists and administrators.[55] Some figures of early prominence in the London society, like Henry Goulburn and Herman Merivale, had been, or would become, members of the Colonial Office staff.[56] For these individuals, political and social concerns were entwined with statistics.

The Board of Trade was the first government department formally to recognise that a more reliable way of collecting and collating information about Britain was needed. In 1832 the Board established a statistical department under the leadership of George Porter.[57] This was followed by a number of financial and administrative parliamentary select committees in the 1830s which examined the collection and collation of information by the British government. The most important legislation of the decade in this area was the Registration Act of 1836 which established the General Registry Office and the civil registration of births, deaths and marriages from 1837.[58] The form of the 1841 census was also substantially revised on the recommendation of government insiders with statistical interests.[59]

It was in this climate that the Colonial Office began to take an interest in the content and utility of returns, as well as their timely production, in the later 1830s. Metropolitan and colonial concern with regulating emigration and land sales suggested new uses for the Blue Books and encouraged the department to make financial and social comparisons between colonies and over time. Quantitative, statistical data overtook the governors' narrative reports in importance. Public interest, especially from potential emigrants, also encouraged the Colonial Office to reconsider the private status of colonial returns: should they perhaps be published? These changes in Colonial Office attitudes demonstrate the interplay between the metropolitan intellectual climate, and colonial and departmental pressures.

The October 1835 circular which limited private correspondence with the Colonial Office and the dismissal of Robert Hay were the final stages of an information crisis which had been building since the 1820s. The volume of official information, both statistical and narrative, arriving in the Colonial Office was overwhelming and poorly archived. This situation was hardly surprising. Little decision-making was delegated to staff below the level of senior clerk (immediately subordinate to the under-secretary), of whom there were only five or six. Moreover, the information collected was often unreliable or in a useless form. As an 1837 select committee discovered, the financial information contained in the Blue Books had not been audited: returns to London were made too soon after the close of the year for auditing to be possible. Consequently – although none of the metropolitan civil servants had carried out any comparison – it was quite likely that the Blue Books differed substantially from the colonial accounts that were returned to the Audit Board (under the Treasury) and then presented to parliament. In fact, no comparison could be usefully made, as the form of accounts submitted to the Audit Board both varied between colonies and differed from that of the Blue Books.[60]

Unofficial accounts arriving through Hay's personal networks addressed many gaps in the Colonial Office's knowledge, despite their recognised bias. When they were banned in October 1835, the department's information crisis was exposed. While matters of delicacy and patronage might still be negotiated via private correspondence (although increasingly with the political, rather than the permanent staff), these letters did not make their way into general departmental circulation as Hay's had, or, for that matter, those of Wilmot Horton and Bathurst in the 1820s. The loss of unofficial colonial intelligence was underlined by the Xhosa–settler war of 1835. Governor D'Urban's failure to keep the Colonial Office officially informed of the war's progress had been exacerbated by Hay's exclusion from decision-making, and the concomitant loss of the private letters he received from D'Urban and others in the colony. Nor had the Colonial Office's archives been of much use: in November 1835 Thomas Buxton reported Stephen as saying he 'never knew' the department had received crucial correspondence from Stockenström, until Buxton told him. Only then had Stephen 'dived into all this neglected correspondence'.[61] The Colonial Office was full of information and correspondence never read or properly digested.

The loss of unofficial intelligence forced the Colonial Office to reconsider the nature of its colonial sources and its metropolitan archive of information. Stephen set about remedying the lack of an accessible archive, encouraging greater vigilance in minuting decisions, tracking documents and arranging papers; he was creating an 'institutional memory'. Grappling with the nature and sources of colonial information was less straightforward: it would involve the more conscientious pursuit and management of colonial information, and entail both greater centralisation and a serious examination of the ways in which information might be used. Two events combined to bring the Colonial Office directly in touch with the era of statistical enthusiasm.

The Select Committee on Colonial Accounts

On 28 April 1837 a House of Commons' select committee was appointed to examine the colonial accounts of receipt and expenditure, and to make suggestions as to how their preparation and presentation might be improved in order to 'introduce uniformity, regularity, correctness and completeness'.[62] The appointment and proceedings of this committee reflected not only the Treasury's desire to secure accurate colonial accounts, but also the growing metropolitan interest in quantitative statistics, a recognition of the importance of centralised control of information, and the need to reform government administration. The committee's membership was biased in favour of pro-reform, free trade liberals, and, in combination with the witnesses called, suggests the influence of the same individuals who were significant in the metropolitan statistical movement.

Reflecting its Treasury backing, more committee members had overtly financial interests than colonial: they included Dr John Bowring, Francis Thornhill Baring, Sir James Graham, Sir Henry Parnell, Sir George Clerk and Sir Thomas Fremantle.[63] On the colonial side, Sir George Grey, the Colonial Office under-secretary, was a member, as were Joseph Hume and Benjamin Hawes.[64] Bowring, the chairman, had previously examined the public accounts of Holland, France and the United Kingdom; and reported on trade relations with the Italian states. He was the first editor of the *Westminster Review*, an intimate friend of Bentham, and would become governor of Hong Kong in the 1850s. Bowring attended all the committee's sittings, while Hume missed only two; others sustaining high attendance rates were Grey, Hawes, Parnell, and John Rundle, MP for Tavistock. The committee's proceedings were efficient, as if underlining the inefficiency of the procedures into which they inquired. After an initial committee meeting on 9 May 1837, evidence was taken on ten separate days, and a report (which consisted simply of the evidence taken) presented to the Commons on 13 July.[65]

The witnesses were drawn mainly from the accounting and financial departments of the metropolitan civil service. The most interesting were George William Brande, the principal clerk for colonial business at the Treasury (and previously of the Colonial Audit Board); and George Richardson Porter, head of the statistical branch of the Board of Trade. Three of the Colonial Office's senior clerks were also called – Peter Smith, T. C. Murdoch and Gordon Gairdner – and three witnesses with first-hand colonial experience. Although the colonists gave relevant evidence, it is likely that their selection as witnesses was in large part due to availability. Philip Souper had filled a succession of official positions in Trinidad which included working in the office of the colonial treasurer, and more recently a period as colonial secretary. William Wemyss had served in the commissariats in New South Wales and Mauritius; while James McQueen, an employee of the Colonial Bank, had extensive experience in Jamaica.

Emerging most clearly from the proceedings was the complete lack of system, centralisation or efficiency in colonial accounting. While, in line with broader Colonial Office changes, colonial accounts were transmitted from the colony via the governor and metropolitan secretary of state, the treasurers of crown colonies had been made responsible to the metropolitan Treasury for the correct and timely submission of audited accounts in 1822. However, the Treasury was unable to communicate directly with colonial treasurers on important matters and no two colonies submitted accounts in the same form, indeed there were 'scarcely any two alike; they are all different!'[66] Brande stated that there were no model cash books, journals or ledgers for the colonial treasurers to follow, and other witnesses made the same point.[67] As a consequence there was a complete lack of comparison between colonies, and no possibility of preparing a budget which encompassed all the colonies (a particular hope of the Treasury since the late 1820s).[68] One of Bowring's first questions for Brande was whether the colonial accounts existed in 'any concentrated shape' other than the abstract which was laid annually before parliament. As Peter Smith told the committee, while the idea of a 'general colonial budget' had been raised in the Colonial Office in the late 1820s, no measures had ever been taken for preparing such a document. There was, he reiterated, 'no general registry or ledger'.[69]

Given the Treasury's existing interest in a pan-imperial budget, it was perhaps surprising that the Colonial Office emerged as the model for the collection of colonial information. The Blue Books were extensively described during the committee's hearings, indicating how important and singular a model they were. Smith explained the history of their introduction and the '22 returns' which they now comprised, while Souper detailed how colonial civil servants collected and organised information for them. That the same headings and format were used for each colony's returns was emphasised both by witnesses and by the committee.[70] But for the Treasury, the Blue Books were a model rather than an answer: although they contained extensive financial information, there was no guarantee that it was accurate. Their contents were 'prepared on a cursory examination of the accounts as furnished to the auditor', and no one was aware of how the two sets of accounts could even be compared, let alone whether this had ever taken place.[71]

The select committee discovered other aspects of the Colonial Office's collection of information that could be improved. Smith was asked to bring in some examples of Blue Books for the committee to examine; he returned with the printed books from 1827, explaining that in general the manuscript returns from the colonies were the only version of the books available.[72] Thus the Blue Books were not generally presented to parliament, nor were they available to other departments of the metropolitan government. This underlined the problems of inter-departmental relations which have long been emphasised by imperial historians.[73] In fact, all the evidence demonstrated that departments operated not only independently but in ignorance of one another. Brande, the Treasury's principal clerk for colonial business, could not tell the committee where Porter at the Board of Trade got his statistics from; while Porter himself merely confirmed that the abstracts he put before parliament did not specify the source of information. He found it easier to leave the attempt to separate civil from military expenditure to Brande.[74]

Discussion returned several times to the Colonial Office's need to implement better methods of controlling information, if it were to use information to control the colonies. In the colonies themselves, control over both money and accounts was still crude. Listing improvements to colonial accounting, Brande reported that colonial treasurers were no longer allowed to keep a colony's money in their own hands: above a certain balance, it was now lodged in a strong room. At a later hearing Wemyss explained to the committee that colonial accounts were the property of the accountant who prepared them. One set was sent to London, and a duplicate set kept in the colony. When an accountant left the colony, he typically took the duplicates with him, leaving the colony without any historical record of its affairs.[75]

When prompted, witnesses from the Colonial Office admitted that they had experienced some difficulty in enforcing the adequate completion and timely return of the Blue Books. It emerged that colonies with representative legislative assemblies were significantly worse than the crown colonies at returning adequate and comprehensive Blue Books.[76] In mid-1837, for example, there were still nineteen colonies from which no financial returns had been received for the year 1834, while fourteen colonies had not returned the figures for 1835.[77] Sir George Grey clearly saw his committee membership as an opportunity to defend the Colonial Office on this point – particularly with regard to the Cape war.[78] Grey asked Smith a number of leading questions about the Colonial Office's attempts to enforce completion of the Blue Books, ascertaining that two letters had been written to Governor D'Urban demanding the missing Cape Blue Book for 1835 'within a few months', and that this was indeed the 'usual course adopted' by the Colonial Office in such a case.[79] Despite such imperfections, the Colonial Office clerks and George Porter, the Board of Trade's statistician, stated that the number of returns received from the colonies had increased and that 'greater pains' were 'taken to insist that those returns should be filled up'.[80]

Porter submitted a report to the committee which identified the colonies that had defective Blue Books, and showed how they were lacking.[81] He suggested that the problems of the legislative colonies' returns stemmed from the relevant officials' hold on their positions. In the legislative colonies some held their offices under patent, while others were non-resident, with incompetent or unmotivated deputies.[82] Even so, for colonies that had experienced disputes with Britain – over slavery or representative government – information was not regarded as neutral, and any collection of it by the metropolitan authorities engendered suspicion. James McQueen, an employee of the Colonial Bank with Jamaican experience, indicated how apprehensive the colonies that enjoyed some local self-government were about surrendering information, particularly financial information, to the metropolitan government. McQueen stressed that the Colonial Office should explain to the colonies that the Government of this country had no view whatever . . . of intermeddling with their internal legislation or taxation, but that it was merely for the purpose of having correct returns of the receipt and expenditure of every colony, and also of their exports and imports, upon a principle the same as that adopted in the mother country.[83]

Colonial concern about the central government's possible use of information mirrors the reluctance of provincial British officials to comply with demands for information in the same period. Eastwood has argued that English magistrates who failed to make returns to London did so partly from 'a strong sense of their territorial power' and a suspicion that the metropolitan government hoped 'to encroach upon and to curtail' provincial independence.[84] Such sentiments were also at work in the colonies.

Most witnesses had a limited conception of the possible uses for colonial information. They advocated the adoption of standard forms for financial returns (as already existed for the Blue Books), which would enable colonial information received by the Treasury and Colonial Office to be reconciled. Aside from standardisation of forms, the majority of witnesses identified the need to encourage fuller and quicker compliance in making returns by colonial administrations, especially those with elected legislative assemblies. Souper, when asked to comment on possible improvements, stated that the Blue Book was 'as complete a document as you can well have; it contains really every information'.[85] The committee did examine Luke Hansard as to the likely expense of printing the Blue Books: he suggested that if they were condensed and rearranged by subject (rather than colony), the annual cost would be about six hundred pounds.[86] This option was not pursued particularly aggressively, nor were any recommendations made on the matter.

Nonetheless, while the suggestions offered to the committee on Blue Books focused on improving the operation of the existing system, they indicated also an appreciation (if rather vague) of the benefits of centralisation and control of information for both metropolitan and colonial administrations. Souper, for example, stated that the duplicate copy of the Blue Book which was kept in Trinidad was 'found very useful as a document of reference'.[87] Peter Smith, in line with departmental comments since the 1820s, emphasised the importance of Blue Books to the Colonial Office.[88] The strikingly basic nature of much of the information provided to the select committee indicates that the mere collection of numerical information was seen as a powerful means of control for the imperial government.[89]

One witness, however, had innovation in mind. George Porter, head of the statistical department at the Board of Trade, vice-president and treasurer of the Statistical Society and brother-in-law of the political economist, David Ricardo, conceived of information rather differently to the other witnesses. Porter not only wanted information to be centralised, but also hoped to be able to use it to make comparisons between colonies, and even more importantly, to allow comparison between the colonies and Britain. To this end, he argued that colonial returns should be based on the same form as returns collected in Britain, and the categories of information collected from the colonies should be extended for the same purpose. 'It seems to me', he told the committee, that:

> there are many facts and circumstances with reference to the colonies, which it is very desirable to have known here and known in a shape to enable us to compare the results in the colonies, so far as they are capable of it, with similar results in the Mother Country.

Porter's evidence showed that, unsurprisingly for one of the leading advocates of statistical investigation, he favoured quantitative over qualitative returns. He was unimpressed, for example, by colonial criminal returns which comprised 'a statement of the condition of the goal'; this could 'hardly be called a criminal return'.[90]

To Porter, faced with seemingly insurmountable difficulties in provincial data collection, the colonial empire provided an opportunity. In Britain there was no network of paid collectors, and, despite the 1836 Registration Act, very little in the way of coercive measures for information collection. The Statistical Society of London, established partly as a way of circumventing the government's problems, was not meeting expectations.[91] The colonies potentially provided a much better sphere for government statistics: the Colonial Office already had many of the structures for collection in place; their data just needed to be refined. Already, Porter used the population figures from the Blue Books, although he admitted that they were incomplete and inaccurate.[92]

Porter made a host of suggestions for improvement reflecting both his passion for statistics and his domestic concerns. Returns on the rates of wages for different types of employment – already collected from the Australian colonies – could, he thought, be beneficially collected across the empire. Criminal returns, if improved, could also be usefully employed in comparison with the United Kingdom. Porter could not believe that it would be 'very difficult' for colonial administrators to make annually 'a criminal statement as nearly as possible in the form of the amended returns now laid before Parliament, as to the state of crime in the United Kingdom'.[93] He argued that the collection and comparison of statistics was a project rightly supported by government, although he saw it as independent of immediate party political concerns. Statistics was a branch of scientific endeavour, he concluded, and the comparisons it would allow between colony and metropole were 'matters of some importance in a scientific point of view'.[94] Porter's views on colonial statistics, as well as his Board of Trade position, connect him with the metropolitan trends in information collection and centralisation identified by Eastwood.[95]

The Select Committee on Colonial Accounts provides several insights into colonial governance. It demonstrates the importance of the Colonial Office's policy of collecting information: from the 1820s a resource was created which could, potentially, be used comparatively. Moreover, information collection was enforced by a variety of coercive and bureaucratic means which were more effective than measures taken to enforce British provincial compliance. The Colonial Office was at the forefront of institutional bodies collecting colonial information, and was certainly ahead of the Treasury. Finally, the ideas presented to the committee in 1837 provided inspiration for the utilisation of colonial information over the next decade.

R. M. Martin colours the empire red

Comparison and collation allowed more sense to be made of the overwhelming diversity of empire. That such techniques of statecraft were quickly adopted also by scientists and missionary societies suggests that they captured some fundamental change of mood. The parallel between the argument presented in this chapter about the Colonial Office and that presented by Janet Browne about biological scientists, in exactly the same period, is striking. As Browne argued, quantitative methods gave scientists

> the feeling that these facts were somehow being collated – synthesised by the mere activity of addition and tabulation. Here a confusing jumble of data could be arranged in neat columns of numbers, perhaps under geographical headings, and certainly under family, or order, giving everyone the satisfaction of doing something apparently useful.[96]

The way in which statistical charts and tables similarly seemed to make colonial difference more manageable for the metropolitan government is perhaps best illustrated by Robert Montgomery Martin's *Statistics of the colonies of the British Empire*.

Martin was variously naval surgeon, newspaper editor, early advocate of vaccination, treasurer of Hong Kong, and indefatigable colonial promoter. He had travelled extensively throughout the British colonies, spending time in east Africa, Ceylon, the Cape Colony, New South Wales, British North America and Bengal, and was the first to describe the British Empire as one 'on which the sun never sets'.[97] Following his return to England in 1830, he began to lobby the government for a colonial position.[98] To sustain himself during this process – but also to increase his chances of success – Martin embarked on a prolific, although by his own account, poorly remunerated, writing career.[99] In 1834–35 he published the five-volume *History of the British colonies*, a mix of geography, history, statistics, economics, ethnography and geology, organised by region and illustrated with maps and pictures.[100] The *History* represented the most significant attempt of the era to delineate – but also to connect – colonial history and geography. Integral to this project were the statistical tables and regional maps included in each chapter.

Two years later, Martin approached the Colonial Office about compiling a volume of colonial statistics based on the Blue Books. Martin seems to have been directly motivated by the work of the Select Committee on Colonial Accounts, as in 1835 he had stated that a 'dry statistical work' on the colonies would not obtain a significant readership in Britain.[101] Presumably the metropolitan interest in 'statistics', combined with the pronouncements of the select committee, convinced him otherwise. The committee's assumption (implicit, rather than explicit, in their report) that publishing the Blue Books was too expensive an undertaking to be justified, encouraged Martin to consider their private publication. Sir George Grey agreed that Martin could have access to the two hundred and fifty volumes of Blue Books and other official documents.[102] The Colonial Office also provided Martin with a room, and agreed that he could describe his work as based on 'official sources', but made no offer to employ Martin nor to defray the publishing costs. Martin additionally sought information from other government departments and independent sources he 'deemed authentic', including the East India Company.[103]

Martin's *Statistics* was quite different in nature to the *History of the British colonies*. The book's preface conveyed both his excitement and the novelty of his undertaking. He explained (a little inaccurately) the history of the Blue Books, before detailing their more mundane aspects for his readers.

> Three blank books, with ruled columns and printed headings, are sent to each Colony every year, the blank columns are filled in by returns from the different departments, under the authority of the Colonial Secretary in each settlement; these returns are then sent in duplicate to Downing Street, and one of the three copies is retained in the Colony for the use of the Governor.

As with the witnesses before the Select Committee on Colonial Accounts, such a basic explanation indicates the novelty of systematic collection of information for the general public. Martin also tapped into the power of 'objective' science. His *Statistics* was 'an official record', independent of comment and interpretation. While it may well have been a wise marketing decision to emphasise the book's 'official' origins (if lack of direct official financial support), and also to keep it to one (large) volume, Martin claimed to have omitted an already prepared introduction on 'ancient and modern colonization and on the political and commercial importance of colonies to England' solely on the basis of the book's status as an official collection of unadorned facts and figures, best understood by themselves.[104] Martin's intention was to 'present consecutive views of the progress or decline of each Colony in . . . every thing which can portray the physical, moral and intellectual condition of so large a part of the British Empire'. The project was also of considerable magnitude: Martin reported proudly that there were 'about *three million* figures in the volume, and a nearly equal number was required to form the additions, subtractions'. Such statements indicated Martin's engagement with the project of comparison, both over time and between regions. Martin recognised that the continued collection and comparison of colonial information on a systematic basis would 'with every future return . . . bring a greater degree of accuracy'.[105] As a whole, however, the *Statistics* concentrated on the immediate past, and included a number of innovative features which allowed comparison between colonies.

These innovations were described in Martin's introductory 'Report'. First, 'a large statistical chart [which] shews, in an aggregate form . . . the condition of the colonies in 1836'. The statistical chart, while using the basic format of the charts in each of the volumes of the earlier *History*, was a far more ambitious undertaking. On one fold-out sheet it characterised every British colony under thirty headings which ranged from 'length and breadth', and 'military strength' to 'expenses of education', 'number of newspapers' and 'salary of governor or chief'. Such a comparative tool allowed the reader to observe that Van Diemen's Land had no 'coloured' population at all, against South Australia's one hundred thousand, while Upper Canada had twenty-five newspapers as opposed to Antigua's one. The second innovation was a 'tabular Index, after a new and compendious plan' which enabled the reader 'to find in a moment' information about any subject across the colonies. Martin emphasised in his discussion of the index how important it was to educate the British public about their colonial empire. In the same vein, the entries in the statistical chart were 'in round numbers, as being more easily retained by the memory'. The tabular index simultaneously demonstrated Martin's commitment to the clearer presentation of information; the influence of statistics; and the rudimentary level at which such methods were employed and understood in the mid-nineteenth century.[106]

The third innovation was a 'map of the world, coloured, to shew the geographical position of our Colonies', which was constructed by James Wyld, geographer to the queen. The imposing image of the British Empire blocked out in red is more commonly associated with the height of late nineteenth-century imperialism than with 1839: many texts on British history or on mapping reproduce an 1886 map produced for the Imperial Federation movement, in which a world map is framed by depictions of some of the empire's subject peoples.[107] Martin and Wyld's world map was one of the first to adopt this iconic colouring. Earlier regional maps (including Martin's in his *History*) had designated British territory by a red boundary;

while others had used colour more randomly to designate the state of civilisation or political boundaries. John Dower's atlases were beginning to mark out British possessions systematically with red in the late 1830s, but neither they, nor the beautifully produced atlases brought out by Aaron and John Arrowsmith from the early nineteenth century, adopted the convention of red to mark British territories on an otherwise uncoloured world map at this time.[108]

Although nearly seven hundred pages long, the *Statistics* was completed by Martin and one assistant inside a year. The Colonial Office responded very favourably. Permanent under-secretary, James Stephen, wrote glowingly to Martin after receiving his (free) copy, that:

> even the pecuniary value of the [*Statistics*], considerable as it is, is as nothing when compared with its utility . . . it contains an almost inexhaustible mine of curious and authentic information on a subject of the highest national importance, . . . your materials have been collected with almost incredible industry and are arranged in the most luminous order.[109]

Stephen's comments demonstrate the extent to which structured observation, such as Martin's classifying, recording and mapping, helped to convince the officials in the Colonial Office that there *was* a British Empire, not merely a difficult and disparate set of colonies.[110] As William Farr, a contemporary statistician wrote, 'classification is another name for generalization'.[111]

Three thousand copies of Martin's *Statistics* were published in January 1839 by W. H. Allen and Co., who also published the second edition in 1843 (confusingly retitled *History of the colonies of the British Empire*). A promotional brochure from the publishers recommended the *Statistics* 'as a work of reference for the Statesman, Philanthropist, and Merchant, . . . indispensable to every Library and Counting House', and included extracts from eighteen favourable reviews published in January and February 1839.[112] The Colonial Office immediately sent a copy to every colonial government with a carefully worded endorsement.[113] The secretary of state's circular emphasised the importance of prompt and accurate colonial returns as Martin's examination of the Blue Books had brought to light their sometimes 'very unsatisfactory' state. 'I must take this opportunity', Glenelg admonished, 'of repeating what I have frequently had occasion to bring before you, the very great importance of having these returns filled up with the utmost precision and exactitude.'[114] In some parts of the empire – notably New South Wales – the volume's considerable inaccuracies provoked heated complaints from both administrations and settlers.[115] But, as the only one of its kind, and with government endorsement, the *Statistics* appeared on a list of necessary and desirable books for that colony's legislative council library within a year of its first publication.[116] So, despite its small print run, the *Statistics* was widely dispersed. Beyond the Colonial Office it was used as a work of reference by metropolitan politicians and officials with an interest in the empire; by colonial administrators; and by lobbyists on imperial affairs.

Moving people and selling land

In the five years following Stephen's appointment as permanent under-secretary, the Colonial Office faced unprecedented public and parliamentary scrutiny. In addition to the rebellions in the Canadas and the end of apprenticeship in the West Indies, this was the period – through the colonisation of South Australia, New Zealand and Western Australia, the select committees on waste lands and transportation, the Durham Report, and relentless parliamentary debates – when the Colonial Reformers attracted most attention and placed greatest pressure on the Colonial Office. The agitation they caused, combined with the colonial crises, underlined the Colonial Office's need to be seen to control the colonies.

The new languages of statistics and systematic colonisation allowed older aspirations – of uniformity in imperial policy and metropolitan control – to be pursued by the Colonial Office. Information, especially quantitative information, whether on land, emigration, convicts, finances or the colonial establishment, more than ever represented a means of controlling recalcitrant colonists and governors. Additionally, it offered a means of subduing metropolitan, and especially the Colonial Reformers', criticism of the Colonial Office: criticism which was not just directed at imperial policy, but at the department's very authority.[117] As Theodore Porter has argued 'the appeal of numbers is especially compelling to bureaucratic officials who lack the mandate of a popular election, or divine right . . . objectivity lends authority to officials who seem to have very little of their own'.[118]

The impact of the Colonial Reformers has been much debated for each area of the globe, and of policy, in which they were interested.[119] This historical scrutiny has been fuelled by the copious evidence of pamphlets, books and parliamentary debates, which the Colonial Reformers left. James Stephen was dismissive about their credentials, but recognised that any parliamentary intervention in colonial affairs was likely to be shaped by 'two or three men intimately connected' with whatever current 'speculation' was under consideration.[120] Undoubtedly, particularly through government insiders like Howick, the Colonial Reformers did influence colonial policy constructively, although on the whole, the aims of colonial policy remained reasonably steady: the metropolitan government was still searching for ways to exert authority and exercise control over the colonial settlements. Moves towards self-government, while seeming probable in pessimistic moments, were not embraced by the Colonial Office staff, any more than they were wholeheartedly embraced by Colonial Reformers whose notion of responsible local government did not entail colonial control over crown lands.[121] Although the Colonial Reformers contributed to the Colonial Office's problems, by drawing attention to existing colonial crises and manufacturing new ones, they also helped shape the government's solution. Contemporary interest in the management of information fitted neatly with the language of systematic colonisation: the Colonial Office could adopt statistics as a way of effectively responding to the Colonial Reformers. What Peter Burroughs described as the Colonial Office's 'distinctly theoretical, if not wholly Wakefieldian, approach' was the manifestation of the Colonial Office's continuing attempt to exert central control in a new climate of information management.[122] The emphasis on uniformity and information was perhaps a way to generate a new sense of empire: empire as a distinct entity, a uniform territory, complete with its own imperial archive.

The Colonial Office's instructions to colonial governors regarding both appointments and information in the late 1830s and early 1840s demonstrate the metropolitan concern for uniformity and central control. Beginning in August 1838, with two despatches which condemned the 'irregularity' and 'want of uniformity' in colonial appointments, continuing with the October 1839 decision to uniformly redefine (and weaken) colonial officials' tenure, and including also a series of restrictions on officials' leave of absence, the Colonial Office was not only exerting metropolitan control, but laying the foundations for the imperial civil service envisaged in the 1820s.[123] The importance of the central collection of information in this process was also clear. Following an 1841 request for returns listing all colonial appointments for the previous three years, in 1842 colonial governors were instructed to return lists of all potential candidates for the colonial service, 'not in reference to any existing vacancy and an actual appointment, but on the more broad and deliberative view of the actual state of the Civil Service'. Both efficiency and surveillance were emphasised in the Colonial Office's request. The secretary of state, having 'before him simultaneously the whole of these Reports' would be able to judge the merits of 'Officers employed in subordinate situations' throughout the empire. The information returned to London would lead to the reward of 'active and efficient service', allow 'local services and experience' to be taken into account, and save time when a vacancy did occur.[124] This request was reiterated in July 1843, and, together with the emerging policy of presenting the Blue Books to parliament, and printing them 'for general information', suggests an effort not just to increase efficiency, but to counter claims of imperial corruption, both in Britain and the colonies.[125]

The Colonial Office's search for imperial uniformity and central control was especially apparent in the areas of land and emigration policy. The ongoing debate about the value of emigration from Britain and Ireland to the colonies had become tied to questions about the disposal of crown land in the 1820s, and was at the heart of plans for 'systematic colonization'. Rising numbers of emigrants during the 1830s led to colonial concern about disease and passenger conditions, and a suspicion that the imperial government was content to ship out British paupers, rather than the skilled labourers the colonies required. The select committees on waste lands and convict transportation of the later 1830s attracted renewed publicity to the Colonial Reformers' schemes, and the question of emigration, and connected the end of transportation to the Australian colonies with land sales' funded emigration.[126]

An agent-general for emigration, T. F. Elliot, was appointed in 1837. Although Oliver MacDonagh argued that Elliot's appointment was a new departure inspired partly by the Colonial Reformers' influence on the Select Committee on Waste Lands, Dunkley has demonstrated that despite the new title, Elliot simply took over the supervision of emigration agents from the permanent under-secretary at the Colonial Office, while 'the main impetus for the further centralization of emigration administration came . . . from inside the colonial office itself'.[127] Goderich had appointed an emigration commission in June 1831, and Elliot, a Colonial Office clerk, had served as the commissioners' secretary, and then overseen emigration until 1833.[128] His appointment as agent-general fitted with Stephen's conception of the Colonial Office in 1837: Stephen thought the larger emigration board advocated by the select committee would be expensive and inefficient; and Elliot was his protégé.[129] Importantly the new position also indicated that the department approached the matter of emigration seriously and systematically.

By 1840 the Colonial Office's ongoing difficulties with the nine-member board that administered South Australia, and the rapid expansion of Elliot's business as agent-general, convinced Stephen and Lord John Russell that combining the two would lead to significant savings and efficiencies.[130] The three-member Colonial Land and Emigration Commission was established in January 1840.[131] Dunkley argues that the Colonial Land and Emigration Commission effectively harnessed 'the field executive's experience' becoming 'a truly integrated centralized administration' for emigration in the 1840s.[132] Once again, criticism from the Colonial Reformers – expressed in select committees, parliamentary debates and Charles Buller's appendix on land and emigration to the Durham Report – could be muted, while existing Colonial Office aims were met.[133] So closely did the new commission appear to adhere to the strictures of 'systematic colonization', that even though criticism of its activities had began as early as February 1840, both Buller and Wakefield conceded its structural strengths during the next decade.[134]

Russell's instructions to the commissioners in January 1840 (which were based on discussions in the Colonial Office during December 1839 as well as Stephen's 1837 analysis of the agent-general's function), [135] made it clear that the new body was to advance the Colonial Office's broader aims: collecting and disseminating information; and exerting metropolitan control over both crown lands and emigration. Of the four principal duties which Russell identified in the commissioners' instructions, two related directly to statistics. Already, the promotion and control of emigration generated reams of annually published statistics and reports, intended to meet the interest of parliament and potential emigrants. But potential emigrants also inspired a wave of non-government publications offering advice, description and statistics – often recognised by the metropolitan or colonial governments as inaccurate. [136] Aside from keeping up financial and statistical returns on the progress of emigration and land sales, Russell emphasised the critical importance of collecting and diffusing 'accurate statistical knowledge' to potential emigrants and land purchasers in Britain. The government was unable to refer people to 'the ordinary sources of popular intelligence' because such sources on the colonies were 'often perverted, and unworthy of confidence'. Russell listed the various types of information which the commissioners were to collect, offered them access to all the Colonial Office's sources, and asked them to alert him to any deficiencies in the Blue Books. He also instructed the commissioners to present their information unadorned, a reflection not only of the responsibility which the government was accepting by providing information, but also an understanding of how powerful a numerical or statistical argument could be. Care must be taken, Russell warned,

> to present such facts in the most precise and determinate form, unaccompanied by any superfluous comment, and still more, to strip them of any language calculated to work on the imagination, or to interfere with the calm and dispassionate exercise of [public] judgment.

In fact, Russell predicted that the Colonial Land and Emigration Office would become 'the depository of all this branch of statistical information, for the assistance, not of private adventurers only, but of this and every other department of State'. [137]

The Colonial Office's attempt to diffuse the demands of the Colonial Reformers by engaging with the new information order can also be seen in imperial policy on crown lands. Duly's criticism of the 1830s as 'the Age of Neglect and Administrative Infancy' in the Colonial Office is unduly harsh; much more convincing is Burroughs' assessment that an essential continuum – albeit shaky, and occasionally reversed – in imperial land policy was apparent from the 1831 Ripon Regulations through to the 1842 Australian Land Sales Act. The imperial government, unlike the Colonial Reformers, thought that only a proportion of the revenue raised from land sales (and in only some colonies) should be used for assisted emigration. Apart from brief experiments in South Australia and Port Phillip, the government also favoured sale by auction; and consistently emphasised the importance of imperial control over both land and emigration.[138]

In its advocacy of systematic colonisation, the Select Committee on Waste Lands did expose the deficiencies of existing arrangements. It was discovered, for example, that the 1831 Ripon Regulations had still not been implemented in the Cape Colony, and that much of the information on land in the Cape's Blue Books was inaccurate. Russell wrote to Governor Napier in November 1840 demanding an improvement and a 'full statistical return' of Cape land transactions going back as far as possible, emphasising the Colonial Office's embarrassment at its 'inability to afford any explanation' to interested parties 'concerning the position and quality of the lands' at the Cape.[139] While the colonial administration prevaricated, detailing special conditions which worked against the sale of land by regulated auction, the Colonial Office continued to press for the colony's conformity with imperial standards.[140] Russell's successor, Lord Stanley, criticised the Cape's Blue Book for 1840 and demanded – against the advice of colonial officials – that an upset price for land be introduced.[141] The Cape's surveyor-general wrote presciently 'I feel how difficult it is to impress any one in England with anything like a correct notion of the character of this country.'[142] He was right; the Colonial Land and Emigration Commission wanted its system of land sales 'universally established throughout the British colonies'.[143] Napier's successor, Governor Peregrine Maitland, left London in 1844 with firm and clear instructions on land: it was only then that the Cape authorities, unwillingly, complied with the Colonial Office's demands to implement imperial policy.[144]

The Australian colonies, more obviously the target of the Select Committee on Waste Lands, and the subject of heated disputes over land sales because of the different systems operating in each colony, the land boom of the late 1830s, and the connection between transportation and free emigration, were not immune from unrealistic metropolitan demands for uniformity and centralisation. One of the Colonial Land and Emigration Commission's first tasks was to investigate the administration of land in the Australian colonies.[145] Burroughs has demonstrated that the Colonial Office, and particularly Russell, had a new land policy in mind even before the commission was established. From 1839 to 1842, imperial policy on Australian land emphasised uniformity across the colonies, and the pre-eminence of metropolitan control, despite strong (and sensible) colonial objections.[146]

Of course, the disparate, difficult colonies did not comply with the metropolitan vision of uniformity, however much the Colonial Office would have liked them to; while the Colonial Office staff, if not the Colonial

Reformers, quickly became aware of the limitations of systematic colonisation. In the Cape Colony, continuing colonial dissatisfaction with what was seen as an inappropriate land policy continued through the 1840s, but it was only after the colony was granted representative government in 1854 that the local legislature was able to repeal the system.[147] In New South Wales, where representative government was introduced in 1843, there was greater success in the 1840s. The fixed price experiment in Port Phillip, implemented against the advice of colonists and governor in 1840, was abandoned within a year, following compelling evidence of emerging problems in South Australia and Governor Gipps's well-constructed objections. (Stephen thought Gipps's critical despatch on the subject 'a very remarkable paper – a kind of triumph of local observation, strong sense and practised ability over mere plausible speculations'.)[148] The Colonial Office did not abandon its efforts to achieve uniformity, nor its adherence to metropolitan control of colonial lands in 1841; it merely changed its uniformly applied policy as embodied in the 1842 Australian Land Sales Act.[149]

Conclusion

In the later 1830s James Stephen and the other permanent staff at the Colonial Office were in charge of cataloguing an ever-increasing volume of quantitative information, albeit with the assistance of bodies like the Colonial Land and Emigration Office. While over the previous twenty years the emphasis had been on the collection of information as a means of alerting colonial governments to the power of the imperial state, there was now an additional emphasis on information's form, management and utility. The imperial government's actions between 1837 and 1842 suggest a belief that statistical information, centrally held, could be used to govern the empire more effectively, seen particularly in the implementation of uniform policies on crown land, the centralisation of emigration administration, and the continued and extended enforcement of penalties for failure to comply with demands for information. The Colonial Office's emphasis on its own bureaucracy and the imperial archive – as noticed by the generation of imperial historians writing in the mid-twentieth century – also marked the change. The collection and comparison of information seemed to give the Colonial Office a way of managing an empire that in other respects was straining against central control.

The government's initial enthusiasm for statistics – colonial or otherwise – was dampened by problems which quickly loomed in statistical inquiry. These problems on the one hand embraced the collection and classification of data; but on the other questioned the ways in which it was to be used.[150] While numbers retained their power as 'neutral' and 'unbiased', collections of numbers – *statistics* – were increasingly seen as confusing, potentially duplicitous and often employed by 'interested parties'. Essentially, numbers were descriptive, while statistics were interpretative.[151] The collection and publication of vast quantities of numerical data may have given the Colonial Office a desperately desired sense of control, but it was soon apparent that figures and facts were being accorded more respect than they deserved. Martin's *Statistics*, for example, was recognised as being riddled with errors: some of his own making, many transcribed directly from the Colonial Office's own records. The lack of possibility of comparison over time was also recognised as a significant drawback. James Stephen, initially so positive, observed as early as September 1839 that Martin's book was actually of little use to the government, 'because the Colonies of which it treats are in such a constant state of progress, or of decay, that the statistics of one year, become valueless in the next'.[152] The colonies also pulled against the notion that uniform imperial policies could be successfully implemented from London, with continuing settler dissatisfaction with imperial control of crown lands merely one indication that rapidly expanding settler societies could not be denied self-government indefinitely.

Nevertheless, while ultimately a degree of political control might be relinquished, through imperial lack of money, manpower or political will, the legacy of the information revolution endured in imperial policy and government practice. Structures of collection, categories of analysis, and a history of implementing imperial policies would all endure. Perhaps the map of the empire in Martin's *Statistics* represented the most important short-term legacy. Maps of the British Empire, boldly coloured in red against a blank background world, spread rapidly during the 1840s and 1850s, used in atlases, by scientists, missionaries and trade societies. These maps represented an important new way of 'seeing' the colonies. Not only did a uniform colour give a superficial sense of uniformity to the empire, but the movement of Britain to the centre of the world (as happened in the *Statistics'* maps between the 1839 and the 1843 editions) allowed the British viewer an unjustified sense of control.[153] Maps perfectly encompass the transition which occurred in the late 1830s and early 1840s: a transition from a conception of Britain's foreign possessions as primarily a collection of diverse colonies; to a conception of a British 'empire' which could be governed (at least theoretically) as a whole.

Notes

1 CUL, Add 7888/II/122, p. 73, James to Jane Stephen, 21 February 1842.
2 GRE/B126/11, Stephen to Howick, 11 January 1836.
3 *Rules and regulations*, 1st edn, preface.
4 Harling, *Old Corruption*, pp. 154–60.
5 *PP 1817*, xvii (129), pp. 231–42, An Account of All Offices; Harling, *Old Corruption*, p. 145; Young, *Colonial Office*, p. 34.

6 *PP 1835*, xviii (507), p. 445, Report of the Select Committee on Sinecure Offices. Also *PP 1823–PP 1835*, annual returns for 'Persons Holding Offices in Colonies absent in Execution of their Duties'.

7 CO 854/1, fos 80, 100, circulars, August 1819, March 1822.

8 Carroll-Burke, *Colonial discipline*, pp. 31, 43–52, 61, 78, 83–6; Foucault, *Discipline and punish*, pp. 184–228; Ignatieff, *Just measure of pain*, pp. 168–9, 187.

9 Eastwood, 'Province of the legislature', 278.

10 Bayly, *Empire and information*, pp. 154–8, 212, 215, 220–1, 245.

11 Woods, 'Bathurst's policy', pp. 236–47; *HRA*, I, x, pp. 4–11, Bathurst's instructions to Bigge, 6 January 1819. On Macquarie's governorship, see: *Hansard*, 1st ser., 1817, xxiv, 920; 1819, xxxix, 1124; Ritchie, *Macquarie*.

12 *HRA*, I, x, p. 8, Bathurst to Bigge, 6 January 1819 [2nd letter].

13 *PP 1837*, vii (516), Qs 145–61, Report of the Select Committee on the Accounts of Colonial Receipt and Expenditure.

14 CO 854/1, fos 113, 253, circulars, 30 April 1823, 1 January 1827.

15 *Ibid.*, fo. 253, 1 January 1827.

16 *PP 1837*, vii (516), Qs 357–9, Select Committee on Colonial Accounts, evidence of Smith.

17 CO 854/1, fo. 251, circular, 11 September 1826.

18 CO 324/85, pp. 35–6, Hay to Buxton, private, 31 March 1826.

19 CO 854/1, fo. 481, circular, 2 November 1836.

20 *Ibid.*, fo. 251, circular, 11 September 1826.

21 CO 324/105, fo. 64, circular, 15 February 1831.

22 CO 324/83, pp. 231–4, Hay to Bell, private, 27 October 1831.

23 Porter, *Trust in numbers*, p. 8; Hacking, 'History of statistics', pp. 183, 192.

24 In 1816, 4,487 letters and despatches were received in London, rising to 5,195 in 1822; 7,491 by 1824; 8,150 in 1830; and 9,754 in 1840. Outgoing despatches increased most sharply in the 1830s, suggesting that while more information was requested by London in the 1820s, the Colonial Office struggled to respond to much of it. This analysis does not account for changes in the length of letters and despatches. Figures for 1822 and 1824: GRE/B143/A6; others: Hall, *Colonial Office*, p. 24.

25 Wilmot Horton, *Exposition and defence*, pp. 39–40. See also Merivale, 'Moral and intellectual statistics', 53.

26 See *PP 1837*, vii (516), Qs 1456–7.

27 CO 324/83, pp. 231–2, Hay to Bell, 27 October 1831.

28 CO 324/105, fos 70, 90–1, circulars, 28 February 1832, 20 August 1833, 21 November 1833.

29 *Ibid.*, fos 62–4, circular, 15 February 1831.

30 *Ibid.*, fos 70, 90, circulars, 28 February 1832, 20 August 1833, 21 November 1833; *Rules and regulations*, p. 50.

31 CO 324/83, pp. 231–2, Hay to Bell, 27 October 1831.

32 *PP 1837*, vii (516), Q 1052.

33 For contemporary discussions see: Merivale, 'Moral and intellectual statistics'; Montagu, *Essays and selections*, pp. 311–32. On 'the discourse of "the real" ' see Vernon, 'Narrating the constitution', pp. 210–11, 228.

34 Cullen, *Statistical movement*; Porter, *Statistical thinking*; Poovey, 'Figures of arithmetic'; Browne, *Secular ark*, pp. 75–6; Levine, *Amateur and professional*, pp. 40–2, 75, 79, 101–4; Cantwell, *Public Record Office*.

35 Drayton, *Nature's government*.

36 *Encyclopaedia Britannica* (3rd edn, 1797), xii, p. 731. Merivale, 'Moral and intellectual statistics', 49.

37 E.g., Merivale, 'Moral and intellectual statistics', 49; Portlock, 'Objects and advantages', 317.

38 Browne, *Secular ark*, pp. 75–9.

39 Cullen, *Statistical movement*, pp. 10–11; Porter, *Trust in numbers*, pp. 8, 78.

40 Browne, *Secular ark*, pp. 58–85.

41 Morrell and Thackray, *Gentlemen of science*, pp. 291–6; and Cullen, *Statistical movement*, ch. 6.

42 Martin, *Statistics*. Tulloch, 'Troops in the West Indies'; Bannister, 'Population of New Zealand'; and Capper, 'Commercial statistics of Ceylon'.

43 MP, A2915, fo. 50, Macarthur to his brothers, 4 January 1842.
44 CO 201/299, fo. 477, Gipps to Russell, 25 October 1840.
45 *Ibid.*, fos 485–6, Report of a committee of the New South Wales Legislative Council, 23 October 1840, encl. in Gipps to Russell, 25 October 1840.
46 CO 201/344, fo. 103, Stephen minute on Gipps to Stanley, 16 March 1844.
47 Nell, 'Public benefit', pp. 101–6.
48 For satire see, e.g., Dickens, 'Mudfog Association', 409–11.
49 McCulloch, 'British statistics', 155–6.
50 'Fourth Annual Report of the Statistical Society of London'.
51 Merivale, 'Moral and intellectual statistics', 50; McCulloch, 'British statistics', 158.
52 Browne, *Secular ark*, p. 77.
53 Altick, *Victorian people and ideas*, pp. 244–5.
54 Cullen, *Statistical movement*, pp. 19–21; Eastwood, 'Province of the legislature', 277; Hacking, 'History of statistics'.
55 This group included Charles Babbage, Thomas Malthus, Charles Poulett Thomson (president of the Board of Trade), J. Deacon Hume, G. W. Wood, Francis Jeffrey, Charles Blomfield (the bishop of London) and Thomas Chalmers: Cullen, *Statistical movement*, pp. 81–7.
56 Cullen, *Statistical movement*, pp. 79–81, 87, 101. Others had Indian interests, including Richard Jones, Colonel William Henry Sykes, and Holt Mackenzie.
57 Brown, *Board of Trade*, pp. 76–93.
58 E.g., *PP 1833*, xii (44 and 717), Select Committee on Public Documents; *PP 1835*, vi (499), Select Committee on Consular Establishments; *PP 1836*, xvi (565), Select Committee on the Record Commission; *PP 1837*, vii (516), Select Committee on Colonial Accounts.
59 Cullen, *Statistical movement*, pp. 96–7.
60 *PP 1837*, vii (516), Qs 32, 34, 112–13, 148–55, 267–8.
61 TFB, vol. 2, pp. 82–3, Buxton to Gurney, 24 November 1835.
62 *PP 1837*, vii (516), p. iii.
63 Baring was joint secretary of the Treasury, and would become chancellor of the Exchequer; Parnell was paymaster-general; Clerk and Fremantle were both secretaries to the Treasury in the 1834–35 Tory administration.
64 Hume's interest in colonial inefficiency dated back to 1821; Hawes had also sat on the Aborigines Select Committee, and was a future under-secretary for the colonies.
65 *PP 1837*, vii (516), pp. ii–iv, and *passim*.
66 *Ibid.*, Qs 10–20, 267.
67 *Ibid.*, Qs 32, 34, 112; see also Qs 1456–7, evidence of McQueen.
68 Young, *Colonial Office*, pp. 194, 238–9. *PP 1837*, vii (516), Qs 22–37. The desire for comparability continued to be frustrated into the 1840s: see, e.g., *PP 1845*, vii (520), Report from the Select Committee on Colonial Accounts.
69 *PP 1837*, vii (516), Qs 34, 148–50, 216. See also, *ibid.*, Q 1214, evidence of Haultain; GRE/B109/5B, fo. 9, Hay to Howick, 10 January 1832.
70 *PP 1837*, vii (516), Qs 155–61, 346.
71 *Ibid.*, Qs 151, 208–11.
72 *Ibid.*, Qs 158–9, 346–59.
73 Young, *Colonial Office*, chs 6–7; Cell, *British colonial administration*, pp. 12, 25; chs 7–8; Knaplund, *Stephen*, p. 42.
74 *PP 1837*, vii (516), Qs 110, 875–80.
75 *Ibid.*, Qs 49, 1537–8.
76 *Ibid.*, Qs 137, 884–5.
77 *Ibid.*, Q 52.
78 See *PP 1836*, xxxix (279), Papers Relative to Caffre War and Death of Hintza; *PP 1837*, xliii (503), Further Papers . . . relative to the late Caffre war, 1836–37.
79 *PP 1837*, vii (516), Qs 165, 167–8.
80 *Ibid.*, Qs 359, 885–7.
81 *Ibid.*, App. 13, Porter to Bowring, 7 July 1837.
82 *Ibid.*, Q 884.

83 *Ibid.*, Qs 1456–7.
84 Eastwood, 'Province of the legislature', 279.
85 *PP 1837*, vii (516), Q 1073.
86 *Ibid.*, Qs 567–72.
87 *Ibid.*, Q 1073.
88 *Ibid.*, Qs 165–6.
89 Other technical and administrative innovations, such as double-entry bookkeeping, were also at a premium. E.g., *ibid.*, Qs 1214, 1227.
90 *Ibid.*, Qs 888, 894.
91 Cullen, *Statistical movement*, pp. 21–7, 91–9.
92 *PP 1837*, vii (516), Qs 889–94.
93 *Ibid.*, Q 894.
94 *Ibid.*, Q 919.
95 Eastwood, 'Province of the legislature'.
96 Browne, *Secular ark*, pp. 75–6.
97 Martin, *History of the British colonies*, v, p. x. There is no full-length biography of Martin, but see King, *Survey our empire!*
98 CO 323/219, fo. 331, Martin to Aberdeen, 8 January 1835; *ibid.*, Martin to Glenelg, 15 July 1835, 8 September 1835; BL, Add 40408, fos 11–12, Martin to Peel, 27 December 1834.
99 Martin, *History of the British colonies*, 1st edn, i, 'Dedication', pp. iii–iv.
100 A second edition of the first volume only was published in 1835, before volume five of the first edition.
101 Martin, *History of the British colonies*, 2nd edn, i, 'Introduction', pp. x–xi.
102 Martin, *Statistics*, p. iii, Grey to Martin, 7 February 1838.
103 *Ibid.*, pp. iii–v.
104 *Ibid.* The second edition, published in 1843, was renamed *History of the colonies of the British Empire* – suggesting that statistics did not sell as well as Martin hoped.
105 *Ibid.*
106 *Ibid.*, p. v.
107 'Imperial Federation map of the world', *Graphic*, 24 July 1886.
108 Dower, *New general atlas*; Arrowsmith, *World on a globular projection*; Arrowsmith, *London atlas of universal geography*.
109 CO 323/225, fo. 296, Stephen to Martin, 17 January 1836.
110 Burnett also makes this point, noting that *terra incognita* was 'above all, a *problem* for imperial administrators' who wanted rather to see 'defined, settled and productive' colonial spaces. Burnett, *Masters of all they surveyed*, p. 10.
111 Quoted in Cullen, *Statistical movement*, p. 34.
112 BL, Add 36470, fos 179–80, encl. in Martin to Hobhouse, 25 March 1839.
113 CO 324/106, fo. 295, Glenelg circular, 29 January 1839; CO 324/105, fos 159–60, Normanby circular (Eastern Colonies), 27 February 1839.
114 CO 324/106, fo. 295, circular, 29 January 1839.
115 Governor Gipps thought it repeated 'some of the errors . . . which pervade other works relating to New South Wales', CO 201/287, fo. 289, Gipps to Normanby, 27 September 1839; Carrington, *British overseas*, p. 506; Balfour, 'Statistical data', 208.
116 The colony wanted books of 'established repute'. CO 201/299, fos 477–86, Gipps to Russell, 25 October 1840.
117 E.g. Buller, *Responsible government*; Molesworth, Colonial Administration Debate, 1838, in Molesworth, *Selected speeches*. For a government response, see Spedding, 'New theory of colonization'.
118 Porter, *Trust in numbers*, p. 8.
119 For example, Duly, *Land policy*; Burroughs, *Britain and Australia*; MacDonagh, *Government growth*; Dunkley, 'Emigration and the state'; Ray, 'Administering emigration'.
120 GRE/B126/11, Stephen to Howick, 1 July 1837.
121 *Ibid.*, Stephen to Howick, 11 January 1836. On Colonial Reformers' view of colonial government, see Burroughs, *Britain and Australia*, pp. 21–2, 29–31.

122 Burroughs, *Britain and Australia*, p. 251.
123 CO 854/2, fos 180–1, 300, 344, 346, circulars, August 1838, 16 October 1839, 3 March 1840, 10 March 1840; CO 854/3, fo. 109, circular, 7 March 1842.
124 CO 854/3, fos 58, 114–15, circulars, 24 April 1841, 15 June 1842.
125 *Ibid.*, fos 170, 273, circulars, 27 July 1843, 24 September 1845.
126 *PP 1836*, xi (512), Report of the Select Committee on the Disposal of Waste Lands. *PP 1837*, xix (518) and *PP 1837–8*, xxii (669), Reports of the Select Committee on Transportation.
127 Dunkley, 'Emigration and the state', 368–70, 375–7; MacDonagh, *Government growth*, pp. 16, 123, 136; Ray, 'Administering emigration', pp. 237–40.
128 Ray, 'Administering emigration', pp. 26, 50 and *passim*.
129 CO 385/17, fos 307–36, Stephen to Spearman, 9 January 1837.
130 Between 1836 and 1839, for example, emigrants leaving England for New South Wales rose six-fold. Burroughs, *Britain and Australia*, pp. 216–19.
131 The commissioners were T. F. Elliot, Robert Torrens and Edward Villiers. Annual reports began in 1842. Martin's application to be appointed a commissioner was rejected. CO 385/19, p. 274, Vernon Smith to Martin, 19 February 1840.
132 Dunkley, 'Emigration and the State', 372.
133 *PP 1836*, xi (512), Report of the Select Committee on the Disposal of Waste Lands; 'Report on public lands and emigration', Appendix B to *Lord Durham's Report on the affairs of British North America*; Duly, *Land policy*, pp. 159–70.
134 Buller, *Hansard*, 3rd ser., lxviii, 6 April 1843, c. 515; and Wakefield, *Art of colonization*, pp. 50–1. See Burroughs, *Britain and Australia*, pp. 220, 224–5.
135 CO 13/15, fos 263–6, Stephen minute, 10 December 1839; CO 385/19, fos 186–201, Russell to lords of Treasury, 30 December 1839; CO 385/17, fos 307–36, Stephen to Spearman, 9 January 1837.
136 See, e.g., Anon., *Observations on the advantages of emigration to New South Wales*; Anon., *Twenty years experience in Australia*; Butler, *Emigrant's hand-book of facts*; Brown, *New Zealand . . . as a field for emigration*.
137 *PP 1840*, xxxiii (35), pp. 3–4, 'Instructions addressed by Lord John Russell to the Land and Emigration Commissioners', 1840.
138 Duly, *Land policy*, p. 141; Burroughs, *Britain and Australia*, p. 250 and *passim*.
139 CO 49/34, pp. 119–23, Russell to Napier, private and confidential, 17 November 1840.
140 *Ibid.*, pp. 115–18, Russell to Napier, 17 November 1840.
141 *Ibid.*, pp. 288–9, Stanley to Napier, 31 December 1841; CA, GH1/29 (Cape), Colonial Land and Emigration Office to Stephen, 27 January 1842, encl. 1, Stanley to Napier, 6 February 1842, cited in Duly, *Land policy*, p. 168; CO 49/36, pp. 34–5, Stanley to Napier, 18 June 1842.
142 CA, GH 28/18, Michell to acting secretary to Cape government, 14 July 1842, quoted in Duly, *Land policy*, p. 169; see also pp. 163, 175.
143 *PP 1843*, xxix, p. 48, Report of the Colonial Land and Emigration commissioners, 24 August 1843.
144 CO 49/36, pp. 389–94, Stanley to Maitland, 4 February 1844.
145 CO 385/19, p. 253, Russell's Instructions to the Commissioners, 30 December 1839.
146 Burroughs, *Britain and Australia*, pp. 222–3, 230–5, 331, 332–7.
147 Duly, *Land policy*, p. 182.
148 CO 201/300, fo. 228, Stephen minute, 7 May 1841, on Gipps to Russell, 19 December 1840.
149 Burroughs, *Britain and Australia*, pp. 236–47.
150 Browne, *Secular ark*, pp. 73–8; Cullen, *Statistical movement*, pp. 11, 14; Tufte, *Visual display*, pp. 32–4.
151 Poovey, *Modern fact*, especially ch. 7.
152 CO 323/225, fos 313–14, Stephen memo to Russell, on Martin's letter of 19 September 1839; see also CO 384/62, fos 409–12, Stephen, minute, 12 February 1840.
153 For a discussion of such 'diffusionist' mapping, see Black, *Maps and history*, pp. 58–61.

CHAPTER EIGHT

Conclusion

> With respect to our right over the [Auckland] islands I see they are coloured red in Arrowsmith's map of the world which I suppose implies some sort of claim on our part. (3rd Earl Grey to James Stephen, 1846)[1]

Earl Grey's casual reference to an Arrowsmith atlas indicates how rapidly new visual and statistical conceptualisations of empire took hold in the Colonial Office. Returning to the department in 1846 as secretary of state, Grey could imagine implementing some of the pan-imperial changes only dreamed of during his term as under-secretary in the early 1830s. The juxtaposition of the changing information order with domestic, colonial and personal politics in the late 1830s had precipitated new ways for the imperial government to control the empire and particularly the settler colonies. Yet during Grey's tenure at the Colonial Office the foundations would be laid for the concession of responsible government to these colonies. This final chapter, which surveys the conclusions reached by *Colonial connections*, considers how these new conceptualisations of empire really affected colonial governance.

By connecting Colonial Office developments in the 1830s with a study of the networks of personal connection that expanded across Britain, New South Wales and the Cape Colony, *Colonial connections* has attempted to conceive a new space in which to study Britain's imperial and colonial past. The 'new imperial history' of the early twenty-first century has stressed the interconnectedness of colonial sites, but sometimes underemphasised the metropolis. Emphasising colonial connections – not just their actual impact, but also their perceived importance – reminds us that for the colonisers (and some of the colonised) Britain remained central to economic, social and political power in the first half of the nineteenth century.

Through its examination of early nineteenth-century networks of personal connection, this book has suggested one way in which the British colonial experience, and the operation of imperial and colonial rule, could be assessed more profitably. Governors, officials, settlers and metropolitan lobbyists not only made their influence felt through personal connections, but also devoted considerable time, attention and anxiety to strengthening their networks and assessing those of their rivals. No group of colonisers was exempt from the concern to strengthen its connections with the metropole, although the avenues open to each group varied according to their financial and social resources, from the excellent connections of Thomas Mitchell or Thomas Buxton to the indirect and shaky network of the Grahamstown settlers. Much more work remains to be done on these networks; there are many connections still to be investigated – especially, for example, within imperial legal and ecclesiastical networks. Even so, *Colonial connection*'s study of New South Wales and the Cape Colony demonstrates that networks of personal connection, whether based on family, military service, attitudes to colonisation, or science, were of both perceived and actual importance to colonial government in the early nineteenth century.

Of course, strong personal connections did not guarantee success; at times, as with the private correspondence between sub-gubernatorial colonial officials and Robert Hay which undermined several governors' authority, or the over-confidence his envoy inspired in Richard Bourke, personal connections even threatened colonial stability. But this does not contradict the fact that almost everyone perceived networks of connection to be a necessary prerequisite for exerting influence. Apart from giving historians a different perspective of these individuals, the study of personal connections highlights the importance to colonial governance of private considerations – patronage, personal ambition or rivalry, and social and financial insecurity – as well as principles and theories.

For governors and colonial officials, the diminished metropolitan reliance on personal networks after 1835 made a significant initial impact. The limits placed on colonial officials' direct personal contact with the Colonial Office favoured those whose existing networks consisted of strong ties – of family, patronage, or friendship – which connected them to the imperial government. Those whose networks depended on weaker ties, of acquaintance or shared interest, were less able after 1835 to develop these connections into stronger links with the Colonial Office. Nevertheless, the impact on sub-gubernatorial officials of restricted contact with London was partly masked in two ways: by the introduction of better-defined conditions of service; and by the appointment in the Cape Colony and New South Wales of more officials who were colonists, rather than metropolitan Britons. Such officials increasingly found that directing their attention to the colonial government was worthwhile.

The transition to greater colonial self-government changed the status of governors too. As Grey would write in 1852: when governors were 'independent of any local [colonial] control', it was important to exercise control over them from London. As governors' powers were limited by colonial legislatures, less 'vigilant superintendence' was required by the imperial government.[2] In the late 1830s, alterations to colonial procedures seemed designed to strengthen the imperial government, rather than governors. More of the decisions once left in practice to governors, such as on subordinates' leave of absence, were now to be made in consultation with colonial councils, while the Blue Books and governors' reports – or their absence – would be exposed to parliamentary and public scrutiny. But, as greater power was transferred to colonists through the 1840s, the need to shore up the status of an 'impartial' governor led to increased emphasis on ceremony and salary increases.[3]

Lobbyists were less affected than officials by the initial impact of the metropolitan government's eschewal of private correspondence; however, the impact was more profound in the longer term. Nor did the introduction of representative (and eventually responsible) government necessarily make lobbying easier. While colonial legislators were more accessible to colonial-based campaigners, victories on either a metropolitan or a colonial front could still prove decisive, as the New South Wales squatters' campaign on crown land administration in 1845 demonstrated. In opposition to Governor Gipps's proposals, the squatters carefully marshalled their evidence, utilising metropolitan newspapers and encouraging British wool merchants and manufacturers to present memorials to the secretary of state, Lord Stanley. Francis Scott, the parliamentary agent of the colony's legislative council, directly lobbied Stanley in a series of private meetings.[4] As Burroughs has argued, it was the squatters' campaign in England that reversed the Colonial Office's position.[5] Despite such victories, it took many lobby groups decades to adapt to the implications of both the statistical revolution and the concomitant depersonalisation or bureaucratisation of government. In the empire, as in Britain, lobbyists' tactics, skills and organisational structures all required reassessment: not only did the methods of collecting, analysing and presenting colonial information change; but they were accompanied by a shift from amateurs and volunteers to experts and professionals. The difficulties of this transition are reflected in the limited progress of 'humanitarian' bodies like the Anti-Slavery Society and the Aborigines Protection Society between 1840 and 1870.[6] These organisations grew out of traditions well established by the 1830s: their standard approach relied on narrative tales collected by missionaries, collated round the kitchen table, and passed on to personal friends within government. While these old campaigners remained in charge, relying on their previous successes and government contacts, it was difficult to adapt to the new information order.

As the experience of lobbyists suggests, the diminished role of personal networks in colonial governance cannot be understood without an appreciation of changes within the government, and within the Colonial

Office particularly. *Colonial connections* has also provided a new interpretation of the Colonial Office in the 1830s; the decade that has attracted such extensive consideration from imperial historians over the last seventy years. Emphasising the continuities, as well as the differences, between Robert Hay and James Stephen reveals important transitions in the metropolitan governance of empire. While the imperial government always attempted to control both governors and settlers, metropolitan understandings of the best way to achieve that control changed during the 1830s. It was information – particularly, statistics – which seemed to offer a means of controlling disparate and difficult colonies by the end of the decade. However, despite the broader intellectual context of the rise of statistics and neo-Baconian thought within which this transition occurred, personal politics also played a part. Hay's alienation from his Whig masters and his rivalry with James Stephen rendered his extensive networks of personal connection unavailable to the government in the mid-1830s, creating a space in which the new quantitative approach could emerge.

The imperial government was affected profoundly by the changing information order: not only did the new sense of empire alter attitudes to the advent of self-government for settler societies; but the very practice of government changed as well. In this arena, the barrier between 'metropolitan' and 'colonial' was broken down. Faced with the administration of a vast empire from a distance of thousands of miles, the Colonial Office was forced to the fore in the wider metropolitan development of a professional bureaucracy. As Eastwood has argued, from the 1830s 'the aristocratic principle in government gave way to the imperialism of the bureaucrat'.[7] This transition was gradual and halting, not merely a product of the 1830s, but the culmination of more than half a century of administrative developments and changing attitudes. While Henry Taylor recognised in 1832 that 'efficiency should be substituted for influence' in government, it took much longer for such attitudes to seep into the general consciousness.[8] The transition from viewing office as property to understanding an appointment as merely the first stage of a career where advancement depended on efficiency and merit was particularly slow.[9] Even John Stuart Mill's 1861 description of a strong executive department with 'proper tests' and rules for appointment and promotion, an open and methodical distribution of business and responsibility, and an efficient and comprehensive archive, would not result in the introduction of recruitment by open examination in the home civil service until 1870.[10] Despite the advances of the early 1840s, Robert Hay's 1826 plan for an imperial civil service had been realised only three years earlier, in 1867.

The transition so long desired by some was precipitated by the information that poured into London – on the poor, the sick, the mad, the Irish and the aborigines. In the Colonial Office, Stephen's intention to keep a personal

[203]

check on every colonial development faded. A much larger cohort of civil servants was required to manage colonial information. In expansion, the certainty that each civil servant would share a certain outlook and approach, cultivated by family, class, club and university, was lost. It was no longer the case that all new recruits could be known personally to a member of the department they entered, although the entrance examination – assessing competence in the classical languages and other, equally relevant, branches of scholarship – went some way to ensuring a certain uniformity in background.

Different types of information, analysed in different ways, called for not only government expansion, but also specialisation within government. Sir Francis Palgrave's 1837 recognition that professional archivists should manage the state records, was matched by developments in other areas of metropolitan government, and similar changes in the colonies. A new class of professional administrators emerged, 'the "statesmen in disguise" who helped inspire and sustain the modern state'.[11] The changing information order not only encouraged professionalisation, but was itself secured by professionals. Under their guidance, the areas to which measurement could be applied, and in which useful experiments might be conducted, expanded every year. As professionals expanded the bureaucracy, the separation between political and permanent staff in government became more apparent, in turn further limiting the impact and potential reach of personal networks.

These changes were both endorsed by and reflected in the colonial sphere. In some respects, as to the statistician George Porter, the colonies represented 'laboratories of modernity' in which data could be collected and theories tested more easily than in the metropole.[12] Colonial governments experienced similar transitions to the metropolitan government's, in terms of professionalisation, centralisation and bureaucratic expansion. Drayton has suggested that it was professionals – in his case, scientific professionals – who actually drove British imperialism in the second half of the nineteenth century. 'Knowledge and technique', he suggests, 'had a charismatic force' which 'garlanded imperial power with a natural legitimacy'.[13]

Although the new emphasis on information was burdensome for the 1830s' Colonial Office, information also offered – via its guise of objectivity, apparent connection with critiques of colonial rule, and impetus to generalisation – an opportunity to implement some of the long-standing aims of Colonial Office policy. In the emerging colonial civil service, as well as in imperial policy on land and emigration, the Colonial Office was able to embrace objectives of centralisation, and colonial uniformity, while stressing the authority of the metropole over the colony. The information revolution, by categorising and mapping the British colonies, allowed metropolitan officials and politicians, like Stephen and Grey, to see that there was an empire, not merely an awkward and diverse collection of colonies.

CONCLUSION

While many of the policies implemented in the late 1830s and early 1840s were ultimately unsuccessful, the way in which Britain's empire was imagined and construed was forever altered. The profound nature of the changes brought about by the information revolution of the late 1830s suggests that later colonial governance could be profitably reassessed in their light; and, in particular, that our understanding of the transition to responsible government might be enhanced. From the 1840s on, settler self-government became an unavoidable, if still unwelcome, reality. The blow was softened for metropolitan authorities, because their central control of colonial information allowed imperial influence, if not imperial power, to be retained. The information revolution gave the imperial government a new language of statistics and expertise with which to meet both metropolitan criticism and colonial crises; while the sense of empire as a unified whole contributed to the Colonial Office's relative effectiveness in administering an ever larger colonial empire through to the end of the century.

Notes

1 CUL, Add 7888/II/10, Grey to Stephen, 2 September 1846.
2 Grey, *Colonial policy*, p. 21.
3 CO 854/2, fo. 346, circular, 10 March 1837; CO 854/3, fos. 49, 273, circulars, 15 March 1841, 24 September 1845; Grey, *Colonial policy*, p. 17; Knaplund, *Stephen*, pp. 52–4.
4 CO 204/16, pp. 415–16, McLeay to Scott, 5 October 1844; CO 204/18, pp. 219–32, correspondence with parliamentary agent, 21 December 1844–11 November 1845.
5 Burroughs, *Britain and Australia*, pp. 315–26.
6 Porter, 'Trusteeship'.
7 Eastwood, 'Province of the legislature', 294.
8 GRE/B143/A8, Taylor to Villiers, 2 April 1832. See also, Taylor, *Statesman*.
9 Silberman, *Cages of reason*, pp. 314, 326–32.
10 Mill, 'Representative government', p. 228.
11 Eastwood, 'Province of the legislature', 293; Levine, *Amateur and professional*, pp. 123–4.
12 Stoler, *Race and the education of desire*, pp. 12–16.
13 Drayton, *Nature's government*, pp. 171–2.

APPENDICES

SENIOR COLONIAL OFFICE STAFF, 1815–50

Secretary of State

Earl Bathurst	Appointed 11 June 1812
Viscount Goderich	30 April 1827
W. Huskisson	3 September 1827
Sir George Murray	30 May 1828
Viscount Goderich	22 November 1830
Hon. E. G. Stanley	3 April 1833
T. Spring Rice	5 June 1834
Duke of Wellington	17 November 1834
Earl of Aberdeen	20 December 1834
Lord Glenelg	18 April 1835
Marquess of Normanby	19 February 1839
Lord John Russell	2 September 1839
Lord Stanley	3 September 1841
W. E. Gladstone	23 December 1845
Earl Grey	6 July 1846

Parliamentary Under-Secretary

Henry Goulburn	20 August 1812
Robert Wilmot Horton	12 December 1821
Hon. E. G. Stanley	15 October 1827
Lord F. Leveson Gower	6 February 1828
H. Twiss	21 May 1828
Viscount Howick	22 November 1830
J. G. Shaw Lefevre	3 April 1833
Sir George Grey	29 August 1834
Hon. J. Stuart Wortley	2 January 1835
W. E. Gladstone	26 January 1835
Sir George Grey	18 April 1835
H. Labouchere	23 February 1839
R. V. Smith	2 September 1839
G. W. Hope	3 September 1841
Lord Lyttleton	8 January 1846
B. Hawes	6 July 1846

Permanent Under-Secretary

R. W. Hay	6 July 1825
J. Stephen	4 February 1836
H. Merivale	3 May 1848

Assistant Under-Secretary

J. Stephen	17 September 1834
	–4 February 1836
F. Rogers	19 May 1846
H. Merivale	3 November 1846
T. F. Elliot	20 November 1847

APPENDIX TWO
COLONIAL GOVERNORS

Cape of Good Hope

1814–26	Lord Charles Somerset
1826–28	Richard Bourke
1828–33	Sir Galbraith Lowry Cole
1834–38	Sir Benjamin D'Urban
1838–43	Sir George Napier
1844–46	Sir Peregrine Maitland
1846–47	Sir Henry Pottinger
1847–52	Sir Henry Wakelyn Smith

New South Wales

1810–21	Lachlan Macquarie
1821–25	Sir Thomas Brisbane
1825–31	Ralph Darling
1831–37	Sir Richard Bourke
1838–46	Sir George Gipps
1846–55	Sir Charles FitzRoy

Other governors mentioned in the text

Adam, Frederick: Ionian Islands, 1824–32; Madras, 1832–37.
Arthur, George: Van Diemen's Land, 1824–36; Upper Canada, 1838–41.
Whitworth-Aylmer, Matthew: Lower Canada, 1830–35.
Campbell, Colin: Nova Scotia, 1834–40; Ceylon, 1840–47.

Colbourne, John: Upper Canada, 1829–36; Ionian Islands, 1843–49.

Cole, Galbraith Lowry: Mauritius, 1823–28.

Darling, Ralph: Mauritius, 1819–21.

Douglas, Howard: New Brunswick, 1824–31; Ionian Islands, 1835–41.

D'Urban, Benjamin: Antigua, 1820–24; Demerara & Essequibo, 1824–31; British Guiana, 1831–33.

Farquhar, Robert: Mauritius, 1810–23.

FitzRoy, Charles: Prince Edward Island, 1837–41; Leeward Islands, 1846–51.

Franklin, John: Van Diemen's Land, 1837–43.

Gawler, George: South Australia, 1838–41.

Grey, George: South Australia, 1841–45; New Zealand, 1845–53 and 1861–68; Cape Colony, 1854–61.

Kempt, James: Nova Scotia, 1820–28; Lower Canada, 1828–30.

Harvey, John: Prince Edward Island, 1836–37; New Brunswick, 1837–41; Newfoundland, 1841–46; Nova Scotia, 1846–52.

Horton, Robert Wilmot: Ceylon, 1831–37.

Maitland, Peregrine: Upper Canada, 1818–28; Nova Scotia, 1828–34.

Phipps, Constantine: Jamaica, 1832–34; Ireland, 1835–39.

Ponsonby, Frederick: Malta, 1827–36.

Pottinger, Henry: Hong Kong, 1843–44; Madras, 1847–54.

Poulett Thomson, Charles: Lower Canada, 1839–41; Canada, 1841.

Sorrell, William: Van Diemen's Land, 1817–24.

Eardley-Wilmot, John: Van Diemen's Land, 1843–46.

APPENDIX THREE
COLONIAL OFFICIALS

Brief details of the colonial careers of officials mentioned in the text

Bannister, S.: Attorney-General, New South Wales, 1823–26.

Bell, J.: Colonial Secretary, Cape Colony, 1827–41.

Bird, C. C.: Deputy Secretary to the Government, Cape Colony, 1818–24; Colonial Secretary, Cape Colony, 1818–24.

Broughton, W. G.: Archdeacon of New South Wales, 1828–36; Bishop of Australia, 1836–53.

Burnett, J.: Colonial Secretary, Van Diemen's Land, 1826–34.

Burton, C.: Master of the Rolls, Cape Colony, 1827–after 1832.

Burton, W. W.: Judge, Cape Colony, 1827–32; Judge, New South Wales, 1832–43; Judge, Madras, 1844–57.

Craig, Mr: Private Secretary to Governor Napier, Cape Colony 1838–42; Clerk to the Councils, Cape Colony 1842–unknown.

Cunningham, R.: Curator of Sydney Botanical Gardens, 1832–35.

Dowling, J.: Judge, New South Wales, 1827–37; Chief Justice, New South Wales, 1837–44.

Forbes, F.: Attorney-General, Bermuda, 1811–16; Chief Justice, Newfoundland, 1816–22; Chief Justice, New South Wales, 1823–37.

Frankland, G.: Deputy Surveyor-General, Van Diemen's Land, 1827–28; Surveyor-General, Van Diemen's Land, 1828–38.

Goulburn, F.: Colonial Secretary, New South Wales, 1821–26.

Hamilton, K. B.: Unknown office, Mauritius, c. 1826–28; Clerk to the Councils, Cape Colony 1828–43; Governor, Grenada, 1846–52.

Hare, J.: Lieutenant-Governor, Cape Colony, 1838–46.

Harington, T. C.: Clerk, New South Wales, 1822; Assistant Colonial Secretary, New South Wales, 1826–41.

Harvey, W. H.: Colonial Treasurer, Cape Colony, 1836–41.

La Trobe, C. J.: Superintendent, Port Phillip, 1839–51; Lieutenant-Governor, Victoria, 1851–54.

Mackaness, J.: Sheriff, New South Wales, 1824–27.

McLeay, A.: Colonial Secretary, New South Wales, 1826–36.

Menzies, W.: Judge, Cape Colony, 1827–50.

Michell, C. C.: Surveyor-General, Cape Colony, 1828–48.

Mitchell, T. L.: Deputy Surveyor-General, New South Wales, 1827–28; Surveyor-General, New South Wales, 1828–55.

Montagu, J.: Clerk of Executive and Legislative Councils, Van Diemen's Land, 1823–29; Treasurer, Van Diemen's Land, 1831–34; Colonial Secretary, Van Diemen's Land, 1834–42; Colonial Secretary, Cape Colony, 1843–53.

O'Connell, M.: Lieutenant-Governor, New South Wales, 1809–14; Commander of the Forces, New South Wales, 1838–47.

Perceval, D.: Clerk to the Councils, Cape Colony, 1825–28; Auditor-General, Cape Colony, January–February 1828.

Plasket, R.: Chief Secretary, Ceylon; Chief Secretary, Malta; Colonial Secretary, Cape Colony, 1824–27.

Plunkett, J. H.: Solicitor-General, New South Wales, 1832–36; Attorney-General, New South Wales, 1836–56.

Porter, W.: Attorney-General, Cape Colony, 1839–64.

Riddell, C. D.: Secretary to the Commission of Eastern Inquiry, Ceylon, 1829–30; Treasurer, New South Wales, 1830–56; acting Colonial Secretary, New South Wales, 1854–56.

Rivers, H.: Wharfmaster, Cape Colony, 1816–21; Landdrost, Cape Colony, 1821–42; Treasurer, Cape Colony, 1842–61; Paymaster-General, Cape Colony, 1851–61.

Robinson, J. B.: Solicitor-General, Upper Canada, 1815–18; Attorney-General, Upper Canada, 1818–29; Chief Justice, Upper Canada, 1829–40.

Scott, T. H.: Secretary to Bigge Commission, New South Wales, 1819–21; Archdeacon, New South Wales, 1824–29.

Smith, H. W.: Deputy Quarter-Master General, Jamaica, 1826–28, and Cape Colony, 1828–40; Adjutant-General, India, 1840–47; Governor, Cape Colony, 1847–52.

Somerset, H.: Commandant of Simonstown, Cape Colony, 1821; Officer in charge of Cape Mounted Rifles, Cape Colony, 1823–52; Commander-in-chief, Bombay army, 1856.

Stapylton, G. W. C.: Assistant surveyor, New South Wales, 1828–40.

Stockenström, A.: Commissioner-General, Cape Colony, 1828–33; Lieutenant-Governor, Cape Colony, 1836–38.

Therry, R.: Commissioner of Court of Requests, New South Wales, 1829–44; acting Attorney-General, New South Wales, 1841–43; Judge, Port Phillip, 1844–46, Judge, New South Wales, 1846–59.

Thomson, E. D.: Clerk to the Councils, New South Wales, 1828–37; Colonial Secretary, 1837–56.

Thomson, J. D.: Naval Storekeeper, Cape Colony, c. 1828–unknown.

Truter, Sir J.: Fiscal, Cape Colony, 1809–12; Chief Justice, Cape Colony, 1812–28.

Willis, J. W.: Judge, Upper Canada, 1827–29; Judge, British Guiana, 1831–36; Judge, New South Wales, 1838–41; Judge, Port Phillip, 1841–43.

Wylde, J.: Judge Advocate, New South Wales, 1816–25; Chief Justice, Cape Colony, 1827–55.

BIBLIOGRAPHY

PRIMARY SOURCES

Manuscripts

Bodleian Library, University of Oxford

Bourke Papers, Rhodes House Library, MSS Afr/t/7/1–25
Thomas Fowell Buxton Papers, Rhodes House Library, Micr. Brit. Emp. 17 (microfilm)
Viscount Melbourne Papers, microfilms 1076/2–4, 6 (Royal Archives, Boxes 5–8, 13)

British Library, London

Add 36470, Broughton Correspondence (correspondence and papers of John Cam Hobhouse)
Add 38763, Huskisson Papers
Add 40408–40410, Peel Papers
Add 40879–40880, Ripon Papers
Add 43236–43237, Aberdeen Papers

Cambridge University Library

Papers of James Stephen:
    Add 7349/1/1–45, Letters from Sir James Stephen to his third son, Sir James Fitzjames Stephen, c. 1834–1859.
    Add 7349/3/1–13, Miscellaneous Letters from Sir James Stephen.
    Add 7888/II/1–53, Letters from the 3rd Earl Grey to Sir James Stephen, 1834–53.
    Add 7888/II/54–77, Letters between Lord Glenelg and James Stephen, 1835–36.
    Add 7888/II/78–89, Letters from Lord Stanley to James Stephen, 1833–47.
    Add 7888/II/104–115a, Miscellaneous letters to and from James Stephen, 1833–56.
    Add 7888/II/118–120, Transcripts of letters of James Stephen to and from various correspondents.
    Add 7888/II/122, Transcripts of, or extracts from, letters of James Stephen to his wife, 1816–45.

Cape Archives, Cape Town

A47, Smith–Godlonton Correspondence.
A50/4, Bundle of letters by Philip, Read, Stretch and Stockenström 1830–46.
A519/1–9, D'Urban Papers, Letters received 1823–47.
A519/18–22, D'Urban Papers, Letters despatched: general 1828–46.

A1415/77, Napier correspondence, and Hare–Napier correspondence.

A1480, John Philip to Thomas Buxton, 1 May 1835.

AY/1/8/24, D'Urban Papers, Letters from the [Cape] Colonial Office received during 1835.

GH/1/107–108, Government House: General Despatches November 1835–February 1836.

LG/9, Commissioner General: Papers re Claim of Natives Eno and Pato concerning Treaties 1835.

Cory Library, Rhodes University, Grahamstown

MS 481–735, Harry Smith Papers.

MS 951, War Journal of Thomas Holden Bowker in 1834.

MS 2712; 8074–77; 8168; 8182–3; 8508–10, John Ross Papers.

MS 3092, Glasgow Missionary Society minutes, 1835.

MS 6768–6809, D'Urban collection.

MS 7131, Thomas Stubbs Journal.

MS 14316, James Collett Papers.

MS 15543, Ayliff's Narrative of Fingo History.

MS 16579, Journal of the Reverend James Laing (including a partial transcript in preparation by Ms Sandy Rowoldt, Cory Librarian).

Durham University Library

Papers, journals and correspondence of Henry George Grey, 3rd Earl Grey:
GRE/B78–130, Correspondence with individuals.
GRE/B135–136, Administration of Army.
GRE/B141, Canada.
GRE/B142, Cape of Good Hope.
GRE/B143, Colonial Office and Colonial Policy.
GRE/B144, Emigration.
GRE/B146, New South Wales.
GRE/B150A, Van Diemen's Land.
GRE/B150B, Transportation.
GRE/B152/1, Catalogue of Books.
GRE/V/C1, Howick's Private Letter Book, 1831–33.
GRE/V/C2–C3, Journals of Viscount Howick, 1827–39.
GRE/V/C7A, Distribution of business in the Colonial Office.
GRE/V/C11/1, Register of applications for employment with minutes of answers, 1834–40.

Liverpool Record Office

Papers of Edward Stanley, 14th Earl of Derby:
920 DER (14) 14/2, Miscellaneous papers relating to colonial business, 1827–34.
920 DER (14) 19/5, Miscellaneous Colonial Papers, 1834.
920 DER (14) 21, Papers relating to the Colonies, especially Canada, 1838–52.

920 DER (14) 23/6, Memorial of the Committee of the APS on behalf of the Aborigines of the British Colonies.
920 DER (14) 24/1, Memoranda on Africa.
920 DER (14) 24/2, Memoranda on Australia and NZ.
920 DER (14) 27/1–5, Cabinet Memoranda 1841–45.
920 DER (14) 100–102, Royal Correspondence.
920 DER (14) 115–142, Special Correspondence.
920 DER (14) 165/3, Drafts of Early Letters.
920 DER (14) 165/5, Stanley to Bishop of London October 1831.
920 DER (14) 167/2–176, Letter Books, 1831–44.

Mitchell Library, Sydney

363.06/1A1, Australian Patriotic Association Subscribers List, 1835.
A290–295, Papers of Sir Thomas Livingston Mitchell.
A357, Papers on Education, etc. c. 1804–68.
A1531/1–3, Edward Deas Thomson Papers.
A1733–1739, Bourke Papers.
A1819, Robert Wilmot Horton's private letters from Sir Francis Forbes, 1825–27.
A2025, Sir George Gipps Papers, 1840–46.
A2167, A2168, A2172, Papers of Sir George Arthur.
A2571, Letters of Colonel Henry Dumaresq 1825–38.
A2913–2915, Macarthur Family Papers: Letters of Sir Edward Macarthur, 1819–54.
A2922, Macarthur Papers.
A4300–4302, Macarthur Papers – W. S. McLeay: Letters from Fanny L. McLeay. 1812–36.
Ae7, Edward Eagar letters.
FM3/789, Letters of William Grant Broughton 1826–1829: Property of the Duke of Wellington (microfilm).
FM4/225–226, Papers of Bishop Broughton (microfilm).
MSS 2328/1, Richard Bourke Papers.
MSS 403/2–9, Bourke Family Correspondence.

National Archives, Public Record Office, Kew

Colonial Office:
   CO 13/15, South Australian Commissioners, Offices and Individuals, 1839.
   CO 48, Cape of Good Hope, original correspondence.
   CO 49, Cape of Good Hope, outgoing correspondence.
   CO 111/98, Memoranda on Constitution and Government.
   CO 201, New South Wales, original correspondence.
   CO 202, New South Wales, outgoing correspondence.
   CO 204/16, New South Wales Sessional Papers, 1844.
   CO 204/18, New South Wales Sessional Papers, 1845.
   CO 323/117–139, Applications for colonial appointments, 1819–30.
   CO 323/140, Applications for colonial appointment (Aberdeen), 1834–35.
   CO 323/144–175, Private letters to Mr Hay, 1825–35.

CO 323/192–230, Secretary of State, Offices and Individuals.
CO 324/74–75, Bathurst's private letters and minutes, 1823–27.
CO 324/76–93, Private letters from Mr Hay, 1825–36.
CO 324/94, Private and unofficial letters from Mr Hay, 1825–36.
CO 324/101, Private letters from Lord Goderich and Huskisson, 1827–28: North America.
CO 324/105–106, Circular despatches, 1826–41.
CO 324/133, Letters from the Chief Clerk, 1810–47.
CO 324/145–148, Letters from the Secretary of State, 1824–47.
CO 325/21–22, Registers of applications for colonial appointments, 1820–32.
CO 325/33, Private Papers: Cape of Good Hope, New South Wales, Mauritius, Sierra Leone, 1826–27.
CO 325/38, Ceylon, Mauritius, Australia, Cape of Good Hope, St. Helena, British Guiana, 1827–48.
CO 325/39, Precis.
CO 384/62, Emigration Original Correspondence, 1840.
CO 385/17–19, Emigration Entry Books, 1836–40.
CO 537/22, Colonial Office Establishment, Minutes, etc. 1832–72.
CO 537/89, Miscellaneous unregistered correspondence.
CO 537/145, Draft of Glenelg Despatch, 26 December 1835.
CO 714, Indexes of governors' correspondence.
CO 854/1–3, Colonial circulars, 1819–47.

Private papers:
PRO 30/22, Papers of Lord John Russell.
PRO 30/43, Lowry Cole Papers.

War Office:
WO 80/2–4, Sir George Murray Papers.

National Library of South Africa, Cape Town

MSB 16, Andrews Family Collection.
MSB 141, Sir Benjamin D'Urban: Papers relating to the Great Trek (copies made by G. M. Theal).
MSB 142, D'Urban–Smith Correspondence (copies made by G. M. Theal).
MSB 590, South African Land and Emigration Association Collection.

School of Oriental and African Studies, London

London Missionary Society Papers:
CWM, Home Office, 1827–36, Boxes 5–7.
CWM, South Africa: incoming letters, 1834–37, Boxes 14–15.

State Archives of New South Wales, Sydney

NSW 2/8017.1, Land held by civil officers, 1829.
NSW 2/8017.8, London Missionary Society re Reverend Threlkeld's Aboriginal Mission, c. 1827.

NSW 4/1285–1314, Despatches from the Secretary of State and Under-secretary of State, 1826–41.

NSW 4/1404–1405, Schedule of Despatches, 1826–42.

NSW 4/1675, Record of appointments of public officers in New South Wales, 1812–28.

NSW 4/7344, NSW Civil Establishment – Returns of the Governor 1831, 1838, 1840, 1842, 1846.

NSW 4/987, Governor's Memoranda, 1831.

NSW 5/1123, Memoranda, Lancelot Edward Threlkeld, Missionary to the Aborigines, New South Wales, 1838.

NSW 5/1161, Miscellaneous Correspondence relating to Aborigines (Burton's Papers).

NSW 5/3822.5, Papers re retirement of Thomas Cudbert Harington, 26 May 1841.

University of Cape Town, Manuscripts and Archives Collection

Correspondence of John Fairbairn.

Printed Primary Sources

Official publications

Select Committees and Royal Commissions:

PP 1828, vii (569), Report of the Select Committee on the Civil Government of Canada.

PP 1831, vii (276), and PP 1831–32, vii (547), Report of the Select Committee on Secondary Punishments.

PP 1833, xii (44 and 717), Report of the Select Committee on Public Documents.

PP 1835, vi (580), Report of the Select Committee on the Conduct of General Darling.

PP 1835, vi (499), Report of the Select Committee on Consular Establishments.

PP 1835, xviii (507), Report of the Select Committee on Sinecure Offices.

PP 1835, xviii (61), First Report of the Select Committee on Printed Papers.

PP 1835, xviii (392), Second Report of the Select Committee on Printed Papers.

PP 1836, vii (538) and PP 1837, vii (425), Report of the Select Committee on Aborigines (British Settlements).

PP 1836, xi (512), Report of the Select Committee on the Disposal of Waste Lands.

PP 1836, xvi (565), Report of the Select Committee on the Record Commission.

PP 1836, xxii (59), Royal Commission for inquiring into the System of Military Punishments in the Army.

PP 1837, vii (516), Report of the Select Committee on the Accounts of Colonial Receipt and Expenditure.

PP 1837, xxxiv (78), Royal Commission on Practicability and Expediency of consolidating Departments concerned with the Civil Administration of the Army.

PP 1837, xix (518) and PP 1837–8, xxii (669), Reports of the Select Committee on Transportation.

PP 1845, viii (520), Report from the Select Committee on Colonial Accounts.

Accounts and papers:

PP 1817, xvii (129), An Account of All Offices, Civil and Military, held under the Crown, either in possession or reversion, in the Colonies and other Foreign Settlements.

PP 1826–27, xxi (444), Communications between Colonial Department and Sir Rufane Donkin.

PP 1826–27, xxi (454), Correspondence between Lord Charles Somerset and the Colonial Department.

PP 1823, xiv (167); *PP 1824*, xvi (440); *PP 1825*, xix (365); *PP 1826*, xxii (388); *PP 1826–7*, xviii (187); *PP 1828*, xxi, (266); *PP 1829*, xxi (167); *PP 1830*, xxi (353); *PP 1830–1*, ix (235); *PP 1831–2*, xxxii (164); *PP 1833*, xxvi (140); *PP 1834*, xliv (151); *PP 1835*, xxxvii (212), Persons Holding Offices in Colonies absent in Execution of their Duties.

PP 1830, xxix (586), Papers explanatory of Charges against Lieutenant-General Darling as Governor of New South Wales by W. C. Wentworth.

PP 1831, xix (328), Royal Instructions to Governors of New South Wales, Van Diemen's Land, and Western Australia for disposing of Crown Lands.

PP 1831, lxiv (589), Papers Explanatory of the Functions of the Crown Agents for the Colonies.

PP 1831–2, xxxii (724), Reports from Commissioners for Emigration to the Colonial Department.

PP 1833, xxiii (215), Return of Sinecure Offices performed by Deputy, held in Reversion or at Will of Crown, in Great Britain and the Colonies.

PP 1833, xxvi (141), Correspondence with Governors of British Colonies in North America and Australia relating to Emigration.

PP 1833, xxvi (434), Accounts of Offices abolished or Salaries reduced in colonies, 1830–33.

PP 1834, xliv (616), Correspondence with Colonial Governors on Emigration and Disposal of Waste Lands.

PP 1834, xliv (617), Papers Relating to the Aboriginal Tribes of North America, New South Wales, Van Diemen's Land, and British Guiana.

PP 1835, xxxix (50), Papers relating to the Aboriginal Inhabitants of the Cape of Good Hope.

PP 1835, xxxix (252), Papers relating to the Condition of Native Inhabitants of southern Africa.

PP 1835, xxxix (87), Correspondence with Governors of Colonies on Emigration; Numbers of Emigrants to British Colonies.

PP 1836, xxxix (279), Papers Relative to Caffre War and Death of Hintza.

PP 1836, xl (76), Correspondence on Emigration between the Secretary of State and Governors of British Colonies.

PP 1837, xliii (503), Further Papers received from the Governor of the Cape of Good Hope relative to the late Caffre war, 1836–37.

PP 1840, xxxiii (35), Instructions addressed by Lord John Russell to the Land and Emigration Commissioners.

PP 1840, xxxiii (113), Report from Agent-General for Emigration; Correspondence between Secretary of State for Colonies and Governors of Australian colonies; General return of Emigration, 1839.

PP 1840, xxxiii (211), Letter to the Secretary of State for the Colonial Department, transmitting Petition from Certain Inhabitants of New South Wales.

PP 1842, xxxi (231), Return of Number of Emigrants from the United Kingdom, 1841; Return of Quantity of Crown Land sold in Colonies of Great Britain.

PP 1842, xxxi (301), Correspondence relating to Emigration between Colonial Office and Authorities in Colonies, on consequences of Emigration.

PP 1842, xxv (567); *PP 1843*, xxix (621), Annual Report of the Commissioners for Crown Land and Emigration.

PP 1843, xxxiv (90), Returns of Emigration during the year 1842.

PP 1849, xxxiv (3), Return of Governors and Lieutenant-Governors of Colonies.

Parliamentary Debates:

Hansard's Parliamentary Debates, *First Series, New Series, Third Series, 1816–1845*.

Articles, books, collections of letters, diaries and pamphlets

Alumni Oxoniensis: the members of the University of Oxford 1715–1886 their parentage, birth place and year of birth with a record of their degrees: being the Matriculation Register of the University, arranged Joseph Foster (4 vols, Oxford and London, 1887–88).

Anon., *Observations on the advantages of emigration to New South Wales for the information of the labouring classes in the United Kingdom* (London, 1836).

Anon., *Twenty years experience in Australia; being the evidence of residents and travellers in those colonies, as to their present state and future prospects; the whole demonstrating the advantages of emigration to New South Wales* (London, 1839).

Arnold, Thomas, *The effects of distant colonization on the parent state* (Oxford, 1815).

Arrowsmith, Aaron, *The world on a globular projection* (London, 1825).

Arrowsmith, John, *The London atlas of universal geography* (London, 1835).

Arthur, Sir George, *The Arthur papers: being the Canadian papers mainly confidential, private and demi-official of Sir George Arthur, KCH, last lieutenant-governor of Upper Canada*, ed. Charles R. Sanderson (3 vols, Toronto, 1957).

Balfour, Edward, 'Statistical data for forming troops and maintaining them in health in different climates and localities', *Journal of the Statistical Society of London*, 8 (1845), 193–209.

Bannister, Saxe, *Humane policy* (London, 1830).

—— *British colonization and coloured tribes* (London, 1838)

—— 'An account of the changes and present condition of the population of New Zealand', *Journal of the Statistical Society of London*, 1 (1838), 362–76.

Beecham, John, *Remarks upon the latest official documents relating to New Zealand* (London, 1838).

Bell, K. N. and W. P. Morrell, *Select documents on British colonial policy, 1830–1860* (Oxford, 1928).

Bentinck, Lord William Cavendish, *The correspondence of Lord William Cavendish Bentinck, governor-general of India 1828–1835*, ed. C. H. Philips (2 vols, Oxford, 1977).

Beverley, R. M., *The wrongs of the Caffre nation; a narrative by Justus with an appendix containing Lord Glenelg's despatches to the governor of the Cape of Good Hope* (London, 1837).

Bland, William, *Letters to Charles Buller, Junior, Esq., MP, from the Australian Patriotic Association* (Sydney, 1849).

Boyce, William B., *Notes on South African affairs, from 1834 to 1838 with reference to the civil, political and religious condition of the colonists and aborigines* (Graham's Town, 1838).

British Association for the Advancement of Science, 'Eighth meeting of the British Association for the Advancement of Science, August 1838', *Journal of the Statistical Society of London*, 1 (1838), 321–4.

British Immigrants of 1820, *Some reasons for our opposing the author of 'The South African Researches', the Rev. John Philip, DD* (Cape Town, Graham's Town and London, 1836).

Brown, William, *New Zealand and its aborigines: being an account of the aborigines, trade, and resources of the colony; and the advantages it now presents as a field for emigration and the investment of capital* (London, 1845).

Buller, Charles, *Responsible government for colonies* (London, 1840).

Busby, James, *Authentic information relative to New South Wales and New Zealand* (London, 1832).

Butler, Samuel, *The emigrant's hand-book of facts, concerning Canada, New Zealand, Australia, Cape of Good Hope, &c.* (Glasgow, 1843).

Buxton, Thomas Fowell, *The remedy; being a sequel to the African Slave Trade* (London, 1840).

—— *Memoirs of Sir Thomas Fowell Buxton Bart with selections from his correspondence*, ed. Charles Buxton (London, 1848).

Capper, John, 'Outline of the commercial statistics of Ceylon', *Journal of the Statistical Society of London*, 2 (1839–40), 424–34.

Chisholme, David, *Observations on the rights of the British colonies to representation in the Imperial parliament* (Three Rivers, 1832).

Coates, Dandeson, John Beecham and William Ellis, *Christianity, the means of civilization shown in evidence given before a committee of the House of Commons on Aborigines* (London, 1837).

Colonial Office, *Rules and regulations for the information and guidance of the principal officers and others in His Majesty's colonial possessions* (London, 1837).

—— *Rules and regulations for Her Majesty's colonial service* (London, 2nd edn, 1843).

Cooley, W. D., 'Cape of Good Hope – the late Caffre War', *Edinburgh Review*, 62 (1836), 455–70.

Crawford, John, *Employment for the million; or emigration and colonization . . . the remedy for national distress* (London, 1842).

Darwin, Charles, *The correspondence of Charles Darwin*, ed. Frederick Burkhardt and Sydney Smith (8 vols, Cambridge, 1985–93).

Dickens, Charles, 'Full report of the first meeting of the Mudfog Association for the Advancement of Everything', *Bentley's Miscellany*, 2 (1837), 397–413.

—— 'Full report of the second meeting of the Mudfog Association for the Advancement of Everything', *Bentley's Miscellany*, 4 (1838), 209–227.

Dictionary of national biography (London, 1885).

Documents relating to the Kaffir war of 1835, ed. George McCall Theal (London, 1912).

Dower, John, *A new general atlas of the world* (London, 1831 and later editions).

D'Urban, Benjamin, *The Peninsular journal of Major-General Sir Benjamin D'Urban, 1808–17*, ed. I. J. Rousseau (London, 1930).

Durham, first Earl, *Lord Durham's Report on the affairs of British North America*, ed. Charles Lucas (3 vols, Oxford, 1912).

Ellis, William, *Polynesian researches, during a residence of nearly six years in the South Sea islands* (2 vols, London, 1829).

Encyclopaedia Britannica, 3rd edn (Edinburgh, 1797); 6th edn (Edinburgh, 1823)

'Fourth Annual Report of the Council of the Statistical Society of London', *Journal of the Statistical Society of London*, 1 (1838), 5–13.

Franklin, Lady Jane, *The journal of Lady Jane Franklin at the Cape of Good Hope, November 1836, keeping up the character*, ed. Brian and Nancy Warner (Cape Town, 1985).

Franklin, Sir John and Lady Jane, *Some Private correspondence of Sir John and Lady Jane Franklin (Tasmania, 1837–1845)*, ed. George Mackaness (2 vols, Sydney, 1947).

Gipps, George, *Gipps–La Trobe correspondence 1839–1846*, ed. A. G. L. Shaw (Melbourne, 1989).

Gladstone, W. E., *The Gladstone diaries*, ed. M. R. D. Foot and H. C. G. Matthew (14 vols, Oxford, 1968–94).

Godlonton, Robert, *A narrative of the irruption of the Kafir hordes into the Eastern Province of the Cape of Good Hope 1834–35 compiled from official documents and other authentic sources* (Graham's Town, 1836).

Grey, Earl, *The colonial policy of Lord John Russell's administration* (London, 1853).

Historical Records of Australia, Series I, Governors' despatches to and from England, ed. Frederick Watson (26 vols, Sydney, 1914–25).

Historical Records of Australia, Series IV, Legal papers, ed. Frederick Watson (1 vol., Sydney, 1922).

Historical Records of New Zealand, ed. Robert McNab (2 vols, Wellington, 1908–14).

'Imperial Federation map of the world showing the extent of the British Empire in 1886', *Graphic*, 24 July 1886.

Kay, Stephen, *A succinct statement of the Kaffer's case . . . in a letter to T. Fowell Buxton, Esq., MP, Chairman of the Aborigines Committee* (London, 1837).

Kitchingman, James, *The Kitchingman papers: missionary letters and journals, 1817 to 1848 from the Brenthurst Collection Johannesburg*, ed. Basil Le Cordeur and Christopher Saunders (Johannesburg, 1976).

Lang, John Dunmore, *Emigration; considered chiefly in reference to . . . New South Wales* (Sydney, 1833).

——*An historical and statistical account of New South Wales* (2 vols, London, 1834).

—— *Transportation and colonization; or, the causes of the comparative failure of the transportation system in the Australian colonies* (London, 1837).

Lewis, George Cornewall, *An essay on the government of dependencies* (London, 1841).

Macarthur, Edward, *Colonial policy of 1840 and 1841 as illustrated by the governor's despatches, and proceedings of the Legislative Council of New South Wales* (London, 1841).

Macarthur, James, *New South Wales: its present state and future prospects* (London, 1837).

Madden, Frederick and David Fieldhouse (eds), *Imperial reconstruction, 1763–1840:*

the evolution of alternative systems of colonial government, select documents on the constitutional history of the British Empire and Commonwealth, vol. 3 (Westport, Connecticut, 1987).

Martin, R. M., *History of the British colonies* (5 vols, London, 1834–35).

—— *Colonial policy of the British Empire* (London, 1837).

—— *Statistics of the colonies of the British Empire* (London, 1839).

—— *History of the colonies of the British Empire* (London, 1843).

McCulloch, J. R., 'The state and defects of British statistics', *Edinburgh Review*, 61 (1835), 154–81.

Merivale, Herman, *Introduction to a course of lectures on colonization and colonies begun in March 1839* (London, 1839).

—— 'Moral and intellectual statistics of France', *Edinburgh Review*, 69 (1839), 49–74.

—— *Lectures on colonization and colonies delivered before the University of Oxford in 1839, 1840, and 1841* (2 vols, London, 1841 and 1842).

Mill, James, *The History of British India* (3 vols, London, 1817).

Mill, John Stuart, 'Considerations on representative government', in John Gray (ed.), *On liberty and other essays* (Oxford, 1991), pp. 205–467.

Molesworth, Sir William, *Sir William Molesworth's speech . . . on the state of the colonies* (London, 1838).

—— *Selected speeches of the Right Hon. Sir William Molesworth on questions relating to Colonial Policy*, ed. H. E. Egerton (London, 1903).

Montagu, Basil, *Essays and selections* (London, 1837).

Moodie, Donald, *The record; or, a series of official papers relative to the condition and treatment of the native tribes of South Africa* (Cape Town, 1838–41).

Mudie, James, *The felonry of New South Wales* (London, 1837).

Philip, John, *Researches in South Africa, illustrating the . . . condition of the native tribes* (2 vols, London, 1828).

Philipps, Thomas, *Philipps, 1820 settler: his letters*, ed. Arthur Keppel-Jones (Pietermaritzburg, 1960).

Portlock, J. E., 'An address explanatory of the objects and advantages of statistical enquiries', *Journal of the Statistical Society of London*, 1 (1838), 316–17.

Powell, John, *Statistical illustrations of the territorial extent and population . . . of the British Empire* (London, 1825).

Pringle, Thomas, *Narrative of a residence in South Africa* (London, 1835).

Records of the Cape Colony: from February 1793 to April 1831, ed. George McCall Theal (36 vols, London, 1897–1905).

Roebuck, J. A., *The colonies of England: a plan for the government of some portion of our colonial possessions* (London, 1849).

Russell, Lord John, *Early correspondence of Lord John Russell, 1805–1840*, ed. Rollo Russell (2 vols, London, 1913).

—— *The later correspondence of Lord John Russell, 1840–1878*, ed. G. P. Gooch (2 vols, London, 1925).

Shrewsbury, William J., *The journal and selected letters of Rev. William J. Shrewsbury 1826–1835: first missionary to the Transkei*, ed. Hildegarde H. Fast (Johannesburg, 1994).

South African directory and almanac for 1834 (Cape Town, 1834).

Spedding, James, 'New theory of colonization', *Edinburgh Review*, 71 (1840), 517–44.

—— 'The expedition to the Niger – civilization of Africa', *Edinburgh Review*, 72 (1841), 456–77.

Stephen, James, *The Right Honourable Sir James Stephen; letters with biographical notes*, ed. Caroline Emelia Stephen (Gloucester, 1906).

Stretch, Charles Lennox, *The journal of Charles Lennox Stretch*, ed. Basil A. le Cordeur (Grahamstown, 1988).

Sydenham, Lord, *Letters from Lord Sydenham governor-general of Canada, 1839–1841, to Lord John Russell*, ed. Paul Knaplund (London, 1931).

Taylor, Henry, *The statesman: an ironical treatise on the art of succeeding*, 1st edn 1832 (Cambridge, 1927).

—— *Autobiography of Henry Taylor*, (2 vols, London, 1885).

—— *Correspondence of Henry Taylor*, ed. Edward Drowden (London, 1888).

Therry, R., *Reminiscences of thirty years residence in New South Wales and Victoria* (London, 2nd edn, 1863).

Thring, Henry, *The supremacy of Great Britain not inconsistent with self-government for the colonies* (London, 1851).

Tulloch, A. M., 'On the sickness and mortality among the troops in the West Indies', *Journal of the Statistical Society of London*, 1 (1838), 129–42.

Ullathorne, William, *The Catholic mission in Australasia* (Liverpool, 1837).

—— *The horrors of transportation briefly unfolded to the people* (Dublin, 1838).

Wakefield, E. G., *A letter from Sydney* (London, 1829).

—— *England and America: a comparison of the social and political state of both nations* (London, 1833).

—— *A view of the art of colonization, with present reference to the British Empire* (London, 1849).

Ward, H. G., *The debate upon Mr Ward's resolutions on colonization in the House of Commons, June 27, 1839* (London, 1839).

Wentworth, W. C., *A statistical, historical, and political description of the colony of New South Wales, and its dependent settlements in Van Diemen's Land* (London, 1819).

Whateley, Richard, *Thoughts on secondary punishments* (London, 1832).

—— *Remarks on transportation and on a recent defence of the system* (London, 1834).

Wilmot Horton, Robert, *Exposition and defence of Earl Bathurst's administration of the affairs of Canada* (London, 1838).

Periodicals and Newspapers

Australian (1834–38).

The Christian Observer, 29–40 (1829–40).

The Colonial Intelligencer, or Aborigines' Friend (1840–45).

Graham's Town Journal (Dec. 1834–June 1836).

Edinburgh Review, 50–76 (1830–45).

Journal of the Statistical Society of London, 1–5 (1838–45).

South African Commercial Advertiser (Dec. 1834–June 1836).

BIBLIOGRAPHY

SECONDARY SOURCES

Articles and books

Altholz, Josef L., *The religious press in Britain, 1760–1900* (New York and London, 1989).

Altick, Richard D., *Victorian people and ideas* (London, 1974).

Arndt, E. H. D., *Banking and currency development in South Africa (1652–1927)* (Cape Town and Johannesburg, 1928).

Armitage, David and Michael J. Braddick (eds), *The British Atlantic world, 1500–1800* (Basingstoke, 2002).

Atkinson, Alan, *The muddle-headed republic* (Melbourne, 1983).

Ballantyne, Tony, *Orientalism and race: Aryanism in the British Empire* (Basingstoke, 2002).

Bayly, C. A., *Imperial meridian: the British Empire and the world, 1780–1830* (London, 1989).

—— *Empire and information: intelligence gathering and social communication in India, 1780–1870* (Cambridge, 1996).

Beaglehole, J. C., 'The Colonial Office, 1782–1854', *Historical Studies*, 1 (1941), 170–89.

Black, Jeremy, *Maps and history: constructing images of the past* (New Haven and London, 1997).

Blakeley, Brian L., *The Colonial Office: 1868–1892* (Durham, N.C., 1972).

Bourne, J. M., *Patronage and society in nineteenth-century England* (London, 1986).

Bowen, H. V., Margarette Lincoln and Nigel Rigby (eds), *The worlds of the East India Company* (Woodbridge, 2002).

Bradley, Ian, *The call to seriousness: the Evangelical impact on the Victorians* (London, 1976).

Brent, Richard, *Liberal Anglican politics: Whiggery, religion, and reform 1830–1841* (Oxford, 1987).

Bridge, Carl and Kent Fedorowich (eds), *The British world: diaspora, culture and identity* (London, 2003).

Brode, Patrick, *Sir John Beverley Robinson: bone and sinew of the Compact* (Toronto, 1984).

Brown, Lucy, *The Board of Trade and the free trade movement* (Oxford, 1958).

Browne, Janet, *The secular ark: studies in the history of biogeography* (New Haven and London, 1983).

Burnett, D. Graham, *Masters of all they surveyed: exploration, geography, and a British El Dorado* (Chicago and London, 2000).

Burroughs, Peter, *Britain and Australia 1831–1855: a study in imperial relations and crown lands administration* (Oxford, 1967).

—— 'The Ordnance department and colonial defense, 1821–1855', *Journal of Imperial and Commonwealth History*, 10:2 (1982), 125–49.

—— 'An unreformed army? 1815–1868', in David Chandler and Ian Beckett (eds), *The Oxford History of the British Army* (Oxford, 1996), pp. 161–86.

—— 'Imperial institutions and the government of empire', in Andrew Porter (ed.),

The Oxford history of the British Empire: vol. 3, the nineteenth century (Oxford, 1999), pp. 170–97.

Burton, Antoinette, 'Who needs the nation? Interrogating "British" history', in Catherine Hall (ed.), *Cultures of empire: a reader: colonizers in Britain and the empire in the nineteenth and twentieth centuries* (Manchester, 2000), pp. 137–53.

Butlin, S. J., *Foundations of the Australian monetary system 1788–1851* (Melbourne, 1953).

Cambridge history of the British Empire (8 vols, Cambridge, 1929–59).

Canny, Nicholas, *The Oxford history of the British Empire: vol. 1, the origins of empire* (Oxford, 1998).

Cantwell, John D., *The Public Record Office 1838–1958* (London, 1991).

Carrington, C. E., *The British overseas: exploits of a nation of shopkeepers* (Cambridge, 1950).

Carroll-Burke, Patrick, *Colonial discipline: the making of the Irish convict system* (Dublin, 1999).

Cell, John W., 'The Colonial Office in the 1850s', *Historical Studies Australia and New Zealand*, 12 (1965), 43–56.

—— *British colonial administration in the mid-nineteenth century: the policy-making process* (New Haven and London, 1970).

Chester, Sir Norman, *The English administrative system 1780–1870* (Oxford, 1981).

Cohn, Bernard S., *Colonialism and its forms of knowledge: the British in India* (Princeton, N. J., 1996).

Colley, Linda, *Britons: forging the nation 1707–1837* (New Haven and London, 1992).

—— 'What is imperial history now?', in David Cannadine (ed.), *What is history now?* (London, 2002), pp. 132–47.

Collini, Stefan, Richard Whatmore and Brian Young, *History, religion and culture: British intellectual history 1750–1950* (Cambridge, 2000).

Cooper, Frederick and Ann Laura Stoler (eds), *Tensions of empire: colonial cultures in a bourgeois world* (Berkeley, 1997).

Coupland, Reginald, *The British Empire: an outline sketch of its growth and character* (London, 1933).

Crais, Clifton C., *The making of the colonial order: white supremacy and black resistance in the Eastern Cape, 1770–1865* (Johannesburg, 1992).

Cullen, Michael J., *The statistical movement in early Victorian Britain: the foundations of empirical social research* (New York, 1975).

Cumpston, J. H. L., *Thomas Mitchell: surveyor general and explorer* (London, 1954).

Currey, C. H., *Sir Francis Forbes: the first Chief Justice of the Supreme Court of New South Wales* (Sydney, 1968).

Darwin, John, 'Imperialism and the Victorians: the dynamics of territorial expansion', *English Historical Review*, 112 (1997), 614–42.

Davidoff, Leonore, *The best circles: society etiquette and the Season* (London, 1986).

Davidoff, Leonore and Catherine Hall, *Family fortunes: men and women of the English middle class 1780–1850* (London, 1987).

De Gruchy, John (ed.), *The London Missionary Society in southern Africa: historical essays in celebration of the bicentenary of the LMS in Southern Africa, 1799–1999* (Cape Town, 1999).

Desmond, Adrian, *Huxley: the Devil's disciple* (London, 1994).

Desmond, Ray, *Kew: the history of the Royal Botanic Gardens* (London, 1995).

Dewey, Clive, *The passing of Barchester* (London, 1991).

Dictionary of South African biography (5 vols, Cape Town, Durban and Johannesburg, 1968–87).

Dracopoli, J. L., *Sir Andries Stockenström 1792–1864: the origins of the racial conflict in South Africa* (Cape Town, 1969).

Drayton, Richard, *Nature's government: science, imperial Britain and the 'improvement' of the world* (New Haven and London, 2000).

Duly, Leslie C., *British land policy at the Cape 1795–1844: a study of administrative procedures in the empire* (Durham, N. C., 1968).

Dunkley, Peter, 'Emigration and the state, 1803–1842: the nineteenth-century revolution in government reconsidered', *Historical Journal*, 23 (1980), 353–80.

Eastwood, David, ' "Amplifying the province of the legislature": the flow of information and the English state in the early nineteenth century', *Historical Research*, 62 (1989), 276–94.

—— 'Men, morals and the machinery of social legislation 1790–1840', *Parliamentary History*, 13 (1994), 190–205.

—— 'The age of uncertainty: Britain in the early-nineteenth century', *Transactions of the Royal Historical Society*, 8 (1998), 91–115.

Eddy, J. J., *Britain and the Australian colonies 1818–1831: the technique of government* (Oxford, 1969).

Edney, Matthew, *Mapping an empire: the geographical construction of British India, 1765–1843* (Chicago and London, 1997).

Elbourne, Elizabeth, *Blood ground: colonialism, missions and the contest for Christianity in the Cape Colony and Britain, 1799–1853* (Montreal and London, 2002).

Ellis, Malcolm Henry, *John Macarthur* (Sydney, 1955).

Finer, S. E., 'Patronage and the public service: Jeffersonian bureaucracy and the British tradition', *Public Administration*, 30 (1952), 329–60.

—— 'The transmission of Benthamite ideas, 1820–1850', in Gillian Sutherland (ed.) *Studies in the growth of nineteenth-century government* (London, 1972), pp. 11–32.

Fitzpatrick, Kathleen, *Sir John Franklin in Tasmania 1837–1843* (Melbourne, 1949).

Fletcher, Brian, *Ralph Darling: a governor maligned* (Melbourne, 1984).

Flint, John E. and Glyndwr Williams, *Perspectives of empire: essays presented to Gerald S. Graham* (London, 1973).

Foster, S. G., 'A piece of sharp practice? Governor Bourke and the office of colonial secretary in New South Wales', *Historical Studies (Australia)*, 16 (1975), 402–24.

—— *Colonial improver: Edward Deas Thomson 1800–1879* (Melbourne, 1978).

Foucault, Michel, *Discipline and punish: the birth of the prison*, trans. Alan Sheridan (London, 1977).

—— *The order of things: an archaeology of the human sciences* (London, 2001).

Francis, Mark, *Governors and settlers: images of authority in the British colonies, 1820–60* (London, 1992).

Fry, Geoffrey K., *Statesmen in disguise: the changing role of the administrative class of the British home civil service 1853–1966* (London, 1969).

—— *The growth of government: the development of ideas about the role of the state and the machinery and functions of government in Britain since 1780* (London, 1979).

Fryer, Alan Kenneth, *The government of the Cape of Good Hope, 1825–54: the age of imperial reform* (Pretoria, 1964).

Galbraith, John S., *Reluctant empire: British policy on the South African frontier 1834–1854* (Berkeley and Los Angeles, 1963).

Gallagher, John and Ronald Robinson, 'The imperialism of free trade', *Economic History Review*, new series, 6 (1953), 1–15.

Gash, N., 'After Waterloo: British society and the legacy of the Napoleonic Wars', *Transactions of the Royal Historical Society*, 28 (1978), 145–57.

George, Marian, *John Bardwell Ebden: his business and political career at the Cape 1806–1849* (Pretoria, 1986).

Goldring, Philip, 'Province and nation: problems of imperial rule in Lower Canada 1820 to 1841', *Journal of Imperial and Commonwealth History*, 9:1 (1980), 38–56.

Gould, Eliga H., *The persistence of empire: British political culture in the age of the American Revolution* (Chapel Hill, N.C., 2000).

Greer, Allan and Ian Radforth (eds), *Colonial leviathan: state formation in mid-nineteenth century Canada* (Toronto, 1992).

Hacking, Ian, 'How should we do the history of statistics?', in Graham Burchell *et al.* (eds), *The Foucault effect: studies in governmentality* (Hemel Hempstead, 1991), pp. 181–95.

Hall, Catherine, *White, male and middle-class: explorations in feminism and history* (Cambridge, 1992).

—— *Civilising subjects: metropole and colony in the English imagination 1830–1867* (Cambridge, 2002).

—— (ed.), *Cultures of empire: a reader: colonizers in Britain and the empire in the nineteenth and twentieth centuries* (Manchester, 2000).

Hall, Henry L., *The Colonial Office: a history* (London, 1937).

Hamilton, C. I., 'John Wilson Croker: patronage and clientage at the Admiralty, 1809–1857', *Historical Journal*, 43 (2000), 49–77.

Hamilton, Douglas, 'Robert Melville and the frontiers of empire in the British West Indies, 1763–1771', in A. Mackillop and S. Murdoch (eds), *Military governors and imperial frontiers c. 1600–1800: a study of Scotland and empires* (Leiden, 2003), pp. 181–204.

Harington, A. L., *The Graham's Town Journal and the Great Trek* (Pretoria, 1973).

—— *Sir Harry Smith: bungling hero* (Cape Town, 1980).

Harling, Philip, *The waning of 'Old Corruption': the politics of economical reform, 1779–1846* (Oxford, 1996).

Harries-Jenkins, Gwyn, *The army in Victorian society* (London, 1977).

Hart, Jennifer, 'Nineteenth century social reform: a Tory interpretation of history', *Past and Present*, 31 (1965), 39–61.

Henige, David P., *Colonial governors from the fifteenth century to the present* (Madison, Wis., 1970).

Hilton, Boyd, *The age of atonement: the influence of evangelicalism on social and economic thought 1789–1865* (Oxford, 1988).

Hirst, John, *The strange birth of colonial democracy: New South Wales, 1848–1884* (Sydney, 1988).

—— *A republican manifesto* (Melbourne and Oxford, 1994).

Hitchens, Fred H., *The Colonial Land and Emigration Commission* (Philadelphia, 1931).

Hollis, Patricia (ed.), *Pressure from without in early Victorian England* (London, 1974).

Hunt, Keith S., *The development of municipal government in the Eastern Province of the Cape of Good Hope with special reference to Grahamstown 1827–1862* (Pretoria, 1961).

—— *Sir Lowry Cole, governor of Mauritius 1823–1828, governor of the Cape of Good Hope 1828–1833: a study in colonial administration* (Durban, 1974).

Hyam, Ronald and Ged Martin, *Reappraisals in British imperial history* (London, 1975).

Ignatieff, Michael, *A just measure of pain: the penitentiary system in the industrial revolution, 1750–1850* (London, 1978).

Immelman, R. F. M., *Men of Good Hope: the romantic story of the Cape Town Chamber of Commerce 1804–1954* (Cape Town, 1955).

Irving, T. H., 'The idea of responsible government in New South Wales before 1856', *Historical Studies Australia and New Zealand*, 11 (1964), 192–205.

Isichei, Elizabeth, *Victorian Quakers* (London, 1970).

Kammen, Michael G., *A rope of sand: the colonial agents, British politics, and the American Revolution* (Ithaca, N.Y., 1968).

Keegan, Timothy, *Colonial South Africa and the origins of the racial order* (Cape Town and Johannesburg, 1996).

Kercher, Bruce, *An unruly child: a history of law in Australia* (St Leonards, 1995).

King, F. H. H., *Survey our empire! Robert Montgomery Martin (1801?–1868) . . . a bio-bibliography* (Hong Kong, 1979).

King, Hazel, 'Richard Bourke and his two colonial administrations: a comparative study of Cape Colony and New South Wales', *Royal Australian Historical Society: Journal and Proceedings*, 49 (1964), 360–75.

—— *Richard Bourke* (Oxford, 1971).

—— 'Pulling strings at the Colonial Office', *Journal of the Royal Australian Historical Society*, 61 (1975), 145–62.

—— 'Man in a trap: Alexander Macleay, colonial secretary of New South Wales', *Journal of the Royal Australian Historical Society*, 68 (1982), 37–48.

—— 'John Macarthur junior and the formation of the Australian Agricultural Company', *Journal of the Royal Australian Historical Society*, 71 (1985), 177–88.

—— *Colonial expatriates: Edward and John Macarthur junior* (Kenthurst, 1989).

Knaplund, Paul, *James Stephen and the British colonial system 1813–1847* (Madison, 1953).

Knox, Bruce, 'Democracy, aristocracy and empire: the provision of colonial honours 1818–1870', *Australian Historical Studies*, 25 (1992), 244–64.

Kociumbas, Jan, *The Oxford history of Australia: vol. 2, Possessions 1770–1860* (Melbourne and Oxford, 1992).

Laidlaw, Zoë, 'Integrating metropolitan, colonial and imperial histories – the Aborigines Select Committee of 1835–7', in T. Banivanua Mar and J. Evans (eds) *Writing colonial histories: comparative perspectives* (Melbourne, 2002), 75–91.

[226]

—— ' "Aunt Anna's report": the Buxton women and the Aborigines Select Committee of 1835–37', *Journal of Imperial and Commonwealth History*, 32:2 (2004), 1–28.

Le Cordeur, B. A., *Robert Godlonton as architect of frontier opinion, 1850–57* (Cape Town and Pretoria, 1959).

—— *The politics of Eastern Cape separatism 1820–1854* (Cape Town, 1981).

Lehmann, Joseph H., *Remember you are an Englishman: a biography of Sir Harry Smith 1787–1860* (London, 1977).

Lester, Alan, *Imperial networks: creating identities in nineteenth-century South Africa and Britain* (London, 2001).

—— 'British settler discourse and the circuits of empire', *History Workshop Journal*, 54 (2002), 24–48.

—— 'Humanitarians and white settlers in the nineteenth century', in N. Etherington (ed.), *Missions and empire* (Oxford University Press, 2005).

Levine, Philippa, *The amateur and the professional: antiquarians, historians and archaeologists in Victorian England, 1838–1886* (Cambridge, 1986).

Lovett, Richard, *The history of the London Missionary Society 1795–1895* (London, 1899).

MacDonagh, Oliver, *A pattern of government growth 1800–60: the passenger acts and their enforcement* (London, 1961).

—— *Early Victorian government 1830–1870* (London, 1977).

Macintyre, Stuart, *A concise history of Australia* (Cambridge, 1999).

—— 'Australia and the empire', in Robin W. Winks (ed.), *The Oxford history of the British Empire: vol. 5, historiography* (Oxford, 1999), pp. 163–82.

Mackillop, Andrew, 'Fashioning a British Empire: Sir Archibald Campbell of Inverneil and Madras, 1785–9', in A. Mackillop and S. Murdoch (eds), *Military governors and imperial frontiers c. 1600–1800: a study of Scotland and empires* (Leiden, 2003), pp. 205–231.

Macmillan, W. M., *Bantu, Boer, and Briton: the making of the South African native problem* (Oxford, revised edn, 1963).

Mandler, Peter, *Aristocratic government in the age of reform: Whigs and Liberals 1830–1852* (Oxford, 1990).

Manning, H. T., 'Who ran the British Empire 1830–1850?', *Journal of British Studies*, 5 (1965), 88–121.

Marshall, P. J., 'Empire and authority in the later eighteenth century', *Journal of Imperial and Commonwealth History*, 15:2 (1987), 105–22.

—— 'Britain without America – a second empire?' in *OHBE*, ii, pp. 576–95.

—— (ed.) *The Oxford history of the British Empire: vol. 2, the eighteenth century* (Oxford, 1998).

Marshall, P. J. and Glyndwr Williams, *The great map of mankind: British perceptions of the world in the age of enlightenment* (London, 1982).

Martin, Ged, *The Durham Report and British policy: a critical essay* (Cambridge, 1972).

—— *Britain and the origins of Canadian confederation 1837–67* (Basingstoke, 1995).

McKenzie, Kirsten, *Scandal in the colonies: Sydney and Cape Town 1820–1850* (Melbourne, 2004).

McLachlan, N. D., 'Edward Eagar (1787–1866): a colonial spokesman in Sydney and London', *Historical Studies Australia and New Zealand*, 10 (1963), 431–56.

—— 'Bathurst at the Colonial Office, 1812–27: a reconnaissance', *Historical Studies*, 13 (1969), 477–502.

McMartin, Arthur, *Public servants and patronage: the foundation and rise of the New South Wales public service, 1786–1859* (Sydney, 1983).

Melbourne, A. C. V., *Early constitutional development in Australia* (London, 1934).

Millar, Anthony Kendall, *Plantagenet in South Africa: Lord Charles Somerset* (Cape Town, 1965).

Moore, D. C., 'The other face of reform', *Victorian Studies*, 5 (1961), 7–34.

Morrell, Jack and Arnold Thackray, *Gentlemen of science: early years of the British Association for the Advancement of Science* (Oxford, 1981).

Morrell, W. P., *British colonial policy in the age of Peel and Russell* (Oxford, 1930).

—— *British colonial policy in the mid-Victorian age: South Africa, New Zealand, the West Indies* (Oxford, 1969).

Mostert, Noël, *Frontiers: the epic of South Africa's creation and the tragedy of the Xhosa people* (London, 1992).

Murchison, Barbara C., ' "Enlightened government": Sir George Arthur and the Upper Canadian administration', *Journal of Imperial and Commonwealth History*, 8:3 (1980), 161–80.

Murray, D. J., *The West Indies and the development of colonial government, 1801–1834* (Oxford, 1965).

Nash, M. D., *Bailie's party of 1820 settlers: a collective experience in emigration* (Cape Town, 1982).

Neal, David, *The rule of law in a penal colony: law and power in early New South Wales* (Cambridge, 1991).

Nell, Dawn, ' "For the public benefit": livestock statistics and expertise in the late nineteenth-century Cape Colony, 1850–1900', in Saul Dubow (ed.), *Science and society in southern Africa* (Manchester, 2000), pp. 100–15.

Newbould, Ian, *Whiggery and reform 1830–41* (London, 1990).

Newman, W. A., *Biographical memoir of John Montagu* (London and Cape Town, 1855).

Olson, Alison, *Making the empire work: London and American interest groups, 1690–1790* (Cambridge, Mass and London, 1992).

Oxford history of the British Empire (5 vols, Oxford, 1998–9).

Parris, Henry, *Constitutional bureaucracy: the development of British central administration since the eighteenth century* (London, 1969).

Peires, J. B., *The house of Phalo: a history of the Xhosa people in the days of their independence* (Berkeley, 1981).

—— 'The British and the Cape, 1814–1834', in Richard Elphick and Hermann Giliomee (eds), *The shaping of South African society, 1652–1840* (Cape Town and Johannesburg, 1989), pp. 472–518.

Poovey, Mary, 'Figures of arithmetic, figures of speech: the discourse of statistics in the 1830s', *Critical Inquiry*, 19 (1993), 256–76.

—— *Making a social body: British cultural formation, 1830–1864* (Chicago and London, 1995).

—— *A history of the modern fact: problems of knowledge in the sciences of wealth and society* (Chicago and London, 1998).

Porter, Andrew, 'Religion and empire: British expansion in the long nineteenth century, 1780–1914', *Journal of Imperial and Commonwealth History*, 20 (1992), 370–90.

—— 'Trusteeship, anti-Slavery and humanitarianism', in *OHBE*, iii, pp. 198–221.

—— (ed.), *The Oxford history of the British Empire: vol. 3, the nineteenth century* (Oxford, 1999).

Porter, Theodore M., *The rise of statistical thinking, 1820–1900* (Princeton, 1986).

—— *Trust in numbers: the pursuit of objectivity in science and public life* (Princeton, 1995).

Pottinger, George, *Sir Henry Pottinger: first governor of Hong Kong* (Stroud, 1997).

Pretorius, J., *The British humanitarians and the Cape eastern frontier, 1834–1836* (Pretoria, 1988).

Pugh, R. B., 'The Colonial Office, 1801–1925', in E. A. Benians, J. Butler and C. E. Carrington (eds), *The Cambridge history of the British Empire, vol. 3: the Empire – Commonwealth 1870–1919* (Cambridge, 1959), pp. 711–68.

Reynolds, K. D., *Aristocratic women and political society in Victorian Britain* (Oxford, 1998).

Richards, Thomas, *The imperial archive: knowledge and the fantasy of empire* (London and New York, 1993).

Ritchie, John, 'Towards ending an unclean thing: the Molesworth Committee and the abolition of transportation to New South Wales, 1837–40', *Historical Studies (Australia)*, 17 (1976), 144–64.

—— *Lachlan Macquarie: a biography* (Melbourne, 1986).

—— *The Wentworths: father and son* (Melbourne, 1997).

Ritvo, Harriet, *The platypus and the mermaid, and other figments of the classifying imagination* (Cambridge, Mass. and London, 1997).

Robinson, Ronald and John Gallagher with Alice Denny, *Africa and the Victorians: the official mind of imperialism* (London, 1961).

Roe, Michael, *Quest for authority in eastern Australia 1835–1851* (Melbourne, 1965).

Ross, Andrew, *John Philip (1775–1851): missions, race and politics in South Africa* (Aberdeen, 1986).

Ross, Robert, *Beyond the pale: essays on the history of colonial South Africa* (Hanover, N.H. and London, 1993).

—— *Status and respectability in the Cape Colony 1750–1870: a tragedy of manners* (Cambridge, 1999).

Sales, Jane, *Mission stations and the coloured communities of the Eastern Cape 1800–1852* (Cape Town, 1975).

Schreuder, D. M., 'The cultural factor in Victorian imperialism: a case-study of the British "civilising mission" ', *Journal of Imperial and Commonwealth History*, 4 (1976), 283–317.

Scott, John, *Social network analysis: a handbook* (London, 2nd edn, 2000).

Shaw, A. G. L., *Heroes and villains: Governors Darling and Bourke in New South Wales* (Sydney, 1966).

—— *Convicts and the colonies: a study of penal transportation from Great Britain and Ireland to Australia and other parts of the British Empire* (London, 1966).

—— 'Orders from Downing Street', *Journal of the Royal Australian Historical Society*, 54 (1968), 113–34.

—— *Sir George Arthur, Bart. 1784–1854: superintendent of British Honduras, lieutenant governor of Van Diemen's Land and of Upper Canada, governor of the Bombay Presidency* (Melbourne, 1980).

—— 'British policy toward the Australian Aborigines, 1830–1850', *Australian Historical Review*, 25 (1992), 265–85.

—— 'James Stephen and colonial policy: the Australian experience', *Journal of Imperial and Commonwealth History*, 20 (1992), 11–34.

—— *A history of the Port Phillip District, Victoria before separation* (Melbourne, 1996).

Shaw, G. P., *Patriarch and patriot: William Grant Broughton 1788–1853: colonial statesman and ecclesiastic* (Melbourne, 1978).

Silberman, Bernard S., *Cages of reason: the rise of the rational state in France, Japan, the United States, and Great Britain* (Chicago and London, 1993).

Stanley, Brian, *The Bible and the flag: Protestant missions and British imperialism in the nineteenth and twentieth centuries* (Leicester, 1990).

—— *The history of the Baptist Missionary Society 1792–2000* (Edinburgh, 1992).

Stewart, Gordon T., *The origins of Canadian politics: a comparative approach* (Vancouver, 1986).

Stokes, Eric, *The English Utilitarians and India* (Oxford, 1959).

—— 'Macaulay: the Indian years, 1834–1838', *Review of English Literature*, 1:4 (1960), 41–50.

Stoler, Ann Laura, *Race and the education of desire: Foucault's* History of sexuality *and the colonial order of things* (Durham, N.C. and London, 1995).

Strachan, Hew, *Wellington's legacy: the reform of the British army 1830–54* (Manchester, 1984).

—— *The politics of the British army* (Oxford, 1997).

Sturgis, James, 'Anglicisation at the Cape of Good Hope in the early nineteenth century', *Journal of Imperial and Commonwealth History*, 11 (1982), 5–32.

Sutherland, Gillian (ed.), *Studies in the growth of nineteenth-century government* (London, 1972).

Swinfen, D. B., *Imperial control of colonial legislation 1813–1865: a study of British policy towards colonial legislative powers* (Oxford, 1970).

Taylor, Miles, 'Empire and parliamentary reform: the 1832 Reform Act revisited', in Arthur Burns and Joanna Innes (eds), *Rethinking the age of reform: Britain 1780–1850* (Cambridge, 2003), pp. 295–311.

Thomson, D. H., *A short history of Grahamstown* (Grahamstown, 1952).

Tufte, Edward R., *The visual display of quantitative information* (Cheshire, Conn., 2nd edn, 2001).

Vernon, James, 'Narrating the constitution: the discourse of "the real" and the fantasies of nineteenth-century constitutional history', in James Vernon (ed.), *Re-reading the constitution: new narratives in the political history of England's long nineteenth century* (Cambridge, 1996), pp. 204–29.

Vickery, Amanda, *The gentleman's daughter: women's lives in Georgian England* (New Haven and London, 1998).

Ward, John M., 'The colonial policy of Lord John Russell's administration', *Historical Studies Australia and New Zealand*, 9 (1960), 244–60.

—— *Colonial self-government: the British experience 1759–1856* (London, 1976).

—— *James Macarthur: colonial conservative* (Sydney, 1981).

Ward, Kevin and Brian Stanley (eds), *The Church Mission Society and world Christianity, 1799–1999* (Richmond, 2000).

Watts, Duncan J., *Small worlds: the dynamics of networks between order and randomness* (Princeton, 1999).

—— *Six degrees: the science of a connected age* (London, 2003).

Webster, Alan, 'Unmasking the Fingo: the war of 1835 revisited', in Carolyn Hamilton (ed.), *The Mfecane aftermath: reconstructive debates in southern African history* (Johannesburg, 1995), pp. 241–76.

Williams, E. Trevor, 'The Colonial Office in the thirties', *Historical Studies*, 2 (1943), 141–60.

Winch, Donald, *Classical political economy and colonies* (Cambridge, 1965).

Winks, Robin W. (ed.), *The Oxford history of the British Empire: vol. 5, historiography* (Oxford, 1999).

Young, Douglas, *The Colonial Office in the early nineteenth century* (London, 1961).

Theses

Bank, Andrew, 'Liberals and their enemies: racial ideology at the Cape of Good Hope' (PhD thesis, Cambridge University, 1995).

Donaldson, M., 'The Council of Advice at the Cape of Good Hope, 1825–34: a study in colonial government' (PhD thesis, Rhodes University, 1974).

Elbourne, Elizabeth, ' "To colonize the mind": evangelical missionaries in Britain and the Eastern Cape 1790–1837' (DPhil thesis, University of Oxford, 1992).

Frye, J., 'The South African Commercial Advertiser and the eastern frontier, 1834–47' (MA thesis, Rhodes University, 1968).

Hickford, Mark, 'Making "territorial rights of the natives": Britain and New Zealand 1830–1847' (DPhil thesis, University of Oxford, 1999).

Lancaster, Jonathon Charles Swinburne, 'A reappraisal of the governorship of Sir Benjamin D'Urban at the Cape of Good Hope, 1834–1838' (MA thesis, Rhodes University, 1980).

Madden, A. F. 'The attitude of the evangelicals to the empire and imperial problems (1820–1850)' (DPhil thesis, University of Oxford, 1950).

McGinn, M. J., 'J. C. Chase – 1820 settler and servant of the colony' (MA thesis, Rhodes University, 1975).

Potter, Simon J., 'Nationalism, imperialism and the press in Britain and the Dominions, c. 1898–1914' (DPhil thesis, University of Oxford, 2000).

Ray, Margaret, 'Administering emigration. Thomas Elliot and government-assisted emigration from Britain to Australia 1831–1855' (PhD thesis, University of Durham, 2001).

Ridden, Jennifer, ' "Making good citizens": national identity, religion and liberalism among the Irish elite, c. 1800–1850' (PhD thesis, University of London, 1998).

Salesa, Damon, 'Race mixing, a Victorian problem in Britain and New Zealand 1830s–1870' (DPhil thesis, University of Oxford, 2001).

Scott, J. B., 'The British solider on the Eastern Cape frontier, 1800–1850' (DPhil thesis, University of Port Elizabeth, 1973).

Ward, Damen, 'The politics of jurisdiction: British law, indigenous peoples and colonial government in South Australia and New Zealand, c. 1834–60' (DPhil thesis, University of Oxford, 2003).

Woods, T. P., 'Lord Bathurst's policy at the Colonial Office, 1812–1821, with particular reference to New South Wales and the Cape Colony' (DPhil thesis, University of Oxford, 1971).

Index